THE ESPN WORLD CUP COMPANION

THE ESPN WORLD CUP COMPANION

Everything You Need to Know About the Planet's Biggest Sports Event

David Hirshey and Roger Bennett

BALLANTINE
BOOKS

ESPN
BOOKS

Published in the United States by ESPN Books, an imprint of ESPN, Inc., New York, and Ballantine Books, an imprint of The Random House Publishing Group, a division of Random House, Inc., New York.

BALLANTINE and colophon are registered trademarks of Random House, Inc.
The ESPN Books name and logo are registered trademarks of ESPN, Inc.

Permission credits can be found on page 251.

Library of Congress Cataloging-in-Publication Data

Hirshey, David.
 The ESPN World Cup companion : everything you need to know about the planet's
biggest sports event / David Hirshey and Roger Bennett.
    p.   cm.
 ISBN 978-0-345-51792-0 (hardcover : alk. paper)
 1. World Cup (Soccer)—History. I. Bennett, Roger, 1970–   II. Title.
 GV943.49.H57 2010
 796.334'66—dc22   2010007273

Printed in the United States of America on acid-free paper

www.ballantinebooks.com
www.espnbooks.com

9 8 7 6 5 4 3 2 1

First Edition

Book design by Henry Lee Studio

For my father
—D. H.

To my dad, for making me a Blue, and to anyone who
has ever pulled on an Everton FC shirt
—R. B.

FOREWORD

BY
STEVE
NASH

Lost in a fit of excitement and emotion, I ripped off my Italy shirt and waved it in circles over my head as though I'd just knocked Germany out of the World Cup myself. Three years later, my Italian buddy who was with me still says my unexpected reaction was as great as the victory itself.

But why was I, a 32-year-old NBA point guard from Canada, going nuts over Italians in Germany?

Although I have devoted my life with a religious fury to the pursuit of basketball greatness, and, for periods of time, wished I had grown up in the Bronx, Compton, or Cabrini-Green, the "beautiful game" has had a strange grip on my life. My wife is from soccer-mad Paraguay, and she can only just survive my love of the game. I don't know whether to be excited or sorry for my two daughters. The sport, after all, will never relinquish its tight grip on my DNA.

I remember sitting in the living room with my dad watching the Mexico World Cup in 1986 on a 16-inch screen for which we needed to use tweezers to change the channel. That little cultural mirror is famous in my family; just recently my dad told his three adult children that when he left it on the curb, it was taken within hours. During the World Cup, that little TV felt like an IMAX theater in our living room, for three very romantic reasons: Canada's improbable participation in the tournament; the capable and inspiring early success of England, my father's nation; and finally, a stubby little wizard named Diego Maradona from a land far away.

Canada battled hard, but went out before scoring a single goal, something for which we would still be waiting if they'd played in every—or any—subsequent Cup. Ouch, I know. But only those who love can criticize.

England—my boys—performed well, but were ultimately defeated by Argentina when we let the cheeky little gaucho, Maradona, dance through us from inside his own half without hacking him down, the customary response to his unbeatable skills. In their defense, it was hot in Azteca for the red-faced Anglos—the stock excuse for England's World Cup failures. (But, I ask you, since when is Germany a tropical nation? They train in a climate similar to England and have had immense World Cup success.)

The outrage was real, but so was my love for the irrepressible Diego. I think my dad secretly felt the same way. He always encouraged us to be creative, subtle, and, at times, audacious. It was from this side of sport that my deep passion grew, and my dad gave me the ultimate gift.

A few years later, I stopped playing soccer because I fell in love with Michael Jordan—and the game he played. Although I have committed my life to the basketball hardwood, I still follow soccer with the very passion that was instilled in me at such a young age.

During the 2002 World Cup, I backpacked with four close friends all around Japan. We lived on Asahi, Pringles, M&M's, and Top Ramen. It was amazing.

Four years later, I went over to Germany during the first week of the 2006 World Cup to see England play my wife's nation, Paraguay. Although I've developed a soft spot for Paraguay, a country I love, England is in my blood. But it was an unexciting game, as England won when Paraguay's Carlos Gamarra put David Beckham's free kick into his own net.

The next day I met a few of my best friends from childhood and we took the train north to Hanover, where we caught a great match between Italy and Ghana. Mere hours after Italy's 2–0 win, we were back on the train to a refurbished Olympiastadion in Berlin to see mighty Brazil play Croatia. The samba boys prevailed on a clean left-footed strike from Kaká. Brazil, the favorites, would never fulfill their dream in this tournament, but it's always a privilege to see the bright yellow shirts buzzing around *la cancha* in their unparalleled rhythm.

After the Brazil-Croatia match, I returned to New York City, where the magic of the world's greatest tournament was pulsating throughout the neighborhoods. Every night my friends and I checked the fixture list and planned to watch the next day's game at the various restaurants and bars of the playing nations. If Argentina was playing, we'd be at Novacento, the Argentine restaurant in Soho, with all the Argies singing *"Vamos, vamos* Argentina!" If Portugal was playing, we'd be at a Portuguese spot. France, a French bar. There's nothing better at 10:30 on a weekday morning. During the World Cup, New York City really makes you believe that soccer will make it in America.

As the tournament progressed, I got word that a friend from Phoenix was taking his family to a villa near Saint-Tropez and was going to pop up to Germany for the semifinals and the final, leaving his family in the stress-free environment of the French Riviera. If there was ever a way of convincing my wife to let me go *back* over to Germany for the World Cup, it was with the lure of the Mediterranean.

I quickly got in touch with my friend, who said there was plenty of room for the Nash family at the villa. All I had to do now was convince my wife that the Riviera was the place to be. Not only could we have a vacation in one of the world's most desirable destinations, but I could also realize my dream of seeing the World Cup semis and final. I explained to her that this was the ideal situation. Still, she wasn't convinced that dragging our twin two-year-old daughters across the globe under my thinly veiled guise of catching the World Cup finals was the best thing to do. We were at a standstill.

I played my last card: I promised I'd take her to the final.

It worked, but I realized what a stupid promise this was—tickets were hard to come by, and I'd already promised four or five to the fellas making the trip. I was desperate to succeed. As my buddies and I watched the

If there was ever a way of convincing my wife to let me go back over to Germany for the World Cup, it was with the lure of the Mediterranean.

tournament unfold in New York, I became anxious for England to advance and wondered how I'd do in my new role as ticket broker. I thought, "If I'm lucky, my friends Alessandro Del Piero or Thierry Henry will make the final, and maybe one of them will have an extra ticket for my wife."

England soon broke my heart, crashing out against Portugal in the quarterfinals by the obligatory penalty shoot-out. But Italy had made it to the final four, and my spirits were lifted by the show that my hero, Zinedine Zidane, put on against Brazil to get France to the semis. Even playing alongside Thierry, one of the best players on earth, Zidane stands out. He's from another planet.

We left New York and arrived in beautiful Ramatuelle along the French Riviera, but not even the warm sun and sparkling reflection from the sea could calm my anxiety. I couldn't wait to be back in Germany, where I'd get to see Alessandro play for a berth in his first World Cup final, Zidane play in a semifinal, Thierry get a chance at his second World Cup trophy, and, perhaps most important, I'd have a shot at getting a spare ticket for my wife. I was beginning to let go of the pain of England's elimination on penalties for the second time in the last three World Cups.

Soon enough, the lads and I were off to Dortmund to see Italy play the German hosts. The stadium held just under 70,000 people, at least 60,000 of whom were chanting with a German accent. The stands were steep, and the atmosphere was incredible.

With the game going into extra time, Italian coach Marcello Lippi put in third and fourth strikers, one of whom was Alessandro. Following Fabio Grosso's late strike with a last minute goal of his own, Alessandro sealed Italy's spot in the final and ran over to us "Italians" to celebrate. And that's when, carried away by my excitement, I ripped off my shirt and waved it over my head like a maniac.

My good friend Thierry Henry and me.

The next day we went to Munich for the second semifinal game, France versus Portugal. The game started off drably, until Zidane scored from the penalty spot to put France in the final against Italy to give them a chance to win their second Cup in the last three tournaments.

I couldn't believe it. Not only would I see two friends play for the biggest trophy on earth, but I also had twice the chance of getting my wife a ticket to the game. I was finally able to get ahold of Alessandro, who, doing his best Santa Claus impersonation, gave me two tickets right next to his wife for the final.

Talk about surreal. On the one hand, sitting with the Italian families for this momentous occasion made me feel like the most privileged guy in the world. On the other, I felt like I was in enemy territory rooting against Thierry. Then I realized I was flattering myself with self-importance, and that I was just like millions of others tuned in to see this battle royale. Undeniably, my situation was unique . . . but I wasn't.

The game had its moments of drama, from Zidane's casual and audacious penalty kick straight down the pipe, off the crossbar, and over the line, to his infamous head butt that I, like thousands of others in the stadium, missed because it happened behind the play. It wasn't until I got to the hotel that night that I learned what he'd done.

When Italy won the World Cup, I was among the celebrating families whose tears were streaming down their faces as their little children played or slept, oblivious to this historic occasion. It is a scene I'll never forget.

But it's just one of countless moments that make up the long, glorious history of the World Cup. Maybe, like me, you've been lucky enough to attend a game in person. Maybe you just glue yourself to the television set every four years. Either way, you can't appreciate the World Cup—or, indeed, soccer itself—without understanding its history. Thanks to David Hirshey and Roger Bennett, *The ESPN World Cup Companion* gives you a front-row seat to the passionate past of this most global of all sporting events.

CONTENTS

INTRODUCTION

When Zinedine Zidane lowered his head and drove it into Marco Materazzi's chest in the dying minutes of the 2006 World Cup final, nearly everyone on the planet recoiled in slack-jawed horror. How could the Great Zizou, one of the game's true geniuses, tarnish his legacy over some run-of-the-mill trash talk? To American viewers, Zidane's *Coupe de Boule* immediately earned a place in the sports pantheon of cheap shots, alongside Kermit Washington sucker punching Rudy Tomjanovich and Mike Tyson snacking on Evander Holyfield's ear.

Yet it also marked the tipping point in the American consciousness of a tournament that had escalated from cult status to can't-afford-to-miss-it-for-fear-of-looking-clueless-around-the-water-cooler Big Event. The final between Italy and France drew an estimated 16.9 million viewers from sea to shining sea, eclipsing both the NBA and NHL playoffs and nearly equaling the audience (17.2 million) for the previous year's World Series. Perhaps most astonishing is the fact that the viewing numbers continued to spike *after* the U.S. crashed out in the opening round. Unlike the Olympics, where the American appetite is largely limited to watching the Red, White, and Blue win a boatload of gold, the World Cup goes beyond chest-thumping patriotism to—dare we say it—an appreciation for

a sport where we're not number 1, or even number 10. (All together now: "We're Number 14!") And yet enough of us played hooky during the 2006 World Cup to account for this staggering statistic: The tournament cost the U.S. $1.2 billion in lost labor because of the number of fans who skipped out of work at all hours of the day to watch the World Cup telecasts.

A couple of years earlier, we got to witness first-hand the roots of this strange phenomenon at our local Irish soccer bar in New York City, where fate originally threw us together as pub mates hungering for the weekly soccer broadcasts from England, Germany, and Spain. Actually, it was almost impossible for us to miss each other, given that, at kickoff time, we were virtually the only customers. Not that we were a match made in soccer heaven, mind you, coming to the game as we did from opposite sides of the field. One of us hails from New York, the other from Liverpool. One bleeds Arsenal red, the other lives and dies with Everton. One of us came of age during the apotheosis of the sport—Brazil's mind-blowing World Cup–winning side of 1970. The other suffered as England found increasingly theatrical ways to shatter the hearts of a nation in the late '80s and early '90s. We were connected simply by our shared love of soccer and all it represents.

After the last World Cup, we realized that something was afoot. The guys who used to parade in around halftime, decked out in their Ohio State or Florida jerseys, and walk straight past the row of TVs in the front room showing English Premier matches on their way to the College GameDay telecasts in the back, actually started to arrive earlier to check out what all the soccer fuss was about. Over the weeks and months that followed, their curiosity intensified:

"What's with all the diving and whining?"

"Where are all the freakin' goals?"

"Why does that dude in goal wear a water polo helmet?"

"Wait, there are two Ronaldos?"

It wasn't long before they began making pronouncements of their own:

"They're playing a 4-5-1? That'll never work against the midfield diamond."

"If Ron Artest played soccer, he'd be Michael Essien."

"Zonal marking on set pieces is insanity!"

When the next season of the English Premier League rolled around, many of our pub mates even adopted a team (that is, if you consider Tottenham a team) and, instead of watching in lunatic isolation, we were surrounded by a rowdy mix of screaming, jumping, expletive-spewing fans who, despite their American origins, knew the words to chants lauding cult figures like Serbia's defender Nemanja Vidic, breaking out on cue:

Nemanja whoa,
Nemanja whoa,
He comes from Serbia,
He'll f***ing murder ya. . . .

These days, if we arrive late at the bar, we're lucky to get a seat.

Imagine, we thought, if we could somehow tap into Americans' wellspring of soccer curiousity and bottle it for the World Cup, so that recent, but tentative, converts to the game could watch the tournament with the same knowledge and passion as the mob at our Irish pub. Or, to misquote the Spanish philosopher George Santayana, "Those who cannot remember soccer's past are condemned to underappreciate it." Thus *The ESPN World Cup Companion* was born to bridge the gap between merely watching the planet's biggest sporting event and understanding it. This book is designed to be your tour guide for the World Cup's rich story lines and national psychodramas that have developed over the course of the last 80 years. You cannot fathom the significance of the World Cup without being acquainted with its backstories any more than you can jump into *Lost* in the middle of season three.

We've been careful in the book to go beyond the crude stereotypes of Brazilian flair, German physicality, and English self-delusion. Within each nation's soccer DNA, lie disparate strengths, tragic flaws, and unshakable conflicts. Teams bring not only decades of fanatical sports history to the field, but the kind of history that made the Nobel Peace Prize necessary. There are blood feuds between conquerors and their former colonies (France vs. Senegal in '02, Portugal vs. Angola in '06), geopolitical showdowns (U.S.A. vs. Iran in 1998), and even civil wars (West Germany vs. East Germany in 1974). And, as a result, a true appreciation of the World Cup can't be limited to what happens on the field. For instance, while we rejoice at an impudent Messi back-heel that cuts a defense to pieces, we also recognize the difference between a good reverse mohawk (Clint Mathis) and a bad one (Christian Ziege).

THIS BOOK CELEBRATES the game for all its beauty and vulgarity, its subtlety and brutality, as an intersection of high and low culture where rogues are to be venerated as much as heroes, and perhaps more. For every mention of *joga bonito*—the "beautiful game" of mellifluous dribbling, no-look passes, and wondrous goals—there's a countervailing example of *joga feio*—the ugly game of physical assaults, diving cheats, and crooked refs. We champion not just the greatest World Cup teams but also the worst; the one-named legends of the game, but also the no-name cult figures; the clean-cut warriors and the hirsute party animals. To us, the World Cup is the greatest soap opera in sports, played out live in front of billions. It has become a singular global event, inspiring high-minded conceptual analysis from intellectuals, statesmen, and poets, while simultaneously providing an endless stream of tabloid gossip for mass consumption.

Now it is upon us again—four long, lonely years after Zidane went nuclear, but just seven months after another beloved Frenchman, Thierry Henry, perpetrated a new scandal by admittedly using his hand to orchestrate the winning goal in extra time of a decisive World Cup qualifier against Ireland, punching France's ticket to South Africa and ensuring that he'd never again walk the streets of Dublin without a police escort. So join us as we explore the glorious madness of the World Cup's 80-year history and the recurring spectacle of 22 men in shorts kicking a ball—and each other—in pursuit of glory. Marvel with us as Fernando Torres suddenly materializes and outraces the Swiss defense to the ball before chipping the keeper. Howl with us as Ronaldo falls down with a look of injured innocence. Exult with us as Landon Donovan scores the winner that vaults the U.S. into the second round. But, most of all, share our love of the game on the eve of South Africa 2010, knowing that, with the help of this book, you'll soon be the most soccer-literate fan around the water cooler.

—*D. H. and R. B.*

We will be discussing these issues and more on our blog at soccernet.com throughout the tournament and look forward to hearing your thoughts as the answers reveal themselves game by game.

AUTHORS' NOTE

Although it seems sacrilegious, given that the sport is called "football" everywhere else, in deference to American English we refer to football as "soccer" in this book, except when "football" appears within a quote or as part of an official name. Similarly, we have replaced the word "pitch" with the American equivalent, "field."

THE ESPN WORLD CUP COMPANION

'30   '34   '38

'50   '54   '58

THE LAND BEFORE TELEVISION

Bolivia, pictured here, crashed out in the first round of the Cup—and didn't fare much better in the spelling bee.

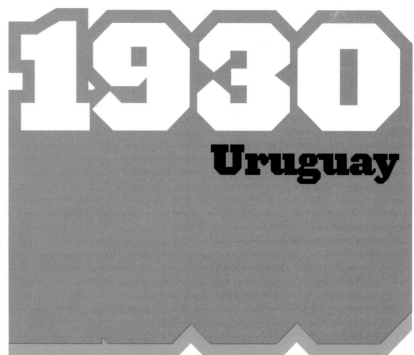

1930
Uruguay

AND GOD SAID, LET THERE BE SOCCER. . . .

The humble origins. South America dominates as few European teams find their sea legs, leaving Uruguay to lift the first Cup.

LONG BEFORE THE DAWN of television, agents, or even highly choreographed goal celebrations, el Campeonato Mundial de Football was established with a simple goal: to unify the various international strains of a sport that had grown rapidly but haphazardly since its emergence on the playing fields of English public schools in the 1800s. Soccer's popularity had spread as fast as

The French team on its slow cruise to Uruguay, where it washed out of the World Cup early.

British mercantile interests were able to carry it across Latin America and Europe. Locals from Rio to the Adriatic were dazzled by British sailors who organized kickabouts in every port of call.

This first tournament was designed to allow international teams to compete at the highest level under standardized rules. However, those who came to watch no more sensed they were witnessing the birth of a global sports colossus than those who saw the Chicago Bears squeeze out a 23–21 victory over the New York Giants in the first NFL Championship in 1933 could envisage the circus that is the modern-day Super Bowl.

Uruguay was given the honor of hosting duties, officially, in celebration of the centenary of its independence, unofficially by virtue of its willingness to single-handedly underwrite all of the organizing expenses. Despite their generosity, only Belgium, France, Romania, and Yugoslavia bothered to make the trip from Europe. The main obstacle was the grueling 15-day ocean crossing from Europe, a journey that forced participants to take a two-month work leave, an impossible luxury for most. A single liner ship left Genoa with three of the four squads aboard. They even graciously stopped to pick up the Brazilians along the way. Frenchman Jules Rimet, the Fédération Internationale de Football Association (FIFA) president and visionary behind the tournament, watched the teams train on deck. The trophy that would later be named for him was tucked safely in his luggage.

This first tournament was big on vision, yet short on details. Participation was by invitation as opposed to qualification, yet an odd number of teams—13—were lined up to play. England, the country that invented the game, was not among them. They saw the French-created tournament as déclassé and beneath them, a position they maintained until 1950. The United States had no such reservations and sent a squad—built around a core of British pros from such powerhouse teams in the American professional league as the Detroit Holley Carburetor, Fall River Marksmen, and the Providence Clamdiggers—that arrived as somewhat of a favorite. This fact alone indicated how very different the tournament was from the World Cups of the modern era.

Actually, the tournament, based entirely in Montevideo, was as different as possible from the global juggernaut of today. The Argentinian captain

(below) Estadio Centenario in Montevideo, venue for the first World Cup final; (right) Uruguay's Pedro Cea scores against Argentina in the final.

1930
RESULTS

SEMIFINALS
Argentina 6 U.S.A. 1
Uruguay 6 Yugoslavia 1

FINALS
Uruguay 4 Argentina 2

missed a game to take his law finals; three members of the Brazilian side played while wearing berets; the Bolivian manager had to perform double duty and step in to act as ref during a few games; the King of Romania selected his nation's team himself. Only 1,000 people saw Frenchman Lucien Laurent volleying home from 12 yards to score the World Cup's first goal, and a mere 300 watched the Romanians outplay the Peruvians. Kickball games in Central Park attract bigger crowds today. But some things were refreshingly similar: The first tournament featured a sex scandal when a Uruguayan

goalkeeper went wild after withstanding eight weeks of isolation in training camp.

By the time Argentina and Uruguay qualified for the final, the region, if not the world, had warmed to the tournament. Thousands of Argentinians crossed the River Plate to Montevideo to cheer on their team against their neighbors and rivals. Organizers searched ticket holders for firearms as 80,000 packed the magnificent Estadio Centenario, a temple of soccer built for this match. The competition boiled over before it had even begun, when the two sides argued over whose ball they would use, as

if the World Cup final was no more dignified than a sandlot touch football game. Officials reached a Solomonic compromise in which the teams agreed to swap balls at halftime. In the match itself, Uruguay came back from 2–1 down to emerge 4–2 victors, with their one-armed center forward, "Manco" Castro, scoring the final goal. Their intoxicated fans celebrated by beating up their Argentinian counterparts, while in Buenos Aires, a mob attacked the Uruguayan consulate, enshrining soccer hooliganism and random acts of violence as integral parts of the World Cup from the very outset.

HÉCTOR CASTRO, URUGUAY

Fifty-six years before Argentina celebrated the goal delivered by the "Hand of God," Uruguay boasted its own one-handed god in Héctor Castro, "El Divino Manco." As a 13-year-old, Castro had channeled his inner *Texas Chainsaw Massacre* and sliced off his right limb at the forearm by playing with power tools. This did not, however, deter him from his dream of playing soccer at the highest level, though it did tend to make him a liability on throw-ins.

In 1924, the man from Montevideo won the first of three championships for his club team, Nacional, and two years later Castro was playing striker for the Uruguayan national team—the first great South American side. The Uruguayans won the Olympic soccer title in 1928 as a prelude to their hosting the inaugural World Cup, where Castro polarized the masses with his on-field thuggery and off-field womanizing and gambling—a flesh-and-blood one-armed bandit.

He scored the first goal of Uruguay's campaign in a 1–0 win over Peru, but waited until the final to make his biggest impact. It wasn't just that he seems to have clubbed the Argentine keeper with his stump while challenging for the ball in the goalmouth, but that his mere presence in the starting lineup was almost scandalous. Castro was a late replacement for beloved but injured forward Pelegrin Anselmo, a move that incensed the numerous supporters of Nacional's archrival club Peñarol, who packed the stadium.

With Uruguay clinging to a 3–2 lead late in the game, and the Argentines pouring forward in search of an equalizer, Castro silenced both the jeers and the opposition with a solo goal that did more than clinch the Jules Rimet Cup for his country; it also affected diplomatic relations between the two nations. Argentina cursed Uruguay in defeat, the Uruguayan embassy in Buenos Aires was stoned and damaged, and the furious Argentines also took their anger out on their own government, using their World Cup loss as a cudgel to help oust their president at the time.

The geopolitical fallout was scary, but just a harbinger of the venomous rivalries and passions run amok that would plague the World Cup for the next 80 years, and probably beyond.

THIEVES LIKE US
A Short History of the World Cup Trophy

Though it stands less than 40 centimeters tall, the World Cup trophy has haunted the dreams of boys and men worldwide, been battled over by the most athletic specimens from every nation, and found itself at the center of an international kidnapping incident. Two versions of the trophy have actually been in play. In a cunning coincidence predating both global sports brands and product placement, the first was cast in 1930 as a sterling silver rendition of Nike, which was, back then, merely the Greek goddess of victory. During the Second World War the trophy was in Italian hands and only the bravery of the country's FIFA vice president's secretary, Otto Barassi, ensured its survival. Suspicious of Mussolini, Barassi kept the trophy under his bed until war's end, becoming the World Cup's equivalent of Oskar Schindler.

But the real threat to the trophy came not in time of war, but in peace. Four months before the 1966 World Cup in England, the trophy was stolen while on display at a London stamp exhibition. Great Britain was in shock for seven days before it was rescued in suburban London by Pickles the dog, who had discovered it wrapped in newspaper and stuffed in a hedge. Pickles became a national hero overnight, and when England won the cup, the dog was guest of honor at the celebration banquet, at which he was allowed to lick the dinner plates clean. A brief career in movies and television followed before Pickles tragically and accidentally hanged himself, having snagged his choke lead on a tree while chasing a cat.

The theft was viewed with particular disgust in Brazil, the country most intimately acquainted with the cup. A spokesperson for the Brazilian Sports Confederation told *The Times* of London, "This shameful theft would never have happened in Brazil. Even Brazilian thieves love football and would never have committed such a sacrilegious crime." But the Brazilians need not have worried, for in 1970 the trophy was in their hands again, and was, on account of Brazil's third World Cup Championship, theirs to keep. FIFA cast a new trophy in Milan, announcing it was an "organic depiction of symbolic exertion coupled with the harmony and simplicity of world peace." English comedians David Baddiel and Frank Skinner disagreed, saying it looked as if the designer had rolled up his sleeve, clasped a grapefruit firmly in one hand, and plunged his arm up to the elbow in a bucket of custard before raising it vertically.

The Brazilians gave the original trophy pride of place in the Brazilian Football Confederation headquarters in Rio, where it was permanently guarded and surrounded with bulletproof glass. But on December 20, 1983, in the middle of the night, a team of thieves broke in, tied up the night watchman, used a crowbar to break into the trophy cabinet, and pinched the world's most coveted trophy. Even Pelé begged for its return, pleading for "the sake of the soul of Brazilian football," but the trophy was never seen again. It is widely thought to have been melted down as the Brazilians pulled off the remarkable feat of winning, and losing, the trophy at the same time. The English Football Association was too diplomatic to give comment, or else wasn't sure about the Portuguese words for "pot," "kettle," and "black."

(above) Brazil and Spain demonstrate the hokey-pokey, putting their right feet (and a couple of left ones) in and shaking them all about; (left) The Cup's well-guarded radio broadcast.

(opposite page) Hoisting the Coppa del Duce.

1934 RESULTS

QUARTERFINALS
Czechoslovakia 3 Switzerland 2
Germany 2 Sweden 1
Italy 1 Spain 1
Italy 1 Spain 0 (replay of tie)
Austria 2 Hungary 1

SEMIFINALS
Italy 1 Austria 0
Czechoslovakia 3 Germany 1

THIRD PLACE
Germany 3 Austria 2

FINAL
Italy 2 Czechoslovakia 1

1934
Italy

WHEN IN ROME, DO AS IL DUCE DOES....

Palms are greased as Italy follows Mussolini's orders to triumph.

THE ITALIAN DICTATOR Benito Mussolini is remembered for many accomplishments, among them establishing a police state, conquering Ethiopia, and making the trains run on time. Less well known is that he was the first global tyrant to recognize the power of the World Cup as the perfect propaganda tool to burnish the image of his regime abroad and promote its domestic popularity. From the very outset, "Il Duce" made it clear to all that he did not just want to host the tournament—he wanted to win. The opportunity to have the *Azzurri* crowned World Cup champions was priceless and he made the lire rain down to ensure that the entire country was a picture-perfect backdrop for their inevitable coronation. Monumental stadia were built across the nation. And the beautification program wasn't limited to Italy. Rumor has it that Il Duce resplendently refurbished the Greek Football Association headquarters in exchange for the Greek team's promise to throw the game necessary to ensure that Italy would qualify for the World Cup.

As one would expect from a totalitarian despot, Mussolini's control of the tournament was absolute. Traveling fans were first lured by offers to cover 75 percent of their travel costs, then issued elaborately designed match tickets, printed on the finest quality paper, that would double as advertisements for the splendors of Italy once they returned home. In addition, he had a creatively titled trophy, the Coppa del Duce, cast to accompany, and tower over, the official World Cup trophy. If that did not provide sufficient motivation to win it all, Mussolini offered highly prized signed photographs of himself for the victors.

The final step in Mussolini's cunning master plan was a twofold strategy to guarantee that Italy won. First, he appointed as coach the short, bristle-haired Vittorio Pozzo, a disciplined tactician. Second, he reinforced the squad by the aggressive repatriation of foreign-born nationals, or *"Oriundi,"* such as Raimundo Orsi, who had actually represented Argentina in the 1928 Olympics. The poor Argentinians, demoralized and disoriented, adopted the unorthodox strategy of leaving their star players at home to prevent further defections, a plan that inevitably led to a quick first-round exit. The poaching Pozzo had no qualms. "If they can

die for Italy, they can play for Italy," he proclaimed, although it should be noted, he did not have a completely free hand. All of his players had to be card-carrying members of the Fascist Party. While Pozzo built the team, Mussolini stayed busy by handpicking (read: bribing) the referees. Their decisions were so consistently one-sided throughout the tournament that no one was surprised when one referee took the extraordinary step of heading the ball to maintain an Italian attack during the opening round.

In the stand-out match of the tournament, the Italians conquered the highly favored Austrian Wunderteam, one of the most fluid sides of their generation, whose strength was negated by a deluge that made their slick interplay impossible. The atmosphere of Italy's final against the Czechs was more suited to a political rally. Mussolini was overjoyed to see journalists from around the world covering the game. The Italians gave a Fascist salute before kickoff and then came back from a goal down to win in extra time and give Il Duce the photo opportunity that might well have been his chief objective.

Sindelar and his girlfriend were found dead in their apartment. There has been no shortage of conspiracy theories.

MATTHIAS SINDELAR, AUSTRIA

Nicknamed "Der Papierene" (the Paper Man) for his slight build and his ability to slip by defenders, Matthias Sindelar is widely regarded as the greatest Austrian player of all time. He was a forward on the celebrated Austrian Wunderteam of the 1930s that ended Scotland's undefeated run on the continent and crushed Germany (twice), France, and Hungary by a combined 23–2. Though the Austrians lost to eventual champion Italy in the semifinals of the 1934 World Cup, they revolutionized soccer by adopting a cerebral, artistic passing game in an era of rugged physicality. As the orchestrator of that free-flowing style, Sindelar became known as "the Mozart of football."

Sindelar and his family were considered "new" Viennese; he and his parents were from Moravia (now part of the Czech Republic), but settled in a poor suburb in the Austrian capital. "In his speech and manner, he was an ordinary Viennese person," said Franz Schwarz, son of the former president of FK Austria, Sindelar's club team. "But he was something very special in his talent."

The striker was an everyman, a hero across the class system; to the Hungarians, Poles, and fellow Czechs who toiled in the factories, as well as to the café-dwelling bourgeoisie. So captivating were his skills that he even attracted interest from Manchester United, which rarely looked beyond British borders for players.

By early 1938, with the annexation of Austria by Germany virtually complete, the Nazis asked Sindelar to join the German national side. He refused repeatedly, claiming a combination of age and injuries, while continuing to play for FK Austria, a team with a Jewish chairman, Dr. Michl Schwarz. When the Nazis came to power, they replaced Schwarz and ordered Sindelar to distance himself from him. But he publicly declared, "The new chairman has forbidden me to greet you, Herr Doktor, but I will always greet you"—earning him a warning of being "very friendly to Jews."

In April of 1938, Sindelar was coaxed out of retirement to play in an exhibition match between the German XI and his Austria (renamed Ostmark by its new masters). The Nazis made it known to the Austrians that the game was to end in a hard-fought, but scoreless draw. For 70 minutes, Sindelar made a mockery of the fix, contemptuously rolling the ball inches past the post. Finally, he scored a goal and assisted on another for a 2–0 Austrian win. And just to make sure that everybody knew how he felt, he raced over to the stands containing the German dignitaries and celebrated with in-your-face defiance.

Months later, Der Papierene and his live-in girlfriend were found dead in their apartment. Though the cause of death was carbon monoxide poisoning, there has been no shortage of conspiracy theories. Romantics claim it was a double-suicide by people unwilling to live under the Nazi regime, but others suggest they were murdered, in part because his girlfriend was suspected of being Jewish. Sindelar's funeral drew a reported 20,000 mourners, a fitting send-off for the Paper Man who danced rings around Hitler.

The great Italian striker Giuseppe Meazza (left) before the final against Hungary. "To have him in your team is to start up 1–0," said his manager.

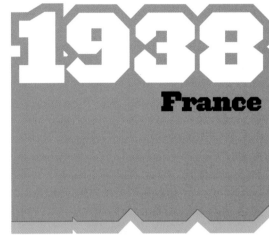

1938
France

BACK IN BLACK

With war on the horizon, Brazil sabotages its own campaign, leaving Italy victorious again.

ITALY ARRIVED TO DEFEND its status as champions with all of the credibility of a professional wrestler, having won its previous title with the referees in its pocket. This time, driven by a determination to prove it was no fluke, Italy won it all the hard way—on merit and away from home, with 10,000 Italian anti-Fascists cheering on every opponent they faced. The tournament was predictably war-stained. With the Spanish embroiled in civil war, the Soviet Union enmeshed in the Great

Purge, and the Argentinians and Uruguayans close to bankrupt and boycotting the tournament on account of FIFA's failure to return it to South America, the teams who absented themselves were as notable as the ones who turned up to compete. Only three non-European teams entered, one of which was micro-power Dutch East Indies (now Indonesia), which seized the opportunity to make its one—and to this point, only—World Cup appearance.

Geopolitical turmoil continued to interfere even after the field had been finalized. The Austrians pulled out between qualification and kickoff after the Nazi's annexation, known as the *Anschluss*, meant that its own team was subsumed by the Germans'. The Führer himself, never much of a soccer fan, demanded his coaches field at least five Austrian-born players throughout the tournament. This team of united *übermenschen* was dispatched by plucky Switzerland in the preliminary round, proving that

the country, unlike Poland and Czechoslovakia, had no fear of the Nazi threat.

The Brazilians opened strongly, powered by the "Black Diamond," Leônidas da Silva, their bicycle kick–pioneering striker who chalked up five goals over the course of the first two rounds. Their challenge faltered after one of the most costly coaching decisions in World Cup history, when the Brazilians benched their rubber-limbed striker to keep him fresh for a final they never reached. Drained as Leônidas may have been after struggling through a replay against a physical Czechoslovakian side (penalty kick tiebreakers would not be instituted until 1982), he might have averted their 2–1 semifinal loss to the Italians.

Mussolini's team had enjoyed its role as the tournament heel, drawing large crowds of vocal, exiled Italian anti-Fascists who jeered their country's every move. Their protests, however, appeared only to

raise Italy's game. In the quarterfinal against host France—which also wore blue—Italy was asked to wear their away jerseys, which were traditionally white. Instead, on Mussolini's orders, they donned black shirts—*Maglie Nere*—to goad the thousands of French and Italian protestors in the crowd. In the final, they patiently picked apart the Hungarians, led by three assists from their legendary captain, Giuseppe Meazza. Italy won the battle, but lost the coming war. They would hold on to the trophy for the next twelve years, as even the World Cup was trumped by the conflict about to consume the continent.

1938 RESULTS

QUARTERFINALS
Brazil 1 Czechoslovakia 1
(Brazil 2, Czechoslovakia 1 in replay)
Sweden 8 Cuba 0
Italy 3 France 1
Hungary 2 Switzerland 0

SEMIFINALS
Italy 2 Brazil 1
Hungary 5 Sweden 1

THIRD PLACE
Brazil 4 Sweden 2

FINALS
Italy 4 Hungary 2

(above) Italy holds aloft the second of its four World Cup trophies; (right) The bloodied Germans—note the swastika crests—leave the field after losing to Switzerland.

14

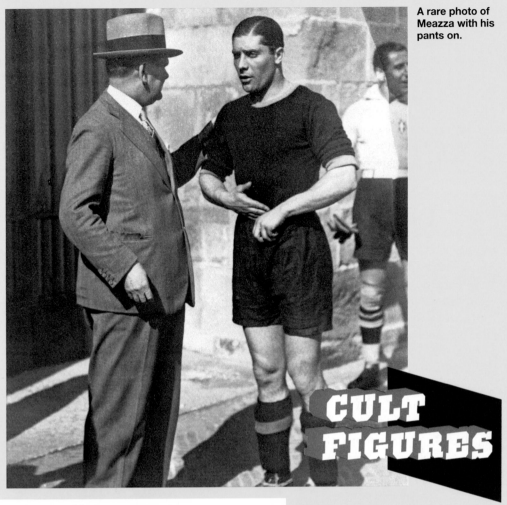

A rare photo of Meazza with his pants on.

CULT FIGURES

GIUSEPPE MEAZZA, ITALY

If grace under fire is a hallmark of the great soccer player, then Giuseppe Meazza has few equals. Imperturbable both on and off the field, his training regimen was, to say the least, idiosyncratic. While his teammates toiled at early-morning practices, Giuseppe preferred to tune up by dancing the tango and sleeping in brothels. And even Italian dictator Benito Mussolini could only smile at such insouciance, as Meazza led the host Azzurri to its first World Cup title in 1934.

Meazza grew up poor on the streets of Milan. His father died in World War I and he learned soccer the same way Pelé did—barefoot, kicking a ball made of rags. By 17, Meazza was a goal-scoring phenomenon for his local team, Inter Milan, and two years later, in 1930, he marked his interna-tional debut with a pair of goals. He would go on to score a total of 33 times in 53 games for the Azzurri, but it was as Italy's creative schemer that he would have his most enduring influence.

With Mussolini looking on, and the team giving him the Fascist salute before every game, the pressure on the host Italians to win the 1934 Cup was enormous. Fortunately, they had Meazza. As legendary Italian coach Vittorio Pozzo put it, "To have him in your team meant to start 1–0 up." Meazza scored the winning goal against Spain in a 1–0 victory, and supplied a steady stream of defense-shredding passes, as Italy advanced to a semifinal showdown with Austria's Wunderteam. The game was played in a downpour at Meazza's home stadium, San Siro (later renamed Stadio Giuseppe Meazza), and Meazza used his intimate knowledge of the slick field to set up Enrico Guaita for the match's only goal.

Midway through the final against Czechoslovakia, Meazza was badly injured in a tackle. Since no substitutes were permitted back then, he soldiered on but he was so ineffective that the Czechs no longer bothered to mark him. The game went to extra time, tied 1–1, when the ball found its way to Meazza on the wing. Shrugging off his injury, he tore open the Czech defense with a perfect pass to Guaita, who slid the ball to Angelo Schiavio for Italy's winning goal.

Meazza went on to captain Italy in the 1938 World Cup, a team that remains the only European one to win back-to-back World Cups. But more than his impressive collection of soccer trophies, it was his hedonistic view of the world that set him apart. Often compared to the Italian sex god Rudolph Valentino, the twice-married Meazza received "hundreds and hundreds of perfumed letters . . . intercepted by his mother," according to the soccer journalist Gianni Brera, who made it his personal mission to track Meazza's lifestyle. As teammate Pietro Rava would recall, "It's difficult to tell if Meazza had won over more girls than the goals he scored." He scored one memorable goal in Italy's 1938 semifinal win over Brazil, when he converted a penalty kick while holding up his shorts. It is said that the elastic waistband had been ripped earlier in the game by a defender but it didn't faze Meazza, who was used to being caught with his pants down. Brera recounts the folktale of how one Sunday afternoon Meazza awoke in an unfamiliar bed with a woman on either side of him. Realizing he was late for that day's game, he took a cab to the stadium, still wearing his pajamas, arrived just before the pregame Fascist salute, and it was only after he had scored two goals that his teammates forgave him.

The Five World Cup Fans You'll Meet in Hell

Rare is the modern tyrant who does not make soccer a central priority of his regime. Romania's Nicolae Ceaușescu dispatched his son, Valentin, to propel Steaua Bucharest to European glory in 1986. Stalin's secret police chief, Lavrenti Beria, was so fanatical about Dynamo Moscow that he had rival players shipped off to Siberia. And Chile's General Augusto Pinochet took time out from making his opponents disappear to serve as honorary president of his beloved club team, Colo-Colo. More effective than a robust domestic policy, soccer is one of the greatest tools a dictator has at his disposal to enhance his popularity. The reflected glory of the victory adds luster to any faltering regime, while a loss can trigger a national uprising, or even an international conflict. Herewith is a rogues gallery of the world's worst soccer fans.

BENITO MUSSOLINI

That Mussolini's ascent to power triggered a golden period for Italian soccer in which the team twice won the World Cup was no coincidence. Il Duce was crazy for the sport, realizing the double propaganda opportunity it offered: It reinforced a sense of Italian unity domestically while burnishing its reputation on the global stage. Mussolini directed his party to remold Italian soccer as a Fascist game, creating a single domestic league to symbolize national unity and installing Fascist bureaucrats to run every important club. When the national team played at home, he enjoyed making a dramatic entrance onto the field riding a white steed, and when they traveled abroad he instructed the players to hold their Fascist salutes until whistling protesters had run out of energy.

ADOLF HITLER

While Hitler appreciated the emotional power and spectacle of soccer, its unpredictable nature left him cold. During the Third Reich's infancy, the national team was strategically employed as an international ambassador for the regime. In 1935 Hitler ensured that 10,000 fans received subsidies to travel to England and cheer the team on for propaganda purposes. The only time he was known to attend a game in person, Germany was defeated 2–0 by the lowly Norwegians in the 1936 Olympics in Berlin. When Norway scored its second goal, Hitler headed for the exit, prompting Goebbels to write in his journal, "The Führer is very agitated. I am almost unable to control myself. A real bath of nerves."

16

Benito Mussolini takes time out of his busy dictator's schedule to pose with his country's team.

GENERAL FRANCISCO FRANCO

The dictator, who ruled Spain from 1939 until his death in 1975, viewed soccer as a game in which, to quote the fascist newspaper *Arriba España!*, "the virility of the Spanish race can find full expression imposing itself over the more technical but less-aggressive foreign teams." But his national team frustrated him with its poor form. Although he delighted in squeezing every ounce of public relations value out of Spain's sporadic wins against Eastern Bloc opposition, the sports newspaper *Marca* was appalled at the team's lack of commitment, claiming that the players were "so conditioned by foreign tactics that it no longer plays like a team of real Spaniards with passion, aggression, virility, and above all, fury." Franco drew solace from the performance of his favorite domestic club, Real Madrid, although their powerhouse status may have had something to do with the director of State Security's regular, intimidating visits to the opponents' locker room before crucial games.

THE ARGENTINIAN JUNTA

The Argentina-hosted 1978 World Cup was used by the military junta as an extended infomercial for their regime. They cut spending in areas like hospitals and schools, diverting it to ensuring victory, allegedly even bribing Peru to throw a critical game with a combination of free grain, forgiving millions of dollars of credits, and allegedly an arms shipment or two. The effort was worth it. When Argentina won, the streets were flooded with people, who cheered the generals as they stood on the balcony of the presidential palace to bask in the acclaim of the nation. To build on its newfound popularity, the junta proceeded to engage Chile in a territorial dispute.

SADDAM HUSSEIN

The Iraqi president, or "Glorious Leader," was not much of a soccer fan, but he recognized the sport's strategic value and so entrusted the national team to his son Uday, who utlilized a series of unique motivational strategies to improve its performance. One of his first acts was to install an iron maiden and a 30-cell prison in the offices of the Olympic federation. Players who were deemed to have underperformed had their feet scalded and toenails ripped off. Squads sent to play abroad were threatened with the possiblity that, in the event they lost, their return flight would explode in midair. The team promptly qualified for the 1986 World Cup. Their failure to qualify in 1994 led to the entire squad being forced to kick concrete balls until the bones in their feet were shattered.

1950
Brazil

RIO NOT SO BRAVO

The English are humiliated by the United States. Prepared for its own coronation,

Brazil falls at the last hurdle. National tragedy ensues.

BRAZIL APPROACHED THE 1950 tournament with all of the confidence of a machine candidate in a Chicago election. Largely insulated from the Second World War and eager to announce itself on the global stage with a victory, Brazil jumped at the opportunity to assume hosting duties. Just assembling a full field of 16 teams proved to be a struggle. Both Germany and Japan were barred from inter-

national competition, the entire Eastern Bloc refused to enter on political grounds, and even India dropped out when FIFA refused to let them play barefoot. Italy, the defending champions, competed only after FIFA agreed to pick up its tab. Their title defense was jeopardized by their insistence on traveling to the tournament by ocean liner after the Turin-based core of the team—eight players—had

perished a year before in an airplane crash. During the long sea crossing, the players and management had so much time to squabble that they arrived embittered and were quickly dispatched.

All of this reinforced Brazil's cockiness. In a country where soccer is a religion, this World Cup was anticipated with all of the fervor of a messianic coming; a national stadium, the Maracanã,

(left) England's team was flying high until it landed in Brazil; (opposite page) Uruguay's first goal in its defeat of Brazil in the final.

was constructed in Rio as a monument both to soccer's importance to the soul of the nation and to the country's global aspirations. It was also a monument to bad planning, as the 200,000-seat national status symbol was not completely finished by kickoff time. It was, possibly, a portent of things to come.

Confidence was also high in the English camp, the too-proud birthplace of soccer, which finally deemed the tournament worthy of its participation. The team behaved as if it only had to turn up to claim the Cup. Demonstrating an arrogance as monumental as the Maracanã, they breezed in a mere two days before kickoff, one of many ill-advised logistical decisions that gave the players no time to acclimate. Instead of choosing a more pastoral training facility, the British struggled to adapt while staying in a tourist hotel amid the chaos of the Copacabana. None of this mattered to the team management, which saw its opponents as target practice, and the Cup as its divine right.

This perspective seemed entirely justified when they lined up against an amateur American team that had been beaten 9–0 in a warm-up game against Italy. Maybe it was the noisy tourist hotel, maybe not, but Joe Gaetjens, a Haitian-born part-time dishwasher (*see Cult Figures, page 22*), headed in a cross from the American captain/gym teacher Walter Bahr to score the match's first goal. Helped by a series of heroic saves from undertaker/goalkeeper Frank Borghi, the United States hung on for the victory, still the greatest single shocker in World Cup history. While English papers proclaimed the death of English football, the American coach, Bill Jeffrey, proudly announced, "This is all we need to make the game go in the States!" It would prove to be just the first of many false dawns for U.S. soccer. Only one journalist, Dent McSkimming of the *St. Louis Post-Dispatch*, saw the game live, and *The New York Times*, at first believing the reported victory to be a hoax when it came through on the wire, buried the story.

BRAZIL JUMPS THE GUN

The final round featured the unusual format of a round robin among four teams, and by the last match, Brazil needed only a draw against its neighbors and global rivals, Uruguay, to fulfill its manifest destiny. The team was so heavily favored that *before the game* it was presented with gold watches inscribed "for the world champions." If that did not instill enough confidence, one of the Uruguayan players actually wet himself with fear while lining up for the pregame national anthems.

The game began according to script when Friaça put the Brazilians ahead. But the Uruguayans did not wilt, first equalizing and then, with eleven minutes to go, scoring the winner as Alcides Ghiggia, all 5'6" of him, slipped the ball past the near post. The 200,000 in attendance fell silent. Brazil couldn't respond to Ghiggia's goal, and when the whistle blew, Brazil's already-engraved winning medals were quickly disposed of. This was unfortunately followed by several World Cup–related suicides across the country. The loss became known as the *Maracanazo*, or the Maracanã blow, and is considered by many to be the greatest tragedy to befall the nation. For a country with few wars, the traditional markers of a nation's history, the World Cups had quickly become the benchmark of Brazil's narrative. The writer Nelson Rodrigues coined the loss "our national catastrophe, our Hiroshima." It's a defeat that none of Brazil's subsequent five victories have come close to healing.

After his team's historic upset of Brazil, Uruguayan defender Schubert Gambetta is swarmed by journalists.

URUGUAY 2, BRAZIL 1
Final

In the annals of pregame pep talks, not even Knute Rockne or Vince Lombardi rose to the oratorical heights of Ángelo Mendes de Moraes, the mayor of Rio de Janeiro. "You players, who in less than a few hours will be hailed as champions by millions of compatriots," he told the Brazilian team before kickoff. "You, who have no rivals in the entire hemisphere! You, who will overcome any other competitor! You, who I already salute as victors!"

You could forgive de Moraes's bravado. The Brazilians were such overwhelming favorites to lift the Cup that the early edition of the Rio paper *O Mundo* ran a picture of the team with the headline THESE ARE THE WORLD CHAMPIONS.

It didn't seem to impress any Brazilian that Uruguay had been the best team on the continent for years, winning not only Olympic gold in '24 and '28, but also the inaugural World Cup in 1930. Close to 200,000 fans crammed into the Maracanã, Rio's majestic new stadium, to witness Brazil's inevitable coronation. The crowd noise was so deafening, so intimidating, that Uruguayan striker Julio Pérez wet his shorts during the pregame national anthems.

The first half was scoreless, but hardly without incident. After 28 minutes, Uruguay's Obdulio Varela, known as "The Black Chief" on account of his dark complexion and imperious style in midfield, bitch-slapped Brazilian left-back Bigode after a collision. When the referee took no action, the Brazilians knew that they would not win the Cup on reputation alone.

They did, however, take the lead just after halftime on a goal that had the Maracanã vibrating even as Varela protested it should have been ruled offside. Despite having no supporting evidence, the Uruguayan captain demanded an interpreter and harrassed the referee long enough to quell the crowd's hysteria. It was a cunning move, allowing his team a chance to regroup before the game started again.

With less than half an hour to go, Varela himself helped craft the equalizer. His pass found Alcides Ghiggia unmarked on the right flank, and the tiny winger skipped past Bigode before crossing for Juan Schiaffino to poke the ball past Brazil goalkeeper Moacyr Barbosa. Then, with 11 minutes remaining, the unthinkable occurred. Once more, Ghiggia got behind Bigode and burst into the box, but instead of crossing as he'd done for the first Uruguayan goal, he pulled the trigger from a narrow angle. Under normal circumstances, it is a cardinal sin of goalkeeping to let the ball squeeze between the keeper and the near post; in a World Cup, it is unconscionable, and Barbosa would come to mourn his mistake for the rest of his life.

Legend has it that then-president of FIFA, Frenchman Jules Rimet, had prepared a congratulatory speech in Portuguese for the home side but had to discard it when Brazil could muster no response, and he was forced to award the Cup to Uruguay in the now dirgelike Maracanã. As the journalist Alex Bellos writes in *Futebol,* his definitive book on Brazilian soccer, the crowd was so deflated that "only one act of violence was recorded: the granite bust of Mayor Angelo Mendes de Moraes was knocked over."

Over time, the fortunes of the game's pivotal figures took disparate turns. In 2003, Varela's boots and shirt from the game were declared to be historical documents that "must remain in Uruguay and be exhibited as an example of its people's highest values."

The Brazilian people, meanwhile, laid the blame for the devastating defeat on Barbosa, even though he had been named the World Cup's top goalkeeper. Video footage of the goal doesn't even show the ball breaching the line, proving that Barbosa wasn't the only one expecting Ghiggia would cross rather than shoot. But it does capture the "heavy, crestfallen" Barbosa slowly rising to his feet after locating the ball in the far corner of the net. The goal triggered a bitter reemergence of Brazil's racial tensions, given that Barbosa as well as Bigode were black. So unforgiving was the national psyche that some believe it's more than a coincidence that no black goalkeeper was picked for the national team until the turn of the 21st century.

Ironically, Barbosa worked at the Maracanã for twenty years (they even let him take home the goalposts from their 1950 defeat, which he then used as fuel for a barbecue), but never escaped the ignominy of July 16, 1950. "The maximum punishment in Brazil is thirty years imprisonment, but my imprisonment has been for fifty," he said. In 1993, Barbosa tried to visit the squad as it prepared for U.S.A. '94, but the Brazilian federation refused to give him access, fearing he would bring bad luck. Barbosa died alone and penniless at age 79; of the 50 people who attended his funeral, it's reported that not one of them was a representative of Brazilian soccer.

As for Uruguay, it faded from the World Cup spotlight, failing to advance past the second round since 1970. Still, their victory at the Maracanã stands as one of the game's greatest upsets, its significance not lost on their goal-scoring hero, Ghiggia. "Only three people have, with just one motion, silenced the Maracanã," he said. "Frank Sinatra, Pope John Paul II, and me."

JOE GAETJENS, U.S.A.

What do you do with a non-U.S. citizen who is studying to be an accountant during the day, washes dishes at night, and had never made an international soccer appearance in his life? Naturally, you make him the starting center-forward for your team and watch him score the only goal in the greatest upset in World Cup history.

Gaetjens had been playing soccer in his native Haiti since he was 14, and when he came to Columbia University on a Haitian government scholarship, he starred for a local semipro team. While he had not been part of the squad that qualified for Brazil, his performance in a tryout game sufficiently impressed the U.S.A. selectors, who added him to the team. "Athletic, unpredictable, a free spirit," was how his teammate Walter Bahr described him. The U.S. Soccer Association's rules permitted him to play if he would declare that he intended to pursue American citizenship. Gaetjens may have had second thoughts when his U.S team tuned up for the World Cup by losing to Northern Ireland, Turkish side, Besiktas, and Italy by a combined 19–0.

With no fanfare, Gaetjens and his teammates took the long flight to Rio de Janeiro. Once there, they did what you'd expect of any group of young, single men on a work/play vacation: drink. "The Americans came strolling into the dressing rooms in Belo Horizonte, surely the strangest team ever to be seen at a World Cup," reported the *Belfast Telegraph*. "Some wore Stetsons, some smoked big cigars, and some were still in the happy, early stages of hangovers." For Gaetjens, this was apparently business as usual. "Joe always swore he played better if he parties—you know, caroused a little—the night before a game," remembered his teammate Harry Keough. "He said he stiffened up with too much sleep."

The first match, against Spain, started brightly with the U.S. taking a 1–0 lead before Spain regained control to win 3–1. The next game against the mighty Lions of England was such a foregone conclusion that a London bookmaker posted the odds of a U.S. victory at 500–1. England dominated the game, but in the 38th minute, Bahr cracked a long-range shot that had "routine" save written on it. Out of nowhere, Gaetjens launched himself headfirst in the direction of the ball and deflected it past an astonished English keeper. Lying face-down on the turf, Gaetjens never saw it go in, and the English media was quick to cast his goal as a piece of dumb luck, claiming that he was trying to duck out of the way of Bahr's drive when the ball struck him in the ear. "Those were the sort of goals that Joe scored," said Bahr. "He always went for the ball."

The U.S. held on for a historic 1–0 win that was later immotalized as "The Miracle on Grass." It was to be the last U.S. World Cup victory for 44 years and Gaetjens was carried off the field on the shoulders of jubilant Brazilian supporters.

After the World Cup, Gaetjens moved to France and played first division soccer for a few years before returning to Haiti, where he became a corporate spokesman for Palmolive, ran a dry cleaning business, and even played for his country in a World Cup qualifying match against Mexico.

Shortly thereafter, he ran afoul of vengeful Haitian despot "Papa Doc" Duvalier, because of his family's support of Duvalier's rival in an earlier election, and in July 1964, at the age of 40, he was kidnapped by the government's notorious secret police, the Tonton Macoutes. "They rushed to his car, put a gun on his head, got in his car, and drove," recalls younger brother Jean-Pierre of the last time he would see Gaetjens. For decades, the family tried and failed to find out what happened to Joe, and it wasn't until 1986, once the Duvalier regime was finally ousted, that they'd learn of his fate: According to a fellow prisoner at the Fort Dimanche hellhole where Gaetjens was taken, he had likely been executed a couple of weeks after his arrest.

"That's what we think . . . but we never knew," Jean-Pierre said. "They had destroyed any evidence on everybody that was killed at the time under Duvalier." It was a tragic and anonymous end for the United State's first soccer hero, but Gaetjens's legacy lives on in a book and movie celebrating that epic defeat of England, a place of honor in the U.S. Soccer Hall of Fame, and even on a Haitian stamp in the late 1990s.

Not bad for a dishwasher who, for one day, on a strip of grass in a Brazilian mining town, was the king of the soccer world.

Hungary and Brazil engage in a precious moment of soccer amid the brawling of the Battle of Bern.

1954
Switzerland

THEY'RE BA-ACK . . . !

The West Germans avenge their World War II loss, shocking everyone, especially the Magical Magyars of Hungary.

THE WISDOM OF MAINTAINING neutrality during global conflict was all too evident as its undamaged economy made Switzerland the only European contender for World Cup hosting duties. The Swiss put its creative financial skills to good use, unveiling two innovations. As a small commercial experiment, the Swiss mint issued a coin as the first official World Cup souvenir. This was also the

first tournament to be televised, with nine games broadcast by the European Broadcasting Union.

These seemingly inauspicious developments would eventually transform both the tournament and the sport itself, but for the moment a great naïveté surrounded much of the competition. The Scottish team's advance research reportedly consisted of skimming *Heidi;* assuming Switzerland to

be an Alpine clime, the Scots equipped themselves with heavy, long-sleeve woolen jerseys, only to wilt in Basel's 100-degree heat as the short-sleeve–wearing Uruguayans ran rings round them.

West Germany was permitted to rejoin soccer's global fraternity just under a decade after it was the enemy of all freedom lovers. Its domestic league was still besieged, but the squad was equipped with

Adidas founder Adi Dassler's revolutionary replaceable studs helped the West Germans to their first Cup.

two enviable assets. The first was their legendary coach, Joseph "Sepp" Herberger, a strategic maestro who focused obsessively on his team's conditioning. The second was the technological edge they derived from the research conducted by the Bavarian-born Adi Dassler and his fledgling sports manufacturer, Adidas. The company had developed a revolutionary boot with exchangeable screw-in studs, offering players the flexibility to adapt boots to conditions even mid-game. This ultimately proved to be a tremendous advantage during the final, which was played in a deluge.

The readmission of the Germans appeared to be just a detail. Hungary, known as the Magical Magyars, entered the World Cup as close to a sure thing as the tournament has ever had. Resplendent in their bright red shirts, they arrived in Switzerland with an undefeated streak of 31 games, a run during which they had become both Olympic champions and, perhaps just as impressively, humiliated England 6–3 to become the first continental team to conquer the nation that invented the game at Wembley Stadium. Inspired by their captain, Ferenc Puskás, a ferocious and creative attacking force known as the Galloping Major, the team was among the first to employ modern tactical formations in which players were able to both attack and defend in numbers. This World Cup was to be their crowning achievement (*see Greatest Teams, page 28*).

Hungary met West Germany early on in a group match. The wily Herberger executed the soccer equivalent of Muhammad Ali's patented rope-a-dope strategy, purposefully benching some of his best players and fielding a reserve team that Hungary quickly dispatched, 8–3. The loss allowed the crafty Germans to continue to fly below the radar while manipulating the tournament bracket to ensure they would avoid both Uruguay and Brazil in the next round. The game had the additional side effect of further swelling Hungary's ego, even though the mighty Puskás limped off the field with a hairline fracture of the ankle that would hamper him for the rest of the tournament.

THE GERMAN MIRACLE

The Magyars withstood more physical punishment during a legendarily brutal quarterfinal matchup against Brazil called "the Battle of Bern." The two sides were among the most artistic in the world. But the Brazilians were still traumatized by their finals loss to Uruguay in 1950 and determined not to go down without a fight—a literal one, it turned out. They elected to negate the craft of the Hungarians by outmuscling them. Two Brazilians and one Hungarian were given their marching orders, as players chased one another around the field, intent on kicking each other rather than the ball. Even the great Puskás, though injured and in

street clothes, entered the fray, using a glass bottle to dispatch an opponent in the locker room with a blow to the head.

Hungary survived and, after nipping Uruguay in extra time, went on to meet the unseeded West Germans in the final at Wankdorf Stadium. Battered, but drawing confidence from their crushing victory over Germany in the opening round of the tournament, they entered the game heavily favored—the equivalent of the Baltimore Colts on the eve of Super Bowl III against the New York Jets. Yet it was impossible for oddsmakers to handicap the intangibles. Both teams were motivated by a domestic wave of nationalist sentiment. The West German's unexpected achievement offered a postwar panacea for a nation suffering a collective depression, while Hungary's success gave its fans, trapped behind the Iron Curtain, an outlet for their feelings toward the communist dictatorship many despised.

(above) Uruguay's Juan Hohberg fainted after scoring his second goal against Hungary in the semifinal, but was revived in time to see his team lose, 4–2; (right) England kicked off its long tradition of losing in the quarterfinals by falling to Uruguay, 4–2.

Within eight minutes of the kickoff, Hungary was ahead 2–0, with Puskás scoring first, confounding those who alleged that the injured Hungarian captain was selected only to collect the cup. The Germans looked dead and buried, but clawed their way back to tie by the 18th minute. After the break, and aided by the driving rain, their Adidas boots, and perhaps by vitamin C injections, they demonstrated the relentless organization and efficiency that would become their hallmark, scrambling across the go-ahead goal with just over five minutes to go. Luck was also with them—another German trait. Hungary hit the post, had a shot cleared off the line, and a second Puskás goal was incorrectly ruled to be offside, helping the West Germans to pull off their equivalent of the Miracle on Ice. On July 4, 1954, 9 years after the collapse of the Third Reich, West Germany was *Weltmeister* once more.

Despite the Hungarian authorities' broadcast of a specially edited version of the game in which Hungary appeared to control the ball for 90 percent of the match, they could not change the final score, and hundreds of thousands of people flooded the streets of Budapest, using soccer as a pretext to demonstrate against the regime. Most of the team went into exile after the Soviets invaded in 1956. The German victory, now known as "the Miracle of Bern," invigorated a nation in recovery. *Der Spiegel* remarked pretentiously that "after 2000 years of taking the wrong path, the Germans have now discovered the true destiny of their national existence." Many historians regard the victory as a key catalyst for the economic miracle that transformed the shattered country into a European superpower.

One can only wonder how the continent's history would have been different had Puskás's disallowed goal actually stood. . . .

1954 RESULTS

QUARTERFINALS
Austria 7 Switzerland 5
Uruguay 4 England 2
Hungary 4 Brazil 2
West Germany 2 Yugoslavia 0

SEMIFINALS
West Germany 6 Austria 1
Hungary 4 Uruguay 2

THIRD PLACE
Austria 3 Uruguay 1

FINALS
West Germany 3 Hungary 2

High bräu: Fritz Walter toasts his World Cup–winning teammates.

CULT FIGURES

FRITZ WALTER, WEST GERMANY

"Not for an instant do I think about the unusual company I play with or what strange ground I'm moving across. For me, the left-winger is just a left-winger. That he's also a Slovak doesn't occur to me. What do I care that the inside-right is from Hungary? We're footballers and nothing else."

Fritz Walter, quoted in one of his many autobiographies, understood the universality of soccer as well as anyone. After all, it saved his life. Drafted into the war in 1943, Walter was captured and interned at an American POW camp. He remained there for weeks, waiting for the eventual handover to the Russians, who were expected to ship out all 40,000 soldiers to Siberia—and almost certain death. Walter was resigned to his fate once he found himself among a trainload of prisoners heading east, with one last stop at a Ukrainian processing center. There he watched a group of policemen playing soccer when a mishit ball ended up at his feet. Still in heavy army boots, he effortlessly lobbed it back into play, a piece of skill that none of the policemen had ever seen before on the prison grounds. It wasn't long before they invited Walter to join their game, which he promptly dominated.

At halftime, a policeman stepped forward. "I know you," he said. "Hungary versus Germany in Budapest, 1942. You won 5–3." That brief exchange spelled the end of his internment—the next day he found his name had been removed from a list of Siberia-bound prisoners—and the beginning of his new position as the trainer of the prison camp's soccer team. Once the war was over in 1945, Walter was released and returned home, where he arguably became the most celebrated German soccer player of all time and the man who captained his country's first ever World Cup championship team.

By the time Germany was permitted to rejoin the interational soccer community in 1954, Walter was 34, but he had become a feared goal-scorer at his club, FC Kaiserslautern, and the leader of the national team. Even with Walter and his younger brother Ottmar spearheading the attack, West Germany wasn't expected to make it out of the group phase. Yet it advanced to the final to play, of all opponents, Hungary's Magical Magyars, who had not lost a soccer match in five years and had already demolished West Germany 8–3 in their opening-round game.

The final, held in Bern, Switzerland, took place during a torrential downpour. This gave West Germany three advantages. The first was that it diminished Hungary's slick ball movement; the second was that Germany's cleats were supplied by Adidas, which had invented the world's first replaceable stud, which gave the Germans superior footing. Finally, the rain and cold helped suppress the symptoms of Walter's malaria, contracted during his POW internment. The worse the weather, the better he played.

The game itself became one of the most hallowed in Cup history—*Das Wunder von Bern*, the Germans named it—in which West Germany stormed back from two goals down to upset the mighty Hungarians. Far more important, though, was its effect on the German people. Director Sönke Wortmann, who shot an award-winning film about the 1954 squad, said, "It was vital for the people who lived in Germany at that time. Everybody who is older than sixty knows exactly where they were on July 4, 1954. That feeling only happened again when the Berlin Wall came down."

In 2004, on the occasion of UEFA's Golden Jubilee, the Germans selected Fritz Walter as their greatest player of the previous 50 years. But perhaps more impressive is his lasting influence on Germany's meteorological small talk. To this day, whenever it rains, German soccer fans smile knowingly and say, "It's Fritz Walter weather."

GREATEST TEAMS

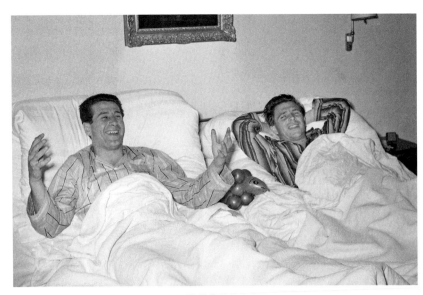

HUNGARY, 1954

In November of 1953, Hungary paid a visit to Wembley Stadium, the English soccer fortress where no team from outside the British Isles had ever been victorious. When the Hungarians were led out by their captain, a squat homunculus named Ferenc Puskás who was known as the Galloping Major, even though he didn't gallop and was only a lieutenant.

"Look at that fat little chap," one English player said. "We'll murder this lot."

The Magical Magyars may have been the reigning Olympic champions and gone 31 games without a loss (still a world record), but the Iron Curtain had hid their true genius from public view. Until now. Six goals, two of them by that small, round fellow with a howitzer for a left foot, silenced all of the skeptics and moved England's Billy Wright to call Hungary "the finest team ever to sort out successfully the intricacies of this wonderful game."

Since the 1954 World Cup was the first in history to be televised, soccer fans outside of Budapest (and England) would finally get to witness how Hungary had revolutionized the game with its visionary 4-2-4 formation. By deploying four men up top and only two in midfield, Hungary turned the prevailing tactical wisdom of the rest of the world on its head. In some respects, Hungary was Brazil before Brazil came along to use the same formation to win back-to-back Cups in '58 and '62. They were also the spiritual forefathers of the Dutch Total Football system that would bedazzle the world in the 1970s with versatility and interchangeability

throughout the lineup. Strikers would retreat deep to pick up possession before launching an attack, and opposing defenses, not knowing whether to pursue, would get sucked out of position, leaving acres of space for the Magyars to run riot.

Responsible for most of the mayhem was the Holy Trinity of Ferenc Puskás, Sándor Kocsis, and Nandor Hidegkuti. Of the three, Puskás was the glamour boy, though he hardly looked the part. "If a good player has the ball, he should have the vision to spot three options," said Hungarian full-back Jeno Buzanski. "Puskás always saw at least five." And that was when he was hungover. His drinking and cavorting were legendary; the Scottish winger Jim Baxter once claimed that the Hungarian knew only two words in England: "vhisky," which is self-explanatory, and "jiggy-jig," which is what a few whiskies often led to at the end of the night.

On the field, however, Puskás was all business, exhorting his teammates to match his intensity. They responded magnificently as Hungary laid siege to the '54 World Cup. Kocsis, known as "Golden Head," scored 11 goals in the tournament, including two hat tricks, but it was Hidegkuti, a converted striker, who was at the heart of the Magyars' passing and movement.The Magyars managed a remarkable 27 goals in just five games (still a World Cup record) while coping admirably with desperate defenses hacking away at Hungarian limbs. Unfortunately, one particularly clumsy attempt in Hungary's group stage romp over West Germany, which would become known as "the tackle that won the World Cup,"

hobbled Puskás for the rest of the tournament.

It remains one of soccer's great injustices that Hungary was not at full strength for what should have been the capstone of its memorable run. While the team started the final against the Germans with a damaged Puskás in the lineup, his presence wasn't enough to prevent defeat. Despite going ahead 2–0 after eight minutes, the Magyars were ground down by a fresher and more resourceful German side and lost 3–2. The result, known as the Miracle of Bern, was a watershed for German soccer and was eventually immortalized in a 2003 movie that is still one of Germany's bestselling films.

Two years later, the Hungarian Revolution of 1956 would convulse the country and scatter the team's players; six of the 11 men who played in the 1954 World Cup final left the national team during the political chaos, while the coaching staff was exiled to all corners of the globe. Constantly harassed, Puskás moved to Spain. The Hungarian government threatened him with treason charges and banned his name from the nation's media for a decade and a half. Goalkeeper Gyula Grosics, whose blunders in the World Cup contributed to Hungary's implosion, was arrested and detained. It was a bitter end to what would be Hungarian soccer's finest era. The closest any generation came to the Golden Team was in the late '70s, when the Hungarians successfully qualified for three World Cups in a row. They exited each tournament in the first round, however, suggesting that the weight of history might simply have been too much for them.

ALFREDO DI STÉFANO

"I don't know if I was a better player than Pelé," Maradona once mused, "but I can say without any doubt that di Stéfano was better than Pelé."

How good was Alfredo di Stéfano? If you were compiling an All-World team from the '50s and '60s, the man known as the Blond Arrow might occupy three spots—in attack, midfield, and defense—because he played them all with devastating versatility in the course of a single game. A deadly finisher? Check. A tireless playmaker with speed and guile? Check. Strong in the tackle and powerful in the air? Check.

Nominally a center-forward, di Stéfano had license to roam everywhere, one minute scoring a goal, the next clearing the ball off his own line. In fact, about the only thing di Stéfano didn't do was play in a World Cup. And because of that hole in his résumé, when it comes to the Greatest Players of All Time, he can do no better than the bronze medal, though his peers would argue otherwise. "I had

never seen such a complete footballer," the English icon Bobby Charlton once remarked. "It was as though he had set up his own command center at the heart of the game."

Trouble was, di Stéfano spent almost as much time in passport offices as on the field. During his glorious 23-year career, he represented three different countries—Argentina, Spain, and Colombia—and didn't make the World Cup with any of them. It didn't matter that he bestrode the summit of European soccer, playing alongside the domineering Hungarian Ferenc Puskás and the electrifying Spaniard Francisco Gento in the storied Real Madrid sides of that era. Together, they won five consecutive European Cups, culminating in the 7–3 carpet bombing of Eintracht Frankfurt in the 1960 final that is generally regarded as the most brilliant display in that tournament's history. Di Stéfano scored a hat trick in that game (Puskás got the other four) and was twice voted European Player of the Year.

But his genius was never certified at the highest level of competition.

In 1950, when di Stéfano was playing for Argentina, his country didn't send a team to the tournament out of protest for FIFA anointing Brazil as World Cup hosts. Four years later, he couldn't outpace the faceless bureaucrats from FIFA, who declared him ineligible for the World Cup because he had switched from Argentina to Colombia. By 1958, di Stéfano had been a Spanish citizen for two years, but his adopted country failed to advance by a single point. He made one last attempt in 1962 at age 36, carrying Spain through qualifying, only to injure himself and miss the tournament. Di Stéfano once said that "a soccer game without goals is like an afternoon without sunshine," yet the man who scored more than 800 goals before retiring never saw the light of a World Cup.

BRAZIL FINDS ITS TEEN ANGEL

France plays "Champagne Football," but Brazil unveils Pelé, and drinks the real thing.

IN THE EYES OF the Brazilian nation, the U.S. and USSR's obsession with the cultural, technological, and ideological dimensions of the Space Race was misplaced. The capture of the Jules Rimet Cup was Brazil's great national project, for which the country's best and brightest were put to work. The president made unprecedented financial resources available to ensure that his team would not repeat the disaster of 1950. Its players underwent intensive preparation, benefiting from pioneering sports psychology and medicine to counter maladies that ranged from intestinal parasites to the syphilis that ravaged the entire squad. More than 300 teeth were extracted from 33 players, who had never been to a dentist. For every player there was an elaborate and revolutionary individualized training regime. There was even room left for a little quackery: One doctor had players trace a vertical line on a piece of paper while being slapped between the eyes.

Brazil left no detail untouched. Female employees were removed from the team hotel, although the Brazilian authorities failed in their efforts to have a nearby nudist camp shut down during the competition. On the field, its graceful soccer utterly dominated the tournament. Its opening-round game against the much-feared Soviet team, which was rumored to have employed rooms of computers to prepare for the clash, proved its potency (and possibly set back the embryonic computer industry). It unleashed the dribbling maestro Garrincha and a 17-year-old waif named Pelé, both of whom had been reserves to that point. They provided the greatest opening three minutes that Brazilian soccer has ever witnessed, taking turns hitting the post before the wonderfully named Vavá finally scored—all in all, a performance akin to a boxer dismantling his opponent in the first round. At one point, Garrincha dribbled through five players. In the words of Brazilian commentator Luiz Mendes, "Russia put the first man in space but they were unable to mark Garrincha."

CHAMPAGNE FOOTBALL GOES FLAT

This was the only World Cup for which each of the "Home Nations"—England, Scotland, Northern Ireland, and Wales—qualified. England, the most serious contender of the four, was hurt when an airplane crash in Munich four months earlier killed eight Manchester United players. France was unheralded, led by the Moroccan-born French forward, Just Fontaine, who arrived as a reserve but seized the moment by scoring 13 goals. The French team rode its attacking "Champagne football" all the way into the semifinal, only to be overwhelmed by Brazil.

In the other semifinal, the Swedes befuddled the West Germans with their unusual gamesmanship.

(left) Brazilian winger Vavá scores his team's first goal in a 5–2 thrashing of France; (below) Seventeen-year-old Pelé would keep his eyes on the prize for three of the next four Cups.

Bite me: Fontaine holds the record for most goals in a single World Cup—13.

CULT FIGURES

JUST FONTAINE, FRANCE

First they prevented German fans from taking their seats, then they employed a frenzied team of cheerleaders to stir up the crowd from the center of the field. The home fans were whipped into an almost riotous state and the match was as good as won before the players took the field. The World Cup Organizing Committee took a dim view of these antics, and the controversial Swedish cheerleaders found themselves banned for the final. Deprived of their muses, the home fans were bereft and the Brazilians strolled to victory, despite falling behind on an early goal. The only unfamiliar aspect of the Brazilians' balletic interplay was the blue jerseys they wore—with team badges haphazardly applied—to help distinguish them from the Swedes. Brazil stroked the ball masterfully around the field while both Brazilian and Swedish fans accompanied each pass with delirious cries of *"Samba! Samba!"* Pelé scored two delicious goals during the 5–2 rout, collapsing to his knees in tears at the final whistle, causing the world to pretty much fall in love with him. The Cup was Brazil's at last. The team graciously paraded around the stadium with the Swedish flag aloft, and as photographers screamed at the captain, Bellini, to make the cup more visible, he raised it over his head, patenting the standard pose for every winner that followed. There was apparently no end to Brazilian creativity.

The legend of the man who holds the record for the most goals scored in any World Cup has two surprising footnotes: He wasn't born in France and he wasn't supposed to be on the team.

Just Fontaine excelled for his club Stade de Reims, notching an astonishing 121 goals in 131 games. Equally imposing with the ball at his feet or in the air, Fontaine claimed he could "jump so high to head the ball that when I come down again, I have snow in my hair." And yet the Moroccan-born striker, originally "discovered" at the obscure club U.S. Marocaine de Casablanca and "repatriated" to France, couldn't hold his place on the national team, thanks to the strength and depth that the French boasted up front.

When the World Cup rolled around in 1958, "Justo" found himself on the bubble until his Reims teammate, René Bliard, picked up a late injury. Fontaine, ever the opportunist, was drafted into the French squad at the last moment and, in his excitement, forgot to pack his shoes. "I found myself with nothing," he would recall later. "Luckily, Stéphane Bruey, one of the second-choice strikers, wore the same size as me and lent me his boots."

Alongside his strike partner Raymond Kopa, the duo, known as *"Le Tandem Terrible,"* obliterated all who stood before them, with Fontaine scoring goals in every conceivable fashion: seven with his right foot, five with his left, and one with his head. After a hat trick in France's opener against Paraguay, he scored at least one goal in every game. While France eventually lost to Brazil in the semis, when a 17-year-old named Pelé knocked in three goals of his own, for Monsieur Dynamite the best was still to come.

In the consolation game against the 1954 champion West Germans, Fontaine struck four times to lead Les Bleus to a 6–3 win and an unlikely third-place finish. All this for a team that, heading into the World Cup, hadn't won a single match in 1958, but had tied often enough to qualify.

Sadly, Fontaine disappeared from the game as quickly as he arrived, after twice breaking his leg in the same place and being forced into early retirement at age 26. Still, the closest anyone has come to his record for a single World Cup was 44 years later. After Brazil's Ronaldo managed eight goals in the 2002 tournament, the 68-year-old Fontaine remarked: "My record still stands. I think I'll take it to my grave!"

As for the boots he borrowed from a teammate? "Six matches and thirteen goals later, I gave them back. I like to think some of my goals were inspired by combining two spirits inside the same shoe."

CAMPEONATO MUNDIAL DE FUTBOL
WORLD FOOTBALL CHAMPIONSHIP
CHAMPIONNAT MONDIAL DE FOOTBALL
COUPE JULES RIMET

CHILE
1962

WORLD CUP

JULY 11 to 30
1966
ENGLAND

MEXICO 70

IX football world championship

may 31 – june 21

'62 '66 '70

THE WORLD CUP GOES GLOBAL

History repeats: Brazil defeats Chile 4–2 in the semis en route to winning their second successive Cup.

1962
Chile

THE EMPIRE STRIKES BACK

Despite a widespread emphasis on defensive soccer and an injury to the world's greatest player, Brazil will not be held back.

CHILE WAS AWARDED the World Cup in 1956, but in 1960 the most powerful earthquake ever made hosting in 1962 inconceivable until the chairman of the country's soccer federation successfully appealed to FIFA, pleading, "You must give us the tournament as we have nothing else." The claim was effective, but not strictly true. The country also had the technology to televise the Cup internationally—

When Garrincha (left) and Pelé were in the lineup together, the Brazilian national team never lost a single game; (right) Yugoslav goalkeeper Milutin Soskic makes an acrobatic save against Chile.

1962 RESULTS

QUARTERFINALS
Brazil 3 England 1
Chile 2 Soviet Union 1
Yugoslavia 1 West Germany 0
Czechoslovakia 1 Hungary 0

SEMIFINALS
Brazil 4 Chile 2
Czechoslovakia 3 Yugoslavia 1

THIRD PLACE
Chile 1 Yugoslavia 0

FINALS
Brazil 3 Czechoslovakia 1

albeit in black-and-white—to a handful of bordering countries. A mere 5,000 people watched one of the semifinals in person, making this the last truly small-scale World Cup.

On the field, the quality of play was compromised by a rule change: Goal differential was adopted as a group stage tiebreaker. Unintentionally, this helped usher in an era of defensive soccer in which teams strived to prevent opponents from scoring rather than actively trying to win. Predictably, the Italians were masters of this dark art, with their *Catenaccio*—or door bolt—defense, designed to stifle opponents by removing the space for them to play. The sinuous Brazilians would have to learn how to adjust on the fly, but their title defense had more immediate problems. Once again they had tried to leave no preparatory detail to chance, even dispatching a medical team to confirm that the government-approved brothels were disease-free. But no amount of planning could have prepared the team for the groin injury Pelé suffered in just the second game. Cometh the hour, cometh the man. Garrincha, no longer forced to share the stage

with his more telegenic partner, stepped up to turn in one of the virtuoso performances in World Cup history. In the quarterfinals against England, he scored two goals and created a third, then capped off this masterful display by adopting a stray dog that had wandered onto the field and urinated on England's star striker, Jimmy Greaves.

PELÉ'S PAIN, GARRINCHA'S GAIN

Against Chile in "the Battle of Santiago," the Italians' reputation for aggression solidified into legend. It was one of the most violent games in World Cup history, more martial arts demonstration than soccer match—a match so shocking that the BBC saw fit to preface a broadcast of the game film with the following warning: "Good evening. The game you are about to see is the most stupid, appalling, disgusting, and disgraceful exhibition of football, possibly in the history of the game." It took just 12 seconds for the first foul to be inflicted and eight minutes for the first player to be sent off—an Italian midfielder, Giorgio Ferrini, who refused to leave the field and had to be forcibly removed by

police. After attempting to officiate the 90-minute riot, referee Ken Aston was inspired to invent yellow and red cards in the wake, admitting that "I wasn't reffing a football match, I was acting as an umpire in military maneuvers." (*See Oh, Behave!, page 39.*)

The Chileans were dispatched by their Brazilian neighbors, or rather by Garrincha, in the semifinal. Again, he scored twice and set up a third, but this time was sent off after retaliating against a defender (and, for good measure, then being hit on the head by a bottle as he walked off the field). The dismissal ought to have meant an automatic suspension for the final, but he was controversially reinstated for the game, in which Brazil repeated their trick of giving up a goal before they handily defeated the Czechs 3–1 and defended their title. Pelé had not been missed. Garrincha was the star, although the adulation he received would contribute to his early demise. He lived a life of increasing alcoholism, debauchery, and destitution for 21 more years. Over time, he would become an increasingly obscure figure in Brazil's ever-more-storied legacy.

LEV YASHIN, USSR

Johnny Cash may have walked the line as the Man in Black, but if he had to stand in front of a soccer ball hurtling toward him at 70 mph, the odds are that he would have ducked. Not so with the legendary Russian Lev Yashin, who, sheathed all in black from his cleats to his signature newsboy cap, defended *his* line with such aplomb that he remains the only goalkeeper to have ever been selected European Player of the Year.

All loose-limbed and heavy-lidded, he appeared so relaxed between the posts that you half expected to see a cigarette dangling from his lips, as one did for most of the 22 hours that he wasn't on the soccer field. Asked once about his pregame preparation, he replied, "Have a smoke to calm your nerves, then toss back a strong drink to tone your muscles."

But his languid appearance belied a fierce intensity and a catlike ability to pounce at the first scent of danger. What drove him was not so much the thrill of a great save, but avoiding the agony of a goal. "What kind of a goalkeeper is the one who

is not tormented by the goal he has allowed?" he once asked. "He must be tormented! And if he is calm, that means the end. No matter what he had in the past, he has no future."

Although there may have been more flamboyant and acrobatic keepers over the years, none revolutionized the game like Yashin. He was the first to athletically command the entire penalty area—punching the ball away on crosses and corner kicks, and marshaling his defenders by bellowing at them so loudly his wife once asked him to stop. Sometimes he even showed his defenders how to do their job, surging out of his penalty area to break up an attack himself. He became the embodiment of the modern goalkeeper—nimble, brave, and supremely confident. And he owed it all to . . . ice hockey.

Unable to break into the starting lineup of his soccer club, Dynamo Moscow, he grew increasingly frustrated and turned briefly to his country's other favorite sport, playing goalie on the team that won the USSR Ice Hockey Cup in 1953. On

the ice, he developed the acute positional sense that his longtime goalkeeping rival, England's Gordon Banks, deemed his greatest strength, one that enabled him to reportedly stone 150 penalty kicks during his storied career. "The joy of seeing Yuri Gagarin flying in space," Yashin famously quipped, "is only superseded by the joy of a good penalty save."

After permanently trading in his skates for soccer boots, he appeared in three World Cups for the USSR and played until he was 41 years old, by which time he had amassed an astonishing 270 career shutouts. When he retired in 1971, he was hailed as his country's greatest athlete and remained a national hero until his death in 1990—which some believe was hastened by a botched surgery four years earlier, when doctors amputated his leg. In 1994, FIFA introduced a new prize to the World Cup for the best goalkeeper of the tournament. To nobody's surprise, they called it the Yashin Award.

OH, BEHAVE!

The Genius Who Gave the World Yellow and Red Cards

Like many great ideas, the card system was born of misfortune: Englishman Ken Aston was at the center of two similar refereeing calamities. He was selected to referee the infamously feisty game between Chile and Italy at the 1962 World Cup, now known as the Battle of Santiago, in which the two teams were at each other's throats before a ball had been kicked. During the match, Aston, who had been a lieutenant colonel in Asia during World War II and was no stranger to conflict, had to dismiss two players, and needed armed police to intervene on three separate occasions.

By 1966 Aston, who had been promoted to oversee all tournament referees, was in a position to do something when a brutality-filled quarterfinal between England and Argentina threatened to descend into farce. Argentina's captain, Antonio Rattín, refused to leave the field after being sent off by a German referee for arguing. How the referee knew exactly what Rattín had said was never established, as the official spoke no Spanish. The communication barrier was all too obvious when Rattín and the Argentinians then argued with the ref for more than 20 minutes. Aston finally came onto the field to talk to the Argentinian captain, before realizing that the only language he would understand was being dragged off the field by two policemen.

On Aston's drive home from the game, he was waiting in his car at a red light on a busy Kensington High Street when he had his bright—and brightly colored—idea for removing all language barriers. He recalled, "I thought, *Yellow. Take it easy. And Red. Stop. You're off.*"

The cards made their tournament debut in 1970 and have since become standard worldwide. The Soviet Union's Evgeni Lovchev went down in history as the first recipient of a yellow card in the opening game, but remarkably, it was not until 1974 that someone—Carlos Caszely of Chile—achieved the dubious honor of being the first World Cup player to see red. The cherry-colored card has seen a lot of action since then. It was held aloft 28 times in 2006 alone.

The Battle of Santiago: before the cards were dealt.

Bigger than Jesus

PELÉ
Brazil: 1958, 1962, 1966, 1970

Jesus. Gandhi. Bono. The truly great are universally known by a single name. Pelé, born Edson Arantes do Nascimento, is no exception. If your knowledge of soccer is one player deep, odds are it's him, thanks to his role as the face of American soccer with the New York Cosmos in the 1970s. But long before his U.S. cameo, he was the finest soccer player the world had ever seen. The gold standard against whom all are measured. A prolific goal scorer who combined power, speed, and masterful control of the ball, to embody the joyous soccer fantasy that was the Seleção Brasileira in its prime.

Pelé's career was a long-running highlight reel of his play for a Brazilian team that was World Champion three times in 12 years. His legend began the instant he made his debut as a scrawny 17-year-old in the 1958 World Cup, where he showed few nerves in the final, nonchalantly lobbing the ball over a defender's head, running around him, and volleying it into the corner of the net for the first of two goals. But perhaps Pelé's ingenuity and audacity were equally well captured by his near misses in 1970. Against Uruguay in the semifinals, he galloped in one-on-one, allowing the ball to run one way while he swept the other, using his body as a decoy to fake out the goalie. While the open goal beckoned, Pelé reconnected with the ball only to slide his shot inches wide of the post—a move that, like the Venus de Milo, was all the more beautiful for its ultimate imperfection.

In his autobiography, Pelé attributed his success to his dazzling control, and his dazzling control to the poverty of his youth. Legend has it he learned to play the game barefoot, using a ball made of worn-out socks. But he was also the beneficiary of great timing. His debut coincided with the advent of live broadcasting of the tournament; that perfect timing, combined with telegenic good looks and otherworldly skills, turned him into the world's first soccer superstar. The only Brazilian of his generation to have an agent and a manager, he became a global brand after he trademarked his name, lending it to MasterCard, Pepsi, Atari, and the John Huston cult film *Victory* (in which he pretty much played himself, predictably scoring a magnificent goal in the final).

He had enough talent to stop a war. His appearance in Lagos for an exhibition game led to a 48-hour cease-fire in Nigeria's civil war so both sides could see him play. More impressive than his 12 World Cup goals in 13 games was his longevity in an era when loose refereeing meant the game was at its most punishing. Despite the beating he received, which led him to threaten to retire on more than one occasion, he dominated the game for over two decades. As Henry Kissinger wrote of Pelé in *Time* magazine's 100 "Most Important People of the Century" issue, "Performance at a high level in any sport is to exceed the ordinary human scale. But Pelé's performance transcended that of the ordinary star by as much as the star exceeds ordinary performance."

THE DNA OF THE WORLD'S GREATEST TEAMS

Brazil is the one dynasty in sport it is impossible to hate. Its soccer tradition does not so much compete with other teams as exist—like the Bolshoi Ballet—on a different level. The *Seleção* has been so dominant, it feels as if it either leaves victorious or having been proclaimed moral victors. Brazil's World Cup performances have been so consistent that they amount to an alternative way of retelling the history of the tournament itself. For supporters, however, winning is not enough. When Brazil loses, flags fly at half-mast, suicides abound, and government inquiries are convened.

For Brazilians, individual precociousness always trumps collective performance. They adore the flick, hip feints, rhythm and movement—soccer forged from samba and Carnaval. Some trace their style to *capoeira*, the martial art invented by African slaves, who originally disguised their fighting style as a dance to fool their masters. Folklore abounds with stories of the *Malandro*, a black or mixed-race rogue who works alone and obeys no one. Poor yet flamboyant, the master of the con, he is irresistible to women—many of the qualities Brazilians love in their soccer players. In 2007, after a World Cup qualifier with Ecuador, petulant striker Robinho was rumored to have ordered a security guard to

The Brazilian team celebrates its 1958 World Cup victory by carrying host Sweden's national flag.

rustle up 40—yes, 40—condoms before heading to an all-night party. The request barely caused a ripple in Brazil; after all, the team had won 5–0 and a man deserves to let his hair down.

The ultimate *Malandro* was Garrincha, the winger who co-starred with Pelé in the first Brazil-ian team to win the World Cup, in 1958. He also reclaimed the trophy four years later without Pelé, who was injured in the first game. Born with bent legs, one curving inward, the other outward, Garrincha never trained, was virtually uncoachable, and, perhaps because he had a famously low IQ,

Italy lifts the Cup after its penalty shoot-out victory over France in the 2006 final.

cared little for tactics. To him, the ball was his "girlfriend" and he played for kicks. His trademark move was to beat a defender, allow him to recover, and then beat him again. The Brazilian writer Nelson Rodrigues summed up his complexities when he offered this backhanded compliment: "He is considered a retard, but Garrincha proved in the World Cup that we are the retarded ones because we think. We rationalize. Next to the prodigious instantaneity of his reflexes we are laggards, bovines, hippopotamuses."

The free-flowing archetype traditionally associated with the *Seleção* has been threatened recently. Brazil has struggled to deliver the beautiful game its fans demand while adjusting to the need for more discipline, speed, and better defense in the more aggressive modern era. In 1966, the world wised up and discovered that the way to beat the Brazilians was not to play them, but to kick them; the battering Brazil received from the European teams forced it to add defensive steel to their offensive flamboyance, a delicate and often unachievable tactical balance. And there are other challenges, like the piles of cash that elite club teams heap on Brazilian superstars, numbing many of them to the glory of representing the yellow and green. When the team plays qualifying games in Brazil, a number of the European-based players have excused

themselves from the long trip home, and when they do play, their joy and spontaneity has noticeably declined. Brazil's 2006 team was loaded with marquee names, but went out with a whimper in the quarterfinals. Cynics would say that the most stylish soccer they have played in the past two decades was in a 1998 Nike promo in which they flipped the ball around an airport during flight delay, chipping it over the baggage carousels and onto the runway hacky-sack style—a visual treat, but the kind of spontaneity that earlier teams could produce live, in one take, without the aid of editing, in the World Cup final proper.

Brazil must also contend with the new reality that soccer players are one of Brazil's leading exports. Over 10,000 Brazilians play around the world every year as the nation acts like a global fish farm, stocking rosters in leagues from Iceland to Israel. These players have begun to shed their Brazilian identities, naturalizing to play for their "adopted" countries at such a rapid clip that FIFA President Sepp Blatter recently predicted, "If we don't take care about the invaders from Brazil, then at the next World Cups we will have 16 teams full of Brazilian players." With Pepe and Deco driving Portugal, Marcos Senna anchoring the Spanish midfield, and Tulio Tanaka holding the line for Japan, he may have a point, but his real

worry are rich fringe teams like Qatar who have taken this to an extreme, littering their teams with Brazilians and even offering stars like striker Ailton a million dollars to represent the state after he lit up the German Bundesliga, despite the fact that he had never set foot in the country.

Combined, these factors place immense pressure on Brazil every time they take to the pitch. The weight of its own history often offers more of a challenge than its opponents. Carlos Parreira, its coach in 2006 (and the coach of South Africa in 2010), vented his frustration to the media with the grandiose lament, "Why does Brazil have to play beautifully and the others don't?" But it is this history that sets them apart. Unless you are from Argentina, it is impossible not to admire and respect them. For everyone else living outside of Brazil, it is their second-favorite team.

ITALY: THE *AZZURRI*
WINNERS: 1934, 1938, 1982, 2006
FINALISTS: 1970, 1994

Man for man, the Italians are the hunkiest-looking team the World Cup has ever seen, as they take the field tight of shirt, olive of skin, and flowing of hair. Their World Cup track record matches their looks. They are the most successful European team in tournament history (they've won the Cup four times to Germany's three), but this record has been built on a negative, defensive style of soccer motivated chiefly by the fear of losing. They are masters of the black arts of the dive and the professional foul. Unpenalized cheating is celebrated. They've even coined a word for it—*Furbo*, gamesmanship—and elevated it to one of the game's highest values.

Even so, the Italian team has become one of the country's few truly beloved national symbols. So central is it to national life that Silvio Berlusconi used his ownership of domestic soccer power AC Milan as a platform for his successful presidential campaign, even stealing a slogan straight from the terraces—*"Forza Italia!"*—for the name of his party, the equivalent of Barack Obama running for the White House as a member of the "Let's Go, White

Sox!" faction. Every four years Italians lay aside their considerable regional rivalries to cheer on a team stocked with players from both north and south. In fact, the nationalist jingoism surrounding the team has become so powerful that the nation was scandalized when fans realized their players were not singing the Italian national anthem, as is the tradition before kickoff. Many accused the players of being ashamed of their own country, and demanded an inquest into why they sang without passion. An embarrassed spokesman was forced to step forward and admit that as the anthem is so rarely sung and the verses are long and tricky, the team simply did not know the words. Hilarity ensued.

The team's emotional following is at odds with its constipated defensive style, designed to produce, if possible, 1–0 victories. Other teams do not share the Azzurri's opinion that the strategy—*catenaccio*, or door bolt—is a thing of beauty. From the 1960s on, their team's calling card has been a highly organized back line: Four defenders shut down opposing attackers while a fifth roams freely among them to put out any fires. Meanwhile, the team relies on breakaways to steal a goal, after which it applies a sleeper hold on the entire game. Watching Italy play at its best is like watching a chess grandmaster play several moves ahead of his opponent. After witnessing AC Milan and Juventus dissect each other in the 2003 Champions League final, even *The Times* of London had to concede that "Football is an Italian game that just happens to have been invented in England."

One of the Italian scheme's downsides, of course, is how it marginalizes brilliant strikers. Improvisers such as Sandro Mazzola and Gianni Rivera in the '60s and '70s, Roberto Baggio in the '90s, and Francesco Totti in the '00s, all achieved far more for their club than their country. The team's steadfast commitment to winning ugly has typically meant the unpredictable genius has either been viewed as an unaffordable extravagance or miscast out of position as a lonely, isolated striker. Strangely, then, Italy has an uncanny ability to discover world-class strikers in the course of the tournament. In 1982, after serving a two-year suspension for match-

Jürgen Klinsmann and the Germans: annoyingly consistent?

fixing, an out-of-shape Paolo Rossi transformed himself overnight into a goal-scoring machine. Most mythically, Salvatore "Totò" Schillaci entered the 1990 World Cup as an obscure, bulbous-eyed benchwarmer and proceeded to crash in crucial goals from all points to end as the tournament's top scorer (*see Cult Figures, page 153*).

The more Italy has been written off, the better it does. In the modern era, its victories in both 1982 and 2006 followed periods when their domestic leagues had been plagued by corruption and match-fixing charges. While the Azzurri often begin tournaments slowly, they are never better than when the Italian game is mired in scandal and the team has nothing to lose.

GERMANY: *DIE NATIONALELF*
WINNERS: 1954, 1974, 1990
FINALISTS: 1966, 1982, 1986 (ALL AS WEST GERMANY); 2002

Germany is the Walmart of world soccer—a highly functioning, but belittled powerhouse. Athletic, pragmatic, and organized, it's been annoyingly consistent, typically dredging a path to the semifinals or beyond, a reality that forced English soccer legend turned television pundit Gary Lineker to quip that

"Football is a simple game—twenty-two men chase a ball for ninety minutes and at the end the Germans win." When you couple Germany's unparalleled determination and preparation—qualities admirable in any other team—with the country's historic propensity to wage war on a global scale, it's no wonder that *Die Nationalelf* has more rivalries than almost every other team combined. The Germans couldn't care less; for them, every match is a grudge match and the team can't wait to wear out all comers.

The legendary 1970s star Franz Beckenbauer cast his long shadow over the team as a player, captain, coach, and bureaucrat, but the team's traits are perhaps best personified by Gerd Müller, the striker who scored the winning goal in the 1974 World Cup final and was nicknamed Der Bomber, a harmless moniker at home perhaps, but provocative for countries who had been on the wrong end of the Blitz. In the same way Dennis Rodman was a rebounding fool, the thick, squat Müller had a gift for, first, getting the ball in the penalty area and, second, doing whatever it took to make sure the ball crossed the line. Beloved in Germany, Müller scored 14 goals in two World Cups, a remarkable record when you consider Pelé scored only 12 in the same number of games—13.

Despite Germany's "us against the world" mentality, its soccer history has been marked by internal strife, especially among player—Beckenbauer lead among them—rebelling against the conservative rigidity of its own soccer federation. The country also has bred a strain of temperamental goalkeepers, like Uli Stein, who turned the tables on Beckenbauer when Beckenbauer became coach in 1986. Stein publicly branded his manager *Suppenkasper*—a deadly insult for Germans meaning "soup clown" or "laughing stock." The politics simmer in good times and bad. When they won the tournament in 1974, the players ditched the official celebrations after their wives were not allowed at the awards banquet. The team decamped to a nearby bar after one official chastised his victorious team, giving rise to the charge that Germans can win a trophy but they cannot throw a good party.

Those who thought the fall of the Berlin Wall and unification in 1990 would make Germany invincible were surprised that, by the time Germany hosted the 2006 World Cup, the team had become so mediocre, it was able to shatter two deeply held stereotypes at the same time. The tournament was the most festive the world had ever seen, proving that Germans could throw one hell of a party after all, and the Germans made an appealing underdog run into the semifinal with a remarkably likable team that—shock, horror—could even be admired by the rest of the world.

ARGENTINA: *LOS ALBICELESTES*
WINNERS: 1978, 1986
FINALISTS: 1930, 1990

If you're partial to *A Clockwork Orange*, the movies of John Woo, Jack Tatum, or the Broad Street Bullies, the violent beauty of the Argentinian National Team is for you. Artful brutality is a natural part of its game. (Even the Paralympic soccer team had a brawl live on national television in 2004.) Like its rivals, the Brazilians, Argentina's passion for soccer is born of poverty, but whereas Brazil fuses the South American and the African, Argentinian football looks to Europe. The working classes inherited the game directly from British sailors, and it spread quickly from the ports to the factories and slums, where workers mastered the slaloming style of dribbling that Argentinians idolize. In the words of Eduardo Galeano, they strum "the ball as if it was a guitar," mixing guile and physicality to create the homegrown *La Nuestra*, or "our style of play."

The team's 1950s editions reveled in its reputation as *Los Angeles Con Caras Sucias* (Angels with Dirty Faces), initiating a long tradition of doing whatever it takes to progress, and exulting in its transgressions. The 1978 team warmed up for the World Cup by playing back-to-back practice scrimmages against England and Scotland, matchups traditionally played at half-pace, akin to an All-Star game, but the Argentinians used the occasions to pummel their opponents' kidneys, groins, and faces. And perhaps most infamously, their 1990 grudge match against hated rival Brazil was won when an Argentinian trainer drugged Brazilian defender Branco by handing him a spiked water bottle as an apparent gesture of goodwill during a break in play.

In fairness to the Argentinians, they never waver from the ethos of respecting those who do whatever it takes to win, even when they're on the receiving end. In 2002, the English avenged a series of controversial losses to Argentina when attacker Michael Owen flung himself to the ground as a defender approached, conning the referee into awarding a penalty that turned out to produce the only goal of the game. Though Argentina had been robbed, Buenos Aires newspapers nodded their approval. "They've learned," wrote one hack.

Yet, just as John Madden's Super Bowl–winning Oakland Raiders were more than a one-dimensional physical team, the Argentinians have also distinguished themselves with the imaginative artistry of their playmakers. While most countries view the offensive creativity of the traditional number 10, free from defensive duties, as an unaffordable luxury, the Argentinians revere the *Enganche*—the hook—and have romanticized the role, played so exquisitely by Diego Maradona; the volatile "Little Donkey," Ariel Ortega; the brilliant, controversial

Maradona jukes West Germany's Schumacher and Förster in the 1986 final.

Juan Román Riquelme; and now the unstoppable dynamo Lionel Messi. El Diez is a national mythical hero. Win and he is beloved. Lose and it is always his fault.

Argentina's tradition of great number 10s looks set to continue. In February 2009, Maradona's daughter Giannina bore a son, Benjamin, to star forward Sergio Aguero, and Lionel Messi became the boy's godfather. Done deal? Hardly. When Maradona's daughter revealed her ambition for her son to become a ballet dancer, Diego cheerily countered at a press conference. "I swear I'll burn down every dance academy in the country! I'm serious," he said, adding, "I am going to put a plaster boot on Benjamin's right leg because I want him to be a lefty like his grandfather!"

ENGLAND: THE THREE LIONS
WINNERS: 1966

The English national team employed a blood-and-thunder style to lift the World Cup on home turf in 1966 and have deviated only marginally from this strategy ever since, but with inferior results. Their performances in subsequent Cups can be summed up best by the title of a popular tome published in the aftermath of the 2006 World Cup, *40 Years of Shite*. The volume celebrates four decades of "the endless torment inflicted upon millions of England supporters doomed to watch endless replays of the only World Cup Final hat trick in history in lieu of any more recent successes."

This hasn't stopped the English, who invented the game, from regarding victory as their right and their destiny. But the island nation often plays as if isolated from the evolution of the sport since its founding. There's still plenty of passion, physicality, and huffing and puffing, but at the expense of modern technique and organization. Fabled soccer writer Brian Glanville nailed it when he called it "the story of vast superiority, sacrificed through stupidity, shortsightedness, and wanton insularity. It is a story of shamefully wasted talent, extraordinary complacency, and infinite self-deception."

The kind of stiff-upper-lip behavior exemplified by defender Terry Butcher—shirt soaked through with blood from a deep head wound in a critical World Cup qualifying game against Sweden in 1989—can get you only so far. English players are renowned for their lack of tactical acumen. The English Premier League may be the world's richest, but the majority of its stars are now foreign, robbing homegrown players of the playing time they need to gain experience at the elite level. Their own superstars remain the most parochial in the world, renowned for their inability to adapt to the highly tactical style of play in the Spanish or Italian leagues. This lack of technical ability, never more evident than in England's flawed penalty-kicking, has become the team's bête noire—a combination of decades of national longing and futility that has crushed the confidence of even the most polished professional.

The English Football Association commissioned a report on their team's consistent failure in 2003, asking, "Why do we always enter tournaments

Jack Charlton and the 1966 English team: Not-so-divine right?

with a belief we will win it, only to be found wanting when the tournament starts to heat up at the quarterfinal stage?" It doesn't help that *The Sun* and the *Mirror* delight in pumping up the team's fragile ego and turning up the pressure on them, the better to eviscerate them the second they lose. Before England's 2002 quarterfinal showdown with Brazil, the *Mirror*'s front page consisted of just the English flag and the caption "This page is cancelled. Nothing else matters." When David Beckham broke his second metatarsal ahead of the 2002 tournament, his status was reported minute to minute, turning the English into a nation of medical experts, intimately familiar with the intricacies of Beckham's rehab.

It is hard to find a more masochistic, gullible bunch than the English fans. In the last 20 years, the core of English support has drifted away from xenophobic hooliganism toward mainstream popular culture. When the team plays, flags fly out the front window of every home as the entire country engages in a mass delusion that the English Premier League's glamour and money predict victory for its lads. In fact, the performance on the field has been drowned out by the soap opera that now surrounds it. No fewer than three members of the 2006 squad pumped out tell-all books as soon as the team was eliminated from the tournament. Controversial midfielder Joey Barton accurately lampooned the mentality of the entire English team as: "I played like shit, here's my book."

Desperate times, desperate measures. The English Football Association has taken the unprecedented step of appointing foreign coaches. Its first, Swede Sven-Göran Eriksson, racked up a number of sex scandals in his six-year tenure; the closest he came to winning a trophy was being named runner-up in the voting for a condom manufacturer's Man of the Year. The job of breaking the vicious British cycle of overconfidence, underperforming, and self-loathing is now in the hands of professorial Italian Fabio Capello. Until he, or someone else, succeeds, the thrill of watching England will remain depressingly similar to that of rubbernecking.

The French experience *joie de victoire* after disposing of Brazil in 1998.

FRANCE: *LES BLEUS*
WINNERS: 1998
FINALISTS: 2006

In 1863, the French Foreign Legion cemented its romantic legend during the Battle of Camarón, when 62 legionnaires and three officers held 2,000 Mexican soldiers at bay until they ran out of ammunition. With three men remaining and not a bullet among them, the legionnaires swore to fight to the death, fixed bayonets, and attempted a futile charge. The wooden prosthetic hand of the deceased leader Capitain Jean Danjou was recovered, and every year it is solemnly sent out on parade, a reminder of his death, the nobility of defeat, and the Legion's motto, "March or Die."

This is French glory. Understand it and you will appreciate the essence of French soccer, which is a product of a culture in which it is better to lose with honor than to win without style, better to bear glorious defeat with stoic dignity than to dully and pragmatically win a trophy.

And although France has bred some of the world's most creative soccer players, defeat has been its customary fate. Perhaps arrogant and superior off the field, the French suffer from a deeply entrenched inferiority complex on it. Early French teams approached every tournament as if it was a small, gallant, fighting force for whom defeat was inevitable, a mental complex grounded in the fact that their domestic league was slow to professionalize. To this day, the vocabulary that pervades French soccer—

or should we say *le football*—is very, very English. "*Les clubs*" make "*les tacles*" and "*ils* shoot" "*le* ball."

The nation's rise to world soccer power has been a very slow burn as a result. Deep into the 1950s, even the greatest French soccer stars still saw the sport as a hobby. Raymond Kopa (born Kopaszewski), the magnificent 1950s playmaker, began his career to avoid going down the mines so he could fulfill his ultimate dream of becoming an electrician. While the French were late to the game, they were early to the administrative side of it. Their proudest tradition was the contribution they made off the pitch as passionate bureaucrats committed to the growth and discipline of the international game, present at the creation of soccer's international governing body FIFA, as well as the World Cup, European governing body UEFA, and all of the early European Cup competitions.

In 1958, the team surprised the World Cup with an extravagant style of play that became known as "Champagne Soccer." Kopa, the son of Polish immigrants and France's first global star, was a visionary and deft dribbler who carved open defenses like a point guard to feed the insatiable Just Fontaine for many of his 13 goals. The tournament transformed France into a nation of soccer fans; radios across the country carried Kopa's faithful declaration to "defend the French colors" and the commentator's cry of "*Vive la France!*" after every goal. Thanks to their pummeling at the hands of eventual victors Brazil in the semifinal, the French team even managed to cement its image as beautiful losers.

France burnished the image in its second semifinal appearance—a heartbreaking loss to Germany in 1982 (*see Greatest Games, page 108*). A journalist for *The Guardian* compared the Michel Platini–led team's dominant yet effortless possession of the ball to a group of "college students sharing a spliff." Their loss to the physical Germans revived, in the words of French commentator Georges de Caunes, "memories of emotions felt during the Second World War." The French, who love their tragic heroes, embraced the team, which confirmed the nation's destiny: to come up short, but always to delight.

The 1998 World Cup, held in France, shattered the country's sense of self, as the victorious multiracial "Black, Blanc, Beur" (black, white, Arab) of Zinedine Zidane and company allowed the nation to instantly reimagine itself as the "*France qui gagne.*" A new myth was forged overnight—one that aligned seamlessly with the political and economic self-confidence that abounded throughout French society at that time. France was now a country that expected to compete and even to prevail. This new image lasted only four years, until 2002, when the favored French were humiliated, losing the opening game to former colony Senegal (*see Worst Teams, page 205*), without scoring a single goal, despite having top strikers from the English, Italian, and of course, French leagues at their disposal. French fans did not mind losing, but they abhorred the lack of effort, honor, or loyalty. The team plummeted in the nation's esteem, only to rebound in 2006, as Zidane led Les Bleus within a literal hair's breadth of winning it all again. The team will travel to South Africa in a ragged state after scraping through the playoffs against Ireland, courtesy of Thierry Henry's handball. According to a national poll, 81 percent of their own fans believed the team did not deserve to qualify. Yo-yoing tournament to tournament has become the new French status quo. France remains a team rife with contradiction: beloved when it loses, scrutinized when it wins; *magnifique* when written off, and *merde* when expectations are high.

Nobby Stiles (in white jersey), pedaling on the way to England's first, and still only, World Cup.

1966
England

WHEN GOD WAS AN ENGLISHMAN

Brazil is booted, Germany muscles in, but plucky—and lucky—England wins it all on the auld sod.

THREE DATES ARE ETCHED in every English schoolboy's brain: the Norman Conquest of 1066, the Battle of Britain in 1940, and the year England won the World Cup—and on home soil—in 1966. Soccer returned to its birthplace, and the proud English saw their team turn in a performance that was all passion and controversy, to claim what they had long believed was rightfully theirs. But the triumph on the soccer field came a little too late to mask England's otherwise diminishing significance on the global stage.

World Cup Willie was the World Cup's first mascot and a sign that the tournament's commercial era had dawned for real. The dashing lion appeared on everything from cigar bands to knickers. But the World Cup's mascot should have been a television set. The 1962 World Cup in Chile had been televised regionally, but European fans still had to wait for game films to be shipped back from South America. In 1966 the whole continent watched live with a deep real-time connection as the story lines—and there were many—unfolded like *Great Expectations*.

The Cup's return to the game's ancestral home caused a bloating of England's self-confidence.

It was whipped up largely by the domestic media after the usually tight-lipped English manager, Alf Ramsey, predicted that his English "Bulldogs" would win it all. Once the opening rounds kicked off, this prophecy was not beyond the realm of possibility. Europe's physicality and stamina trumped the guile and flair of South America. Portugal, led by Eusébio, the sad-eyed star who could seemingly score from anywhere on the field, battered Brazil, giving Pelé such a beating that he threatened to retire. The defending champions were eliminated after their worst performance ever, although they were quick to point out that it was an English referee, George McCabe, who had offered their players

no protection, permitting them to be, almost literally, kicked out of the tournament.

The North Koreans overcame attempts by the British foreign office, still smarting over the Korean War, to deny them visas. The foreign office relented when North Korea agreed not to play its national anthem before games. The Koreans went on to record one of the great outside runs the tournament had ever witnessed. Opening the tournament as 1000–1 outsiders and forced to play away from the media glare in the unglamorous northern hinterlands of Middlesbrough and Liverpool, the team used its three years of intensive preparation to great effect. Against Italy, Pak Doo-Ik scored to

(far left) The Swiss team practices neutral frivolity; (top left) Willie the Lion was modeled on the son of the mascot's creator, artist Reg Hoye; (below left) Portugal's Eusébio, the second best player in the world behind Pelé . . . but not by much; (right) Defending champion Brazil was eliminated after their worst performance since 1934.

secure a shocking 1–0 victory. Such was the Italians' disgrace that, despite taking the precautions of flying home in the middle of the night and landing at an airport different from the advertised one, they were still met by hundreds of disgusted fans who welcomed them with a barrage of rotten tomatoes. Meanwhile, the Koreans had the temerity to go three-up inside 25 minutes against the mighty Portuguese, only to lose their nerve and the game before exiting valiantly. They remain cult heroes to this day throughout parts of the North of England (*see Greatest Games, page 54*).

England progressed through the tournament, dispatching team after team with passionate, pugnacious, uncultured soccer. Its rivalry with Argentina was cemented after an ill-tempered, often violent, game in which the only goal, scored by the English, was disputably offside and the German

referee dismissed one of the Argentinians because, in his own words, "I did not like the way he looked at me." Alf Ramsey ran out onto the field at the end of the game to ensure his players did not swap shirts with opponents who he branded as "animals." The Argentinians were outraged. For them the game was *el robo del siglo*, the robbery of the century, even though there were still 20 years left to go until Maradona truly defined that term (*see 1986*). "First they steal the Maldives from us, now they steal the World Cup," wrote the *Cronica* newspaper, which went so far as to send an airplane to plant an Argentinian flag on one of the islands.

It was only fitting that West Germany was England's opponent in the final—a game to be played at Wembley Stadium in London, a city the Luftwaffe had tried to blitz off the map just 26 years earlier. The 93,000 who packed the stands

were augmented by 400 million others tuned in to television sets around the world, to witness these two rivals play their first non-friendly game since World War II ended. Ramsey's total control of his squad ultimately paid off. He minimized risks with his roster choices. There would be no room for flair or fancy stuff. This was a solid, reliable team personified by the hardworking midfielder Nobby Stiles, who could be counted on to stifle the opposition's creative players in the middle of the field. The game was a classic. The Germans scrambled the ball over the English line in the second-to-last minute, possibly with the aid of a hand, to tie the game at 2–2. In the break before extra time, Ramsey ordered his exhausted team to stand up in order to demoralize the Germans with its charade of tirelessness.

West Germany's Wolfgang Weber and England's Martin Peters perform aerial maneuvers in the final.

TWO WORLD WARS, ONE WORLD CUP

In extra time, striker Geoff Hurst completed the only hat trick in the history of World Cup final matches, the second goal of which remains controversial to this day. His shot from close range cannoned off the underside of the bar and appeared to bounce either over the line or exactly on it—depending whether you were English or German. The only opinion that mattered, though, was that of Soviet linesman Tofik Bakhramov, who awarded the goal. (There is an apocryphal story that when asked how he was so sure it was a goal, Bakhramov gave the one-word reply "Stalingrad," referring to the bloody World War II battle in which more than a million Soviets died.) Hurst completed his hat trick and put the game beyond doubt with a definitive drive for a stunning fourth goal. The British

commentator's triumphant call to accompany the shot—"Some people on the pitch, they think it's all over. It is now!"—has echoed for Englishmen ever since. The victory—the English still crow about winning "two World Wars and one World Cup"—has become a kind of national salve to ease the pain of postindustrial and colonial decline.

This was a World Cup that had something for everyone. The African continent lionized the Portuguese Eusébio, orginally born in Mozambique. Asia marveled at North Korea's pluck. And the Cup's first English-language winner made headlines in Australia and even in America. The forces of technology, sports, nationalism, and commerce had joined up to make the World Cup's existence felt around the world—or at least anywhere there was a television set.

FANTASY FOOTBALL

How Scotland Became World Champions

The World Cup is a banquet of 64 games in a month. But once the trophy is awarded, soccer fans have to endure roughly 1,370 days of famine until the next feast. FIFA has long contemplated the creation of international tournaments to feed the masses, but the experiments have floundered. The Nations Cup in Brazil in 1964 was a grandly named trophy for a competition for which only four teams showed up. In 1980 the *Mundialito,* or Little World Cup, celebrated the 50th anniversary of the tournament by convening all previous champions to compete in Montevideo. Only England declined the invitation, but the competition felt manufactured, a cheap reproduction of the World Cup's magic.

A number of reasons have been offered to justify holding the tournament only as often as leap years and U.S. presidential elections. The prohibitive logistics of the qualifying process, which now stretches over two years in six continental groupings, is as convincing an argument as any. Eccentric French goalkeeper Fabien Barthez has tendered a more poetic explanation. "The World Cup is like a woman," he said after his French team lifted the trophy in 1998. "The longer you wait for one, the more you appreciate it. Four years is perfect."

Nature, however, abhors a vacuum, and so fantasy has moved in with a fix for hardcore fans: The Unofficial Football World Championships uses boxing-style calculations to determine a world champion, whose title becomes the property of the next team to beat it. The idea hails from Scot-land, a country whose fans have, in the words of one English journalist, become "accustomed . . . over the years to returning from major tournament finals ahead of their postcards home." Its roots lie in the 1966 World Cup. It was England's finest hour, yet a triumph that turned the average Scotsman's stomach more than a dodgy batch of haggis. Nine months later, Scotland faced the English in London when their "Auld Enemy" were not only World Champions, but on a 19-game unbeaten run. Only a man with money to burn would have bet on Scotland, given its history of glorious failure. But in a blood-and-thunder game, Scotland pulled off its most significant victory since Bannockburn in 1314, shocking its rivals 3–2. The team's fervent and inebriated fanbase, the Tartan Army, swarmed onto the field and dug up pieces of the turf to carry across the border as a memento of the occasion. They pro-claimed their team to be the "Unofficial Champions of the World."

Their jubilation lasted exactly 25 days, whereupon USSR traveled to Glasgow and thumped Scotland 2–0, a defeat that tabled the notion of Unofficial World Champions until 2002. In that year, when a Scotsman called in to an English sports talk show and asked about the current titleholder, the media resurrected the concept and a team of stat heads set up a Web site, UWFC.co.uk, to retroactively crown every Unofficial World Champion since the birth of the sport. This neccessitated combing through the result of every international game played since the very first, an 1872 clash between England and Scotland. The UWFC team's passion and patience proved contagious and the concept quick-ly achieved cult status among soccer cognescenti in championship-challenged countries. Wales, Bolivia, and Zimbabwe may not win the World Cup in our lifetimes, but they have all managed to become Unofficial World Champions, as have such minnows as the Dutch An-tilles (via a 2–1 victory over Mexico in 1963), Israel (thanks to a resounding 4–1 victory over Russia in 2000), and Angola (after beating Nigeria 1–0 in 2004). Even the U.S.A. once held the title, albeit for a mere three glorious days following its 1950 World Cup shocking win over England.

The researchers have even established a metric to determine the World Champion of all time. And the winner is—fittingly, if not convincingly—Scotland.

PORTUGAL 5
NORTH KOREA 3
Quarterfinal

In the summer of 1961, Bela Guttman, the coach of Portuguese superclub Benfica, was getting his hair cut in Lisbon when he overheard another coach in the next chair talking excitedly about an "outrageous teenage talent" he had seen in Africa. The soccer world has been forever grateful that Guttman risked decapitation by suddenly leaping out of the barber's chair and into an airplane seat. Five years later, Eusébio, whom Guttman had plucked from the former Portuguese colony of Mozambique and brought back to the motherland, would produce one

The North Koreans, before Portugal threw them under the bus.

of the most memorable individual performances in World Cup history. To put it in perspective, Pelé in four World Cups never had as dominant a game as Eusébio did in his one and only tournament.

Nicknamed the Black Panther for his power and grace, Eusébio had given a hint of his coiled menace at the end of the group stage, when he scored twice in Portugal's 3–1 dismantling of Pelé's Brazil, winners of back-to-back World Cups. And now the Portuguese were in the quarterfinals, playing against an unknown North Korean team that had just sent heavily favored Italy home to a barrage of rotten fruit from its angry fans.

Still, against a European powerhouse like Portugal, which in addition to Eusébio boasted his prolific strike partner José Torres and the tall, elegant midfielder Mário Coluna, the pint-sized Koreans—whose average height was 5'5"—were considered dog meat. However, it was Portugal that was being feasted on during the game's first 25 surreal minutes, the length of time it took North Korea to carve up the Portuguese defense and score three thrilling goals. No one, least of all Eusébio, could believe what had just happened. How did this Korean team, shrouded in mystery and just emerging from the trauma of war, come out of nowhere and shock the world?

Eusébio decided to take matters into his own hands—or, rather, feet—specifically his thunder-

ous right one. Two minutes after the Korean's third goal, he calmly collected a cross and blasted it into the top corner. Then, after Torres was chopped down as he was about to shoot, Eusébio converted the penalty kick. When Eusébio left his marker reeling in his slipstream to hammer the ball past the helpless Korean keeper, the score was tied 3–3 with half an hour remaining. It was a magical, improbable comeback, and one for which the North Koreans had no answer. Tactically naive, they lost all sense of cohesion between defense and midfield and were reduced to flailing at Eusébio as he tore them apart.

"Every time I scored it was just a question of picking the ball out of the net, carrying it to the center circle, and getting on with looking for another one," Eusébio recalled. "There was no time for celebrating goals." Running full-tilt at the now terrified Korean backline, Eusébio was hacked down in the box and coolly dispatched the penalty kick to give Portugal a 4–3 lead. But the North Koreans would go home heroes, a supernova that flashed across the soccer sky (and not to be seen again in a World Cup until 2010, when they earned another shot at Portugal).

At the final whistle, the crowd stood and applauded both teams. An English boy sprinted onto the field and chased after Eusébio, but had no more luck catching him than did the North Koreans.

The foul that led to the third—and the eventual winner—of Eusébio's four goals.

(opposite) Hail Kaiser: In 1970, a 24-year-old Franz Beckenbauer tried to carry Germany to the final on his injured right shoulder.

FRANZ BECKENBAUER
West Germany: 1966, 1970, 1974

Franz Beckenbauer embodied just about every stereotype of the German people: The defender was logical, aloof, arrogant, conservative, consistent, and efficient—so utterly Teutonic that his nickname was "Der Kaiser." It is perhaps the greatest testament to his reengineering of the modern game that it is impossible to hold any of this against him. In five World Cup finals as either player or coach, he never finished below third place and he remains the only man to lift the trophy as both captain and manager.

Technical yet graceful, rugged yet elegant, he was physical enough to do battle with his arm strapped to his side after dislocating a shoulder in a semifinal against Italy in 1970, but his greatest attribute was his mental control the game. He always seemed to be several moves ahead of his opponent. A midfielder-turned-defender, he popularized a new role called *libero,* a creative force who would carry the ball from the back, fusing the midfield with the line. Before the *libero,*

defenders were generally large and so awkward on the ball that they were unlikely to leave their own half. Beckenbauer changed the categories of the game, taking advantage of the fact that he was rarely closely checked to storm out of the defense with trademark runs that were as revolutionary as defenseman Bobby Orr's rink-length rushes in the same decade with the NHL's Boston Bruins.

Beckenbauer became the pop star of German football, cementing his fame by recording a hit single called "True Friends Can't Be Separated," a hurdy-gurdy track—part Donovan, part Hasselhoff—with lyrics that summed up the team-first ethos of the West German teams he marshalled:

Good friends—no one can tear apart
Good friends are never alone
Because in life one can
Be there for one another

History has not recorded whether the 1974 squad listened to the song in the locker room before matches, but the team's well-organized and ruthlessly efficient performances undressed the highly favored Dutch team in a final that saw Beckenbauer combine with prolific goal-scorer Gerd Müller to shock the world and lift the trophy. Beckenbauer's influence during that campaign was evident off the field, where he picked players, shaped tactics, handled media in his coaches' stead, and even negotiated the win bonus.

All of this was the ideal preparation for 1990, when he successfully managed the German team to victory in Italy. As a coda, he returned to the World Cup to chair the organizing of the tournament in Germany in 2006. Ever the control freak, he used a helicopter to crisscross the country and attend 46 of the 64 games, even managing to squeeze in his third marriage between matches. The tournament, predictably, ran like clockwork.

WHO OWNS THE '66 BALL?

GERMANY, ENGLAND, AND THE BATTLE OVER THE WORLD CUP'S MOST CONTESTED SOUVENIR

The bright orange leather ball from the epic 1966 final between England and West Germany is, like Maris's 61st, McGwire's 70th, and Bonds's 73rd homerun balls, an artifact of great sentimental and financial value, but it had something else going for it: two countries still fighting over it 30 years later. In the ensuing bedlam at the end of the only World Cup England has ever won, Helmut Haller, scorer of the opening goal, wrested the ball away from head referee, Gottfried Dienst, later explaining, "I ran off with the ball because it is an old German tradition—if the winners get the Cup, the losers keep the ball." Haller took it back to West Germany, where it resided peacefully in his son Jürgen's basement amid other family heirlooms, albeit none signed by Pelé.

Then, in 1988, Sir Geoff Hurst, knighted for his three goals in the '66 final, ran into Haller at a soccer function and said, "I want my ball back," reminding him of the long-standing tradition that a player who scores a hat trick gets to keep the game ball. Haller responded with yet another German saying, "No, the first man to score in the final always gets to keep it." And there it stood until 1996, when, on the eve of the 30th anniversary of the final, two English tabloids decided to go to war over the ball. Under the guise of righting an historical injustice—shouldn't England get to keep the most famous souvenir of its soccer glory?—but really looking for a way to boost circulation, *The Sun* and the *Mirror* battled each other with the

same dogged ferocity that marked the England-Germany rivalry on the field.

The Sun drew first blood, claiming that after a long investigation (it had actually read about the ball's whereabouts in *Total Football* magazine) it had tracked down England's most storied orb and was negotiating to bring it home. But before the paper could arrange to get Haller onto a plane, the *Mirror* had swooped in with an offer of 120,000 pounds (positioned as a donation to charity, of course) and stripped the ball—and the attendant fanfare—from *The Sun*. As the next day's triumphant headline blared:

DAILY MIRROR 1, THE SUN 0:
THE GREATEST WIN SINCE 1966

NOBBY STILES, ENGLAND

When you grow up as a Smurf named Norbert in a working-class Manchester neighborhood, wearing thick-rimmed specs because your vision is so bad, you either learn to "get stuck in" or consign yourself to a life in the shadows. No Englishman of a certain age goes to sleep at night without thanking the soccer gods that Nobby could do both.

Long before the term "defensive midfielder" entered the soccer lexicon, Stiles sacrificed his body to that least glamorous of roles on England's 1966 World Cup champions—patrolling the area between the back four and the five attacking players. It fell to the aesthetically and dentally challenged midfielder to make that swath of turf his own and hang out his shingle: *Thou Shalt Not Pass if Thou Values Thy Family Jewels.*

On England's march to glory, Stiles clamped down—despite the absence of front teeth—on the opposition's best player, including his iron-clad job on Eusébio in the semifinal. Afterward, as a testament to how comprehensively Stiles marked the Portuguese superstar out of the game, television commentators would remark that they had barely mentioned either player for most of the 90 minutes.

Stiles was more than just the mortar that held the English defense together, he was the personification of its selfless grinding. No longer looking to make style points on the field, Stiles frequently spooked opponents merely by removing his dentures before a game. The sight of this tiny madman with bare gums and a feral gleam in his eye made players think twice before tangling with him.

Though he ended his career with a modest 28 appearances for England—the least of any of the 1966 starters—Stiles is one of only two Englishmen to ever win both a World (1966) and European Cup medal (he was the defensive mainstay on the Manchester United winning side in 1968).

But by far the most enduring image of him remains his post-championship celebration, a dementedly boyish jig that has been burned into the collective English consciousness, as every four years a clip of this giddy, toothless, dancing dwarf is trotted out as part of the World Cup video package. "It was absolutely spontaneous," Stiles said of his famous boogie. "I don't know what I was thinking. I'm a bloody awful dancer anyway."

One-hit Wonders: Ball, Charlton, Moore, and Cohen leave the field, but this time with the Cup.

ENGLAND, 1966

You know how the U.S. acts during every Little League World Series or World Baseball Classic? That *step-off-we-invented-this-game* 'tude? Well, that's how the English had always felt about the World Cup. There was just one problem: They hadn't won anything. So when England was selected as the hosts for the 1966 Cup, the nation went bonkers. The English manager, Alf Ramsey, predicted that his side would "most certainly" win the World Cup. Cue a frenzy of flag-waving and irrational hopes that would have overwhelmed any reasonable team.

Therefore the 1966 England team is deservedly worshipped because it met, and ultimately exceeded, the berserko dreams of its fans. Never before, and never again, was so much expected of a squad that was, in reality, less talented than many of the teams it faced. Argentina, Portugal, and West Germany were all more gifted than the English, and yet, in the face of immense, unyielding pressure, they could not be beaten.

Yes, the team was brave, strong, bold, and whatever other homage to fortitude English sportswriters could find in their thesauri. But it was also gloriously, magnificently, exquisitely lucky. In the history of the tournament, no team has been as fortunate as England in 1966—and not simply because the winning goal in the final probably shouldn't have counted.

Normally the English were blessed with just one or two transcendent players every generation, surrounded by blue-collar grafters to make up the numbers, but heading into '66, they had a handful of alpha dogs to call upon: the small, dynamic Bobby Charlton orchestrating the attack; the regal captain Bobby Moore coolly marshaling the defense; the indefatigable Nobby Stiles snapping and snarling at German ankles like an English terrier on steroids; and the opportunistic forwards Jimmy Greaves and Roger Hunt poaching goals. By defying conventional tactical wisdom and opting to employ three energetic midfielders in the center to squeeze opposing playmakers rather than stationing two players out wide to spread the field, the English became known as the "Wingless Wonders." What they lacked in trickery or verve, they made up for with tireless running and inexhaustible belief.

After a dreary 0–0 draw with Uruguay, wins against Mexico and France propelled them into the knockout portion, and from there, the soccer gods took over. A fortuitous sending-off in the Argentina quarterfinal deprived their bitter rivals of their captain for 55-plus minutes, and turned the game in England's favor, culminating in Geoff Hurst's late winner. In the semis, English World Cup organizers made sure to take care of their own. Adhering to a decision made before the tournament—that if England won its group, its knockout games would be at the spacious and home team friendly Wembley—the semifinal with Portugal was moved from the claustrophobic Goodison Park, a place that had grown fond of Eusébio's heroics. In front of 94,000, the Portuguese labored after the exertions in their quarterfinal (*see Greatest Games, page 54*), and England advanced to the final against West Germany.

Their hat-trick hero on that historic day, Geoff Hurst, almost wasn't even on the field. In the face of relentless media pressure to restore England legend Jimmy Greaves to the lineup after he had recovered from an injury early in the tournament, Ramsey kept faith with Hurst even though Greaves's speed posed the greater danger to the stolid Germans. In the end, of course, Hurst's immortal non-goal—the Ricochet Heard Round the World—gave the English their one and only World Cup championship and, in so doing, appears to have exhausted their good fortune forever.

The boys from Brazil: Pelé is mobbed by teammates after their stunning 4–1 victory over Italy in the World Cup final.

1970
Mexico

GREATEST OF ALL TIME

Africa returns and Italy shows it still has flair, but Brazil is brilliant.

FEW THINGS IN LIFE are perfect. The Great Star of Africa diamond. Michael Phelps in Beijing. Or, if you're a fan of cinematic tearjerkers, the movie *Beaches*. And then there's the 1970 World Cup, the tournament's leading candidate for the pantheon. It was widely considered the finest ever, replete with passion, beauty, imagination, and numerous firsts. The attack-minded Moroccans were the first African

They don't call it "The Beautiful Game" for nothing: (below) England's Norman Hunter gets a pedicure; (left) A Peruvian defender gracefully fouls a Moroccan forward.

(far right) Brazil and Italy at attention before the final; (near right) World Cup mascot Juanito shows off a different kind of hat trick.

team to qualify since Egypt in 1934; yellow and red cards made their first appearance; Adidas provided its first official tournament ball, the Telstar, with its distinctive black and white panels that branded the company on televisions across the globe; and it was the first (and the last) to have a World Cup rally as a curtain-raiser. Ninety-six drivers, including former England star Jimmy Greaves, "drove" from London to Mexico City, crossing the Atlantic and traversing 25 countries over the course of 39 days. Even more significant, this was the first Cup to be broadcast in color, lending the footage a magical quality. Brazil's trickery, mastery, and golden shirts were captured forever in all their splendor.

Brazil's greatest challenge turned out to be the playing conditions. Matches were played in the thin air of venues 7,000 feet above sea level. To make matters worse, the games were scheduled for the convenience of prime-time television audiences in Europe, forcing players to endure midday kickoffs in temperatures that approached 100 degrees.

The military government, which had come to power in Brazil in 1969, took no chances with this World Cup campaign, dispatching the team to train at high altitude in Mexico under the eye of a NASA-influenced military physical education specialist. They need not have worried, as their squad was one of the finest ever assembled, equipped with so much firepower that mono-named star strikers packed even the midfield—Pelé arrived for his fourth and final World Cup, joined by Tostão, Gérson, Rivelino, and Jairzinho, *Furacão* da Copa (the World Cup Hurricane), who remarkably scored in every game. This was stylish, flamboyant, explosive soccer. The sport played as if it had been choreographed by Cirque du Soleil.

FROZEN MEALS, SUPERHUMAN SAVES

England may have been defending champion, but it was despised across Latin America. The entire continent was still simmering over the last World Cup, which, it was believed, had been fixed by the

squad commonly referred to in the media as "that team of thieves and drunks." The English even flew in frozen meals from home to avoid the local cuisine's inevitable aftermath, Montezuma's revenge. Things came to a head when Bobby Moore, the English captain and national talisman, was apprehended for allegedly stealing an emerald bracelet on his way to Mexico and was placed under house arrest for four days in Colombia. The incident, which became known as the "Bogota Bracelet Scandal," served to further unsettle a squad already sleep-deprived, thanks to a flotilla of cars that spent the wee hours honking its horns as it circled the Guadalajara Hilton, the English base camp.

In the opening round, Brazil and England met in a legendary game billed at the time as the Clash of the Champions. The great English goalkeeper, Gordon Banks, flew across the face of his goal to make a superhuman save on a point-blank Pelé header, as the Brazilian was already wheeling

away to celebrate. Brazil, however, went on to win 1–0 and England was knocked out in the quarterfinals by West Germany, which thereby gained a measure of revenge for 1966. This time, Banks was missing from the lineup after being defeated by a bottle of local beer and falling desperately ill. His replacement, Peter Bonetti, known as "The Cat," played more like a mouse and was at fault for all three German goals, as his team gifted Germany a victory by surrendering a two-goal lead and then losing in extra time.

The Italians began the tournament, in the words of British soccer historian David Goldblatt, "hardwired for deep defense"—so much so that even their own fans booed their tedious tactics. They came out of their shell in a fabulous semifinal against Germany, in which they outscored the Germans 3–2 in extra time, emerging 4–3 victors, earning the right to be patsies for the Brazilians in the final. The *Seleção* were almost perfect. Their 4–1 victory was sealed with one of the greatest team goals the

sport has seen. Eight out of the ten outfield players touched the ball as they swept the full length of the field, tormenting their opponents along the way, before Pelé laid off a pass for Alberto to smash home. It was an exquisite exclamation point on a dazzling display. Brazil had worked out how to counter the brutish soccer that had befuddled them in England 1966, and became "Tri-Campeão"—three-time champions. Its third Cup gave them the right to keep the trophy permanently. As its fans mobbed the field, Tostão was robbed of every garment except his blue underpants—an act of thievery that foreshadowed the disappearance of the Jules Rimet Cup itself from its display box in the headquarters of the Brazilian Football Confederation.

Like Tostão's uniform, it has never been seen again.

1970 RESULTS

QUARTERFINALS
Brazil 4 Peru 2
West Germany 3 England 2
Italy 4 Mexico 1
Uruguay 1 Soviet Union 0

SEMIFINALS
Brazil 3 Uruguay 1
Italy 4 West Germany 3

THIRD PLACE
West Germany 1 Uruguay 0

FINAL
Brazil 4 Italy 1

Brazil parades its third World Cup trophy through Brasilia, the nation's capital.

BRAZIL, 1970

In 1966, Brazil's wonder team had been hacked, cleated, gouged, elbowed, and basically mugged out of the tournament. Leading the parade of the aggrieved was Pelé, who vowed never to play in the World Cup again unless some of his thuggish opponents were dragged before the equivalent of a soccer war crimes tribunal. But, three years later, Pelé bowed to the impassioned pleas of his worshipful countrymen, reconsidered his World Cup retirement, and in 1970 Brazil meted out its own special brand of justice by assembling the most talented group of players ever.

Its outspoken coach, "Fearless" João Saldanha, a former journalist, had expressed reservations about selecting Pelé and Tostão together because he regarded their abilities as "too similar"—and he brooked no interference, not even from Brazil's president: "I do not mess with his cabinet; he will not mess with my team."

Saldanha was summarily canned and replaced by Mário Zagallo, a World Cup–winner as a player in '58 and '62, who took the position that you can never have too many superstars in your team. Zagallo played Tostão as a striker, which freed up Pelé to dictate from his favored position out wide. This gave Brazil a mesmerizing attack force balanced by a poised defense, which had never been a Brazilian hallmark. It was no mere juggernaut, but something rarer: a soccer team's Platonic ideal—beauty, brains, and brawn, all wrapped in the gold, green, and blue.

In addition to Pelé, there was Rivelino, known as "King of the Park" for his powerful dribbling and shooting; Tostão, a diminutive money player, aptly nicknamed "The Little Coin"; Jairzinho, the turbo-charged winger who scored in every game (still the only man to ever perform the feat in a World Cup), and Gérson, whose left foot was so cultured that an England player once said, "He could stir his tea with it." Captain Carlos Alberto was the composed heart of the backline and the agile midfielder Clodoaldo knit together defense and offense. Clodoaldo had the ignominy of being the one Brazilian without that signature brio, and yet, without him, they'd have been lost. Known as *cabeça de alho* (or "head of garlic"), his dominance of midfield allowed the Brazilians to unleash their devastating counterattacks. Even the goalkeeper, Félix, was a solid shotstopper, an anomaly in a nation that had suffered so much angst at the bumbling hands of its keepers (look no further than the 1950 final for proof; *see Greatest Games, page 21*).

The Brazilians gave up seven goals in six games and were rarely in danger of losing as they dismantled all opposition, netting a preposterous 19 goals in the most dazzling display of attacking soccer that the world had ever seen.

Four of those goals came in the 4–1 final against the Italians—who, by packing the penalty area, allowed the Brazilians space on the flanks in which to run amok. And, oh, how they did. Brazil dis-

played a different facet of its breathtaking skill and technique with each of the first three goals—Pelé's soaring header, Gérson's left-footed scud, Jairzinho's walk-the-ball-into-the-net finish—and then brought all of their disparate qualities together for the defining moment of *joga bonito* in the 86th minute. It involved eight Brazilian players, all of whose touches were perfectly weighted and played into space. How ironic that it was the unheralded Clodoaldo who would be at the heart of the interplay. It was the Brazilian midfielder's error that gifted Italy the tying goal in the first half, but here he was dribbling past four Italians, including one he faked out without touching the ball. It was Jairzinho's turn next; the winger maneuvered down the left flank before sliding the ball to Pelé, whose cool hold-and-release sucked in the entire Italian defense as he waited for Carlos Alberto to race the length of the field from his right fullback position. Pelé's pass and Alberto's right foot arrived at the same spot, and without breaking stride the Brazilian captain lashed the ball into the net.

Brazil had now won its third World Cup in four straight attempts, earning them the right to keep the Jules Rimet Cup for eternity. Technically, a new trophy would have to be made for the 1974 tournament, but did anyone really think at the time that it would end up anywhere but Rio?

ENGLAND VS. GERMANY

Any discussion of the rivalry between England and Germany in soccer should start with the words of Basil Fawlty: "Don't mention the war." But to this day, games between the two are still viewed by the English as extra time in the match that was World War II. The Germans, on the other hand, are too busy playing high-tempo, skillful, and above all winning soccer to care. That they lost to England in the 1966 World Cup final, and in London to boot, is neither here nor there to many Germans; thanks to recent forensic testing (we're not making this up), the world now knows that Geoff Hurst's shot didn't actually go in. And since that injustice, it's been pretty much one-way traffic on the autobahn.

For two nations who share a love of beer and, well, beer, there is precious little *Gemütlichkeit* between them on the soccer field. That's because each country likes to think of itself as Europe's dominant power, even though Italy probably has more of a legitimate claim to that title than either of them. England enjoyed a solid superiority over Germany from 1919 to 1966, with two World War wins and a World Cup triumph in 1966. From 1950 to 1967, the two nations played five matches and the English won all of them. The games between the two followed an established plotline: English pregame confidence, English on-field dominance, English postgame arrogance. Great rivalries do not arise from such constant beatdowns.

To compensate for their silverware deficit, the English like to refer to their battlefield supremacy whenever possible, so much so that the English Football Association has begged fans to lay off his-

torical trash talk, such as chanting, "Stand up if you won the war," and singing, to the tune of "She'll Be Coming 'Round the Mountain" with arms outstretched, "There were ten German bombers in the air." Of all the terrace tunes, perhaps the most painful note was "the greatest goal that never was," the one that gave England their one and only World Cup trophy in 1966 at West Germany's expense.

That final, which drew a record 400 million viewers, was the most significant cultural moment in England's postwar recovery. In front of 93,000 rabid fans, England lifted the Jules Rimet Cup, unaware it was beginning a long and agonizing soccer decline. Its stubborn manager Alf Ramsey felt the victory vindicated all of his antediluvian tactics and bizarre personnel selections in the following years. While the rest of the world was learning soccer the Brazilian way—and to devastating effect—England got left behind.

Since that glorious summer day, though, the Germans, long reviled by the Brits for their mechanical approach to the beautiful game, have mechanically broken the English spirit several times on the World Cup stage.

In 1970, led by the magisterial Franz "Der Kaiser" Beckenbauer, West Germany rallied from 2–0 down in the stifling Mexico heat to win 3–2 in the quarterfinals, giving them its first win over the English in 38 years. Aided by boneheaded Ramsey substitutions—including the removal of midfield general Bobby Charlton, prompting Beckenbauer to erupt in glee ("How glad I was to see the back of Charlton!")—and the dead-eye sniper Gerd Mül-

ler up front, the Germans gained immediate revenge for their Wembley humiliation. After leading for close to an hour, the champions had imploded when their reserve goalkeeper Peter Bonetti made two crucial and brutal errors that led to West German goals. The gritty midfielder Alan Ball was incensed—"It wouldn't be so bad if we had lost to a great team, but they were nothing"—while Ramsey thought "The whole thing was unreal, a freak of nature." Four days after the match, the reigning Labour Party was ousted in England's general election, and its leader, Harold Wilson, blamed the loss on the English defeat.

In 1990, the West Germans tormented the English again in the semifinals, derailing their strongest World Cup performance since '66. Back then, English department store Rumbelows essentially offered free TVs to its customers by guaranteeing full refunds on all sets purchased right before the tournament, provided the nation's heroes come back as champions. It was a move that could have bankrupted them. After taking a freakish early lead via a deflected shot off defender Paul Parker's butt, Beckenbauer's men sat on their 1–0 advantage until a late Gary Lineker equalizer necessitated extra time, and the two sides hurtled toward a penalty shoot-out. Before knocking them out 4–3 from the spot, the Germans made beloved midfielder Paul Gascoigne cry like Mike Tyson on Barbara Walters's hot seat; after picking up a yellow card during extra time for a reckless tackle, "Gazza" sobbed and dried his eyes on the Three Lions badge upon realizing he'd be suspended from the final if England

Before West Germany's 1970 quarterfinal victory, England's fans (right) had plenty to cheer about: five straight triumphs over the Germans and their faithful (below).

advanced. It was typical of the tragicomedy that was England's 1990 meltdown that the subsequent inability of professional soccer players to find the net from 12 yards out (stand up, Stuart Pearce and Chris Waddle) was forgiven by the fact that the country's best player was having a bit of a blubber.

The loss sent fans back home into a funereal state; two people died and over 600 hooligans were arrested as the police faced rioting in 30 towns. Even politicians exuded anti-German animosity. Right-wing Cabinet member Nicholas Ridley used an interview about the German-proposed European monetary union to throw in some Nazi jibes: "I'm not against giving up sovereignty in principle, but not to this lot. You might just as well give it up to Adolf Hitler, frankly."

Eleven years later, the English exacted a measure of retribution, even if no German needed a Kleenex, with a 5–1 beatdown in a World Cup qualifier—in Munich, no less. This led to—what else?—a hit song, this time by the English punk band The Business, with the clever title "England 5, Germany 1." Still, in the World Cup their momentum carried them only into the quarterfinals, where they fell to a 10-man Brazilian team.

The rivalry has cooled somewhat in recent years, living on largely in the glossy tabloids that pander to each nation's lowest common denominator. It's mostly on the English side, to be honest. Nazi nicknames—Jerrys and Krauts—are fodder for the English headline writers. On the eve of their 1990 encounter, *The Sun* ran the banner HELP OUR BOYS CLOUT THE KRAUTS! complete with several manipulated WWII photos and a handy, cut-out wall chart illustrating the changes in Germany since 1966—including average income, beer consumption, and bra size. The paper concluded its coverage with a helpful history lesson: "We beat them in '45, we beat them in '66, now the battle of '90. Herr we go again."

Ahead of England's semifinal with Germany in the 1996 European Cup, the *Mirror* ran the headline ACHTUNG! SURRENDER! FOR YOU FRITZ, ZE EURO 96 CHAMPIONSHIP IS OVER atop a mock article that mimicked a report of the 1939 declaration of war between the two countries.

In 2010, after Germany unveiled their new all-black jerseys, *The Star* ran the headline RETURN OF ZE BLACK SHIRTS. The German press shot back; *Bild* called the comment the "absolute summit of tastelessness" while *The Cologne Express* chimed in, "Nothing goes on on The Island without Nazi comparison."

As German politician Gebhardt von Moltke put it, "England's teaching of German history stops at 1945." But in some ways England's memory stopped even earlier; in May 1938, prior to an exhibition game on German soil, the English players had performed the Nazi salute during the anthems before battering their hosts 6–4.

Jairzinho launches one against England's Bobby Moore and Martin Peters.

JAIRZINHO
Brazil vs. England, Group Stage

They called it "the final that might have been"—at least the English did, when the defending champions faced off against the champions-to-be in a group stage match. The two best teams in the world didn't disappoint, the game offering up both a master class of Brazilian ball control and a robust demonstration of good old British derring-do. As early as the 10th minute, it was obvious that this was one for the soccer historians to cherish.

Jairzinho had galloped down the right flank, skipped past a tackle, and from the right touchline delivered a looping cross to the far post, where Pelé rose to powerfully head down toward the intersection where the post meets the goal line. This is the one spot in the 24-foot width of the goal that is generally considered unguardable by goalkeepers. Place it there and 99 times out of 100, it's in. Certainly Pelé was convinced it was a goal, but as he was already wheeling toward his teammates in the early stages of celebration, English keeper Gordon Banks hurled his body across the goal to meet the ball just as it hit the turf. Somehow he managed to flick the ball over the bar—the physics of it still defy belief. Had a Martian fallen out of the sky at that moment, Pelé would not have looked more incredulous. Apparently, it would take an otherworldly play to beat Banks on this day.

Now, in the 59th minute, Pelé was in the middle of it once again. Tostão split two English defenders and dribbled to the edge of the box. The Brazilian striker, who had suffered a detached retina a year earlier, had no trouble seeing Pelé approach the penalty spot and chipped the ball to him. Figuring that Pelé would surely pull the trigger from such close range, the English defense collapsed in on him. But out of the corner of his eye Pelé glimpsed Jairzinho bursting down the wing again. Now it was Pelé's turn to return the favor. The defense froze as he swiveled ever so slightly to his right, opened up his body, and flicked the ball into Jairzinho's path. The winger took a touch to steady himself and from a tight angle ripped a fierce rising drive off his right foot that even Banks was helpless to keep out of the top corner.

The goal, like so many Brazilian highlights, consisted of one exquisite, improvised moment of skill after another until the ball was in the net. England's defense, composed and unyielding all game, had lost its focus for no more than 10 seconds, the time it took from Tostão's surge to Pelé's layoff to Jairzinho's thunderous finish. It broke the English spirit and reestablished the hegemony of Brazilian skill over European brawn.

GEORGE BEST

Doing what he did best: juggling balls and women.

The high-flying, hard-partying winger from Northern Ireland was soccer's bad boy decades before David Beckham sanitized the celebrity lifestyle with his sarongs and hair gels. Hardly a day went by when Best's swarthy, hungover mug wasn't staring up, bleary-eyed, from an English tabloid, a Miss World or two usually wrapped around his neck. "I spent a lot of money on booze, birds, and fast cars," he once quipped. "The rest I just squandered."

On the field, though, Best lived up to his surname. There wasn't an opponent alive he couldn't turn inside out—defenders suffered from "twisted blood"—and unlike today's superstar floppers he didn't go to ground under every hard challenge, but rode the tackles straight to goal. At Manchester United, where he was European Player of the Year in 1968, he scored at the rate of one goal every three matches, including, in 1970, six in one game alone, albeit against a fourth division team. To avoid humiliating the opposition any further, he ended that game playing left back. (One opposing defender lamented: "The closest I got to him was when we shook hands at the end of the game.")

But no moment better personifies Best's audacious style than when Northern Ireland played Holland in a 1976 World Cup qualifier. Asked before the game by a journalist what he thought of the Dutch maestro Johan Cruyff, to whom he was often compared, Best conceded he was an outstanding player but not superior to him. And to prove it, he added, he would nutmeg the world's reigning soccer deity the first chance he got. It was a preposterous boast, reminiscent of Ali in his prime, but coming from a man who once claimed that "if I'd have been born ugly, you'd never have heard of Pelé," it made perfect sense. So when he received the ball five minutes into the match, he set out in pursuit of Cruyff across the field instead of homing in on goal. Never mind that he had to evade at least three Dutch defenders in order to reach his prey; Best was on a mission. Slipping the ball between Cruyff's legs with insolent ease, he glided past the slack-jawed Dutchman and pumped an I-told-you-so fist in the direction of the press box, as if to say, "Johan Cruyff isn't fit to lace my boots, let alone my drinks."

It was his drinks, of course, that were the problem. Unlike his goals, there is no score sheet as to how much booze Best consumed, but it was enough to drown a career as brilliant as any in the history of soccer in the United Kingdom.

"Wednesday till Saturday is murder," he said. "I know I've got to stay off the town and get to bed by eleven. The only thing that keeps me sane is remembering that there'll be a party on Sunday and Monday and Tuesday."

On one memorably debauched weekend, he skipped United's game with Chelsea so he could shack up with an Irish actress in London as paparazzi camped outside. But such was his artistry with a soccer ball that his managers always welcomed him back—until Manchester United started to lose and unravel around its totemic star. "When the bad times started, I couldn't bear the thought of going out on the pitch," he said. "I used to drink so I didn't have to think about it. What came first? The bad times then the drinking, or the drinking then the bad times?"

He left United on January 1, 1974, and soon sought peace and relative privacy in the soccer backwater of the United States where he bounced around the NASL, playing for three teams before stumbling back across the pond. Overweight and underwhelming, Best had become a bloated, slow-footed shadow of his former self as the '82 World Cup beckoned. Though Northern Ireland qualified for just the second time in its history, he was long past his sell-by date and, to no one's surprise, manager Billy Bingham left him off the team.

From there, it was all one sad and inexorable descent into alcoholic oblivion until his liver finally gave out in 2005, when he was 59. His death triggered an orgy of grief worthy of Princess Diana. And yet, unlike Di's shocking end, there was nothing surprising about George Best's denouement. According to English television personality Michael Parkinson, one of Best's biographers, who had befriended the player when he was at the top of his game, it was as if "all his life since then has been a suicide note."

Berlusconi was so incensed by Rivera's behavior that he tried to have his name stricken from the record books.

CULT FIGURES

GIANNI RIVERA, ITALY

Before the 1970 World Cup, Alf Ramsey, coach of defending champion England, was asked to name the four strongest players on the Italian squad. "Rivera, Rivera, Rivera, Rivera," he replied. It made sense since Gianni Rivera was the reigning European Player of the Year, and yet, bizarrely, the 26-year-old midfielder from AC Milan couldn't even get a complete game for his national team. Rivera, and his crosstown rival, Sandro Mazzola (the captain of Inter Milan), were so similar in their playing style that Italian coach Ferruccio Valcareggi, opted for a controversial "relay" system whereby Mazzola and Rivera would each play one half of the game.

Rivera was a gifted attacker who was more interested in moving forward than tracking back on defense (yes, this made him quite unusual in Italian soccer). The media criticized him for being only half a player, and he was regarded as a diva who was out solely for individual glory. That reputation was underlined by a dreadful lapse in the semis against West Germany, when Gerd Müller's header off a corner flew by Rivera, who stood riveted at the post. If that wasn't bad enough, his response to the goal—sprinting back to the center circle for the restart—was seen by the media as a craven act of self-preservation in order to avoid the wrath of his goalkeeper, who was raging at him over the German equalizer.

Afterward, Rivera would explain that he was simply eager to atone for his error. History is certainly on his side as he coolly notched the game-winner less than 60 seconds later. In one of the more egregious slights in World Cup history, Coach Ferruccio Valcareggi abandoned his 50/50 split in the final against Brazil, and didn't deign to put Rivera on the field until the 84th minute, with Italy hopelessly behind. Valcareggi was unapologetic, feeling that he had endured enough of Rivera's egocentric behavior. It was a calculated and humiliating cameo for the "Golden Boy of Italian Soccer," and it belied his extraordinary success at club level, where he led AC Milan to three league titles and two European Cups. But even in Milan, Rivera was bedeviled by controversy. The Italian tabloids took great delight in his affair with a young actress, whom he dumped while she was pregnant, and later reveled in his feud with Milan owner Silvio Berlusconi, a man whose ego dwarfed even Rivera's. Berlusconi, who would go on to become the Italian Prime Minister, was so incensed by Rivera's outspoken behavior that he tried to have Rivera's name stricken from Milan's record books.

Yet even Berlusconi couldn't extinguish the legend, and Rivera was ultimately vindicated when an international panel voted him the best Italian soccer player of the 20th century.

Fußball-Weltmeisterschaft 1974
FIFA World Cup 1974
Coupe du Monde de la FIFA 1974
Copa Mundial de la FIFA 1974

13.6. - 7.7.1974
Hamburg   Düsseldorf   Frankfurt
West-Berlin Gelsenkirchen Stuttgart
Hannover   Dortmund   München

XI
Campeonato
Mundial
de Fútbol

Junio 1978

Buenos Aires
Córdoba
Mar del Plata
Mendoza
Rosario

Argentina '78

ESPAÑA

'82

'74 '78 '82

THE GAME'S GLORY DAYS

Puffed up: Gerd Müller and Paul Breitner savor West Germany's World Cup championship.

1974 Germany

SMOKIN'!

Total Football wins the world's affection, but West Germany lights up the Oranje.

THE DECISION TO SELECT West Germany as the host of a global tournament in the early seventies was as curious as choosing Vegas as the venue for a convention of church organists. Since 1968, the entire continent of Europe had been plunged into chaos as terrorist gangs such as the Red Brigades, ETA, and the Baader-Meinhof Gang took turns committing chilling acts of random violence, culminating in the murderous attack on the Munich Olympics by a Palestinian group two

(far left) The 12-year-old who randomly pitted the Germanys against each other; (above) Jürgen Sparwasser scores the only goal of the game as East Germany trumps West in the opening round; (near left) World Cup mascots Tip and Tap; (right) Brazil's Jairzinho skips through Zaire's woeful defense.

Nothing said it better than this: Pelé was now a pitchman for Pepsi.

years before the World Cup. Fear and vulnerability were compounded by the Cold War, in which a divided Germany was the front line, and which intruded before the tournament had even begun. The Soviets were eliminated during the qualifiers after refusing to play in Chile at the Estadio Nacional, once a World Cup stadium but also used as a clearing station for political prisoners under Pinochet's military regime. The East Germans' defense of the Soviets—by asking whether a Western nation would contemplate playing a game at Dachau—fell on deaf ears. Chile took the field unopposed to kick the ball into an empty net, securing their qualification.

At a tournament with so troubled a political subtext, the two teams that ultimately dominated were perfectly typecast. The magnificent Dutch side played *"Total Voetbal,"* a radically progressive, free-thinking style of soccer. Their players were versatile, long-haired progressives. The stoic Germans were secretive, setting up camp in fortress-style settings in which their players were incarcerated like prisoners, left to ponder the expectations of a nation. The teams were distilled to the essence of their respective stars—the revolutionary Dutch master Johan Cruyff, and the ultra-conservative Franz Beckenbauer, known as Der Kaiser.

Money was also a central theme. Soccer historian David Goldblatt refers to 1974 as the "tipping point in the history of the tournament, perhaps in all global sport . . . a shift in political geography of global football of tectonic proporations and the herald of an era of hyper-commercialization." The charge was led by Adidas, which set up an entire division to oversee sponsorship and television rights. The number of credentialed journalists doubled from four years before in Mexico, although attendance was up only slightly. From this point on, the television spectacle was what mattered most.

All of this trickled down to the players. The Germans and the Dutch, as it turned out for good

reason, and the Scots, for no fathomable reason whatsoever, arrived already squabbling over win bonuses and revenue share. Where once the honor of representing the nation had sufficed, the players were now part of a money-making machine, and getting their share was worth the distraction it caused. Scotland committed the ultimate in sacrilege, blacking out the Adidas brand on their boots throughout their less-than-auspicious appearance. They failed to emerge from the opening round.

Nothing said it better than this: Pelé was in attendance, not on the field, but up in the corporate boxes in his new role as a pitchman for Pepsi. Also, England was absent after failing to qualify, victims

of a deadly cocktail of insecurity and overinflated national expectations. It would not reappear in the tournament for eight long years.

FIRST MUSSOLINI, THEN MOBUTU

The World Cup draw had been made by a 12-year-old boy from the Schöneberger Sängerknaben Boys' Choir. The planners had no way of knowing that a hand so innocent would trigger a major Cold War incident by pitting East and West against each other in the opening group stage. East Germany defied the odds, winning the battle 1–0, but didn't survive the next, killer round. The national shame heaped upon the West German squad ultimately forced it

to execute a series of drastic tactical realignments that would pay dividends in the long run.

Another opening-round performance of note belonged to Zaire, the first sub-Saharan team to qualify. President Mobutu followed the example of fellow despots Mussolini and Hitler by using the World Cup as a public relations coup. (*See The Five World Cup Fans You'll Meet in Hell, page 16.*) He renamed the team the Leopards (they had been the Lions) to reflect his trademark hat, then purchased on-field billboards, typically reserved for multinational sponsors, that proclaimed ZAIRE—PEACE. But their play could not match the high expectations of the entire African continent; their perfor-

Gerd Müller, aka Der Bomber, detonates the second and final West German goal against Cruyff's Holland in the final.

The Dutch commentator uttered the now-legendary words of helpless horror: "They have tricked us again!"

mance in a 9–0 drubbing by Yugoslavia cemented the stereotype of African teams as comical fodder. (*See The New World Soccer Order, page 234.*)

The Dutch were a revelation. Their previous lack of world-stage pedigree allowed them to play without pressure, enhancing their carefree and deceptively effortless *"Total Voetbal."* In a bruising second-round game, they dispatched a Brazilian team that had strengthened its traditional free-flowing style with some real muscle, and the tension had begun to build. The West German tabloid *Bild Zeitung* alleged that the liberated Dutch squad prepared for that game by hosting a "naked party" with German *mädchens* around their hotel pool. Photographs were promised, but never delivered.

Whether or not they met Germans around the pool, the Dutch definitely met them—the West German variety—in the final. The meeting between Cruyff and Beckenbauer promised greatness. The Dutch sensed all was not right when the tape for their ritual pregame sing-along, by the Volendam rockers The Cats, went strangely missing and they were forced to replace it with David Bowie's "Sorrow." But the game started well for them—almost too well. It took only 90 seconds for Holland to score, courtesy of the first-ever penalty shot in a

World Cup final after Cruyff had been brought down in the box without the Germans even touching the ball. As the English-born referee Jack Taylor pointed to the spot, Franz Beckenbauer invoked recent history by reminding him that "Of course you gave a penalty. You are an Englishman!"

As sometimes happens in soccer, the early advantage put the Dutch off their game. They stroked the ball around the field, playing keep-away, without building on their lead, and neglecting to score a second goal. Twenty-four minutes later, with Beckenbauer's comment no doubt still ringing in his ear, the referee awarded the Germans a dubious penalty of their very own, evening the score. The rest of the game, according to *The Guardian*, was as if "somebody had ploughed over a tulip field." Fitting, then, that it was Gerd Müller, the stocky German goal machine with the uncanny knack of scoring ugly but critical goals, who bundled the ball in for the winner in typical style. As the ball trickled across the line, Dutch commentator Herman Kuiphof recognized the national trauma it was about to trigger; he compared the goal, and the game, to the Nazis' surprise 1940 invasion of Holland with a few now-legendary words of helpless horror: "They [the Germans] have tricked us again!"

There are certain constants in soccer. Among them, a player can't use his hands to touch the ball (goalkeepers, Maradona, and Thierry Henry are the exceptions), each team consists of 11 men, and England always chokes in a shoot-out. But almost everything else having to do with how the players perform, think, and train has been altered and tweaked more times than Victoria Beckham.

PHYSIOLOGY
THEN: DRINK A KEG

On the field, the throwback Lotharios played the game in super slo-mo, using primitive equipment—heavy boots, sodden ball, wool jerseys—and were trapped by their circumscribed roles. There was virtually no cross-pollination of duties; defenders defended, midfielders dribbled and distributed, and strikers shot at goal. Players thought nothing of arriving at games hungover, glassy-eyed, or reeking of women's perfume. And the effects of their late night high jinks were barely noticeable when it came to those hedonistic giants like Meazza, Puskás, and Best. Of course, this was before the introduction of random postgame drug tests (*hola*, Diego) and coaches requiring players to be at the training ground by 8 A.M. for a series of tests aimed at eliminating toxins from the body, either voluntarily or involuntarily.

NOW: DRINK A KEG, MAINTAIN A SIX-PACK

Amazingly, even though the modern player needs to be harder, sleeker, and fitter than his ancient counterpart, his commitment to debauchery hasn't wavered, and this despite the fact that YouTube instantly and globally showcases the slightest transgression. In 2009, English winger Ashley Young and Brazilian striker Pato were both caught in an "offside" position on private webcams, and Italian striker Antonio Cassano boasted in his autobiography that he enjoyed sex with a succession of women in his hotel room before helping himself to an assortment of pastries—no doubt the greater violation of training rules.

Their indiscretions aside, today's players have a healthier respect for both their hearts and their

CHANGING POSITIONS

It's not your grandfather's game anymore

livers due to the exacting physical standards they're held to, not to mention the stratospheric amounts of money at stake. Players are often weighed before each training session to measure the ratio of body fat to muscle. The renowned Arsenal coach Arsène Wenger, whose use of scientific methods in training revolutionized England's soccer culture, mandates that any player whose body fat is above 12 percent cannot practice with the squad until the excess blubber has been turned into muscle.

Diet and nutrition, which used to consist of washing down steak and fries with a light beer, is now fetishistically monitored as well. Organic vegetables, pasta, and fruit are the new training meal staples and the go-to drink is a recovery shake full of vitamins and minerals that help replenish muscles.

Of course, any training regimen, no matter how sophisticated, is built on one simple premise—winning—which is why the best teams in the world have always led the way. When it comes to the World Cup, it all begins with the Dutch and *Total Voetbal*, a system that required 90 minutes of balls-out commitment. Given the Oranje boasted as many party animals as a Seth Rogen movie, they set the modern bar for hard work and harder play.

Total Football's be-everywhere-at-once dictum ushered in an athletic Darwinism that has since only become more unforgiving. As soccer evolved and grew, so too did the way players were evaluated. The catalyst was a joyless Ukrainian named Valery Lobanovsky, who believed that tactical superiority could be measured with the help of computers. After meticulously tracking players' performances during practice, he'd pick his team based on the accumulated data. Every run, pass, shot, and tackle was logged, and his players were put through rigorous physical training and dietary modifications in order to become "perfect" soccer specimens. The results were reflected in the success of the two teams he managed. Dynamo Kiev won everything in sight during his tenure, while the USSR finished second in the 1988 European Championships.

Today, the tobacco-fueled lug (Bulgaria's Dimitar Berbatov remains a notable exception) has been replaced by chiseled freakazoids like Holland's Dirk Kuyt and South Korea's Park Ji-Sung, who hustle, chase, and switch positions with *Kama Sutra*–like dexterity. Teams demand a fluid position-agnostic effort from their players, many of whom will run six to eight miles in a single match. In 2003, OPTA Sportsdata emerged as the world leader in soccer statistics, furnishing coaches with vital information such as passes completed, tackles attempted, and distance covered. These, and other data points, are the holy scripture of the modern game.

GOALKEEPERS
THEN: SUMO WRESTLERS

"Put the fat kid in goal." It's a cliché in sports movies and often a reality on the playground. William

Foulke, an English goalkeeper at the turn of the 20th century, tipped the scales at a Shaq-like 336 pounds. Although he was 6'4", he bore as much resemblance to the modern keeper as the elephant does to the giraffe. Once, during a match for his club team, "Fatty" Foulke broke the wooden crossbar after swinging on it. And it wasn't until the late 1940s that any goalkeepers wore gloves. Try stopping a Cristiano Ronaldo free kick with your bare hands and see if you have any sensation in them for the next week.

NOW: NINJAS

These days, it's rare to find a goalkeeper who doesn't look like he could compete in the NBA. Italy's Gianluigi Buffon, Czech Republic's Petr Cech, and Dutchman Edwin van der Sar tower above everyone in front of them and can bend and

bow their frames into spectacular twisting shapes to deny goals. They are tactically sound, come equipped with condorlike wing spans, and dominate the aerial space.

There's another subset of shot-stoppers who use their raw athleticism to make up for their occasional positioning blunders. France's daredevil Fabien Barthez was the avatar of this style, while Tim Howard is the latest in a string of high-reflex U.S. keepers (Kasey Keller and Brad Friedel are part of that proud tradition) who honed their hand-eye coordination playing American sports. Long gone are the days when the keeper effectively taught himself, learning on the job. The training of goal-

keepers has become so comprehensive that in addition to pounding the ball from goalbox to goalbox, they are now capable of accurate long-range passing, dribbling out of danger, and defending with their feet when lured out of their penalty area. This is both a good and bad thing for soccer. On the positive side, goalkeepers now possess a skill set equal to most outfield players. The problem is, risk-averse managers have become overly reliant on them to dominate a match. How else to explain Italy's coach Marcello Lippi's response, when asked by a journalist why he hadn't bothered to replace the team's creative lynchpin, or *fantasista*, Francesco Totti, who retired after the 2006 World Cup: "We have our own *fantasista*. In goal. His name is Gigi Buffon. A great goalkeeper like him does nothing for an hour and then comes up with a decisive intervention."

In other words, why take a chance entrusting your team to a temperamental goal scorer or free-spirited playmaker when you have a multifaceted rock in goal who can keep your opponent off the board?

DEFENSE

THEN: IMMOVEABLE OBJECTS

Traditionally, the last line of field players, the fullbacks, were the least skilled players in the game. The conventional wisdom was that if you could dribble, you were placed in midfield and if you were good in the air, they'd put you in central defense. Thus, players who were masters of neither skill were stuck out wide on either side of the goal and left to fend for themselves. There, they made up for their lack of finesse with brute force and an ability to instill pants-soiling terror in opposing strikers who dared twinkle-toe into their area. Several of these mongrels tormented opponents at the 1954 World Cup; Scotland boasted the no-nonsense hardman Tommy Docherty, while eventual champions West Germany was anchored by its rock of nastiness, Herbert Erhardt. Of course, any soccer player stuck with a first name like Herbert is bound to have an edge to him.

NOW: PERPETUAL MOTION MACHINES

The Brazilians brought two extra attackers to the World Cup in 1958 and disguised them as fullbacks

to devastating effect. Djalma and Nilton Santos were as likely to be seen galloping forward to support Garrincha and Pelé as they were to be glimpsed defending their own goal. Nilton scored a wonder goal against Austria early in the tournament when he embarrassed several would-be tacklers, and prepared to shoot. His coach, Vicente Feola, could be heard screaming at his fullback to pass the ball and retreat. Instead, Nilton uncorked a wicked shot to give Brazil a 2–0 lead.

By 1974, the attack-from-the-back approach was all the rage. The "libero" or sweeper, so-called for his deep-lying perch behind the rest of the

defense that allowed him to clean up any balls that got through the rearguard, began to make surging runs up the field. Germany's Franz Beckenbauer and Holland's Ruud Krol were at the forefront of the sweeper revolution, gliding through the middle to join the attack and even occasionally scoring from long-range. But it was the wingbacks who enjoyed the most freedom. West Germany conquered the Dutch in 1974 with Paul Breitner and Berti Vogts marauding up the flanks, and it's no coincidence that the last five World Cup winners have featured forward-thinking wingbacks. Of those, Brazil's Roberto Carlos, a star in 2002, is the gold standard for the new breed, combining grace, supreme athleticism, and a thundering repertoire of free kicks. The Brazilians, once a leading proponent of the separation of church (defense) and state (attack) are now the world's leading exporter of attacking wingbacks, though it rarely seems to matter that many of them, Carlos included, are barely adequate as defenders. In fact, some of the most noted backs of the modern era (José Bosingwa, Maicon, and Dani Alves) are as well known for their tentativeness in defense as for their dynamism moving forward.

MIDFIELD

THEN: JACK-OF-ALL-TRADES CENTER-HALVES

Before World War II, a soccer team was commanded by its center-half, an all-purpose midfielder who served as brain, general, and judge all in one. It was his job to cue the attack or dictate that his teammates drop into a defensive posture. He did the thinking and he alone decided who was going to receive the ball.

In the inaugural World Cup final in 1930, Uruguay and Argentina were both heavily dependent on their center-halves. Even though he was on the losing side, Argentina's Luis Monti was widely regarded as the first great player in that position. Nicknamed *doble ancho* ("double-wide") for his ability to cover so much space, Monti was both engine and bulldozer, crippling opponents' attacks with his tackling. His side fell to Uruguay in the final, but four years later Monti switched allegiances, moved to Italy, and helped his new countrymen win the 1934 Cup.

NOW: ONE DEFENDS, THE OTHER ATTACKS

The injection of speed during the '70s, thanks in large part to the urgent fluidity of Total Football, meant that no longer could one man marshal the middle, as the workload was simply too demanding. The game no longer hinged on flashes of individual brilliance; a fast, quick-witted midfielder can easily be neutralized by two or three well-disciplined, brawny opponents. This led to the birth of the midfield specialist: the outside midfielders like France's Franck Ribéry and Spain's David Silva who can tear down the flanks and cross a ball with GPS accuracy; the frenetic, bullying defensive midfielder (Ghana's Michael Essien and Argentina's Javier Mascherano) charged with negating the opponent's best player; and the attacking midfielder (Brazil's Kaká and Portugal's Cristiano Ronaldo) equally comfortable annihilating you with their passing, shooting, or dribbling.

These days, World Cups are rarely won without these key ingredients; while France's run through the elimination rounds in 1998 was credited to the mercurial genius of Zidane, he in turn owed a considerable debt to the rock-solid Didier Deschamps in the defensive third and his tricky offensive counterpoint, Youri Djorkaeff. Zidane's two-game suspension during the tournament, long thought to be enough to break the French resistance, proved a minor speed bump on their march to Paris.

In 2002, it was Ronaldinho's omnipresence as the attacking midfielder (anchored by the twin tacklers Kleberson and Gilberto Silva, winning balls behind him) that was the driving force behind Brazil's title, just as Italy's success in 2006 was largely attributable to the forward-moving Andrea Pirlo and his bulldog defensive foil Gennaro Gattuso.

In this new soccer century, national and club teams would sooner give up the free money from their shirt sponsors than risk losing their two-headed, four-footed midfield duopoly. The split midfield is here to stay.

STRIKERS

THEN: ONE-DIMENSIONAL GLORY HOUNDS

In the game's early days, the center forward would just lollygag around the penalty area waiting for service as though he was His Royal Highness at teatime. Germany's short, squat, and ungainly Gerd Müller was rarely encouraged to venture much farther than six yards from goal, where he was absolute money. The iconic English forward Gary Lineker was lethal when shooting yet inept when tackling.

The archaic division of labor meant that strikers were unconcerned with tracking back and helping out on defense. Instead, their job was to take up residence near the opponent's goal until the ball came their way, at which time they'd pounce. But the ability to finish isn't enough anymore to ensure a striker's place in the modern game. Today, goal-hanging predators like Müller and Lineker would be little more than late second half, damn-the-torpedoes-and-get-me-the-equalizer substitutes.

NOW: FORWARDS WHO GO BOTH WAYS

The laws of mathematics changed the strikers' role. If the fullbacks were charging forward, and multiple midfielders were making runs, then there simply weren't enough players in the back to corral the stampede. Once again, it was the Dutch who were the first to demand defensive aptitude from their forwards. As Johan Cruyff and successive midfield senseis took up more of the scoring burden, the traditional striker-as-goal-scorer-only eventually became an endangered species. Cameroon's Samuel Eto'o is as valued for his willingness to track back and help control the ebb and flow of the game as he is for any goal-scoring gifts.

The English Premier League is the most physically demanding in the world, so it is not surprising that the personification of this new breed of striker is England's fiery Wayne Rooney. Rooney's dribbling and shooting skills sometime mask the other equally fearsome weapons in his arsenal. Even when he doesn't have the ball, Rooney flies around the entire field like an angry wasp, chasing down opposing strikers and providing extra cover when necessary. His work rate and leadership are relentless in both halves of the field, reminiscent of the Ukrainian Andrei Shevchenko in his prime. For club and country, "Sheva" worked tirelessly when not scoring goals, prompting the dour Lobanovsky to label him the first "universal player."

To make life even more challenging for the modern striker, many teams now play with just one player up front to ensure sufficient coverage in defense and midfield. The one thing that hasn't changed, though, is the the core mission of the striker: to put the ball into the net by *any* means possible, as Germany's Mario Gómez demonstrated when he scored a goal for his club with a part of his body that he claimed "is big and it was hurting." And he didn't mean his ego.

JÜRGEN SPARWASSER, EAST GERMANY

Despite its reputation for churning out a cyborg-like assembly line of superhuman swimmers, bobsledders, and female shot putters in the '70s, the German Democratic Republic, or East Germany, was regarded in the soccer world as the poor communist ragamuffins living on the wrong side of the Berlin Wall. It was democratic West Germany that had the talent and trophies, not to mention the economic and social freedoms.

In 1974, West Germany also had the World Cup. The luck of the draw placed the two Germanys in the same group, and the Cold War was symbolically enacted by 22 men in tight satin shorts. When they met, West Germany had already qualified for the next group (East Germany needed a tie), but the event was considered so culturally significant that the Soviet-controlled GDR permitted 3,000 carefully selected East Germans to cross through the checkpoints and attend the match in Hamburg.

Though the East Germans had taken home a bronze soccer medal in the 1972 Olympic Games and qualified for their first World Cup, they were given little chance against a West German juggernaut with three of the greatest German players of all time—the magisterial sweeper and captain Franz Beckenbauer, the goal-scoring dynamo Gerd Müller, and the legendary goalkeeper

Sepp Maier. Not surprisingly, West Germany enjoyed the run of play, but in the 77th minute East German midfielder Jürgen Sparwasser nodded a crossfield pass past two defenders, calmly settled the ball, and lobbed it over Maier to give the GDR a 1–0 victory in the only international match ever played between the two Germanys. The only goal Sparwasser would ever score in a World Cup gave the "other Germany" bragging rights for all-time over their more affluent, powerful neighbors. "Inscribe 'Hamburg 1974' on my tombstone," Sparwasser said. "Then everybody will know who's in that grave."

Contrary to popular opinion, the goal did not lead to a life of riches and acclaim for Sparwasser. On their return home, he and his teammates were declared Meritorious Champions by the government, but there was no ticker tape parade, no gifts, no perks. "Rumor had it I was richly rewarded for the goal, with a car, a house, and a cash premium," said Sparwasser, who escaped to the materialistic nirvana of the West in the late-'80s, "but that is not true."

If Sparwasser's defection was the final irony of the whole episode, it was by no means the only one; in defeating their bitter rivals, East Germany inadvertently ended up helping them. The loss dropped the West Germans to runners-up in the group, leading to a second round that saw them pitted against the lame, the halt, and Poland. Meanwhile, the victory vaulted the GDR into the group's top spot, putting them in a meat grinder of a draw against Holland, Brazil, and Argentina. East Germany was eliminated in the round of eight and Sparwasser's historic goal was reduced to a footnote amidst the euphoria as West Germany hoisted its first World Cup since the raising of the Berlin Wall.

HAITI, 1974

WHY THEY MADE THE LIST: Playing their final qualifying match at home in front of the country's feared military dictator, "Baby Doc" Duvalier, Les Grenadiers of Haiti beat Trinidad and Tobago to earn their spot in the tournament, only after the Soca Warriors had four goals disallowed for various infractions. Chief among them, evidently: showing up in Port-au-Prince.

THE HIGH POINT: Ending Italy's world-record shutout streak of 19 straight when Emmanuel "Manno" Sanon scored in the 46th minute to give Haiti a short-lived 1–0 lead.

THE NADIR: Haitian defender Ernst Jean-Joseph became the first player ever to fail a doping test at the World Cup. He claimed that he wasn't aware that his asthma medication contained a banned substance. Not everyone was convinced, and he was dragged off and reportedly beaten by Haitian officials.

THE FALLOUT: Following their three first-round thrashings by a combined score of 14–2, Les Grenadiers have yet to be heard from again in the World Cup. As for Jean-Joseph, he ended his career with a punishment that not even the barbaric "Baby Doc" could have conceived of—playing for the Chicago Sting of the North American Soccer League (NASL).

HOLLAND, 1974

What Brazil sparked in the heat and humidity of Mexico in 1970, the Dutch set on fire. Brazilian soccer was about beating your man on the dribble, and since almost every Brazilian player was better than the defender across from him, opponents usually lost their will to live after being schooled for the third or fourth time. In 1974, the Dutch brought the same swagger and skill to the game, but added a revolutionary tactic grandiosely called *"Total Voetbal."*

It was a bold and risky system. When it worked, Total Football devoured opponents whole—a feat made even more surprising since it was accomplished by an assortment of shaggy-haired free spirits from the most liberal nation in Europe. For 50 years, soccer had been an allegory for military action. Teams used the flanks and superior firepower to break down their opponent. They lined up in static, rigid formations. But Total Football was a seamless, cerebral blend of movement and interplay that required all ten field players to be able to play all ten positions. Teams were drilled in the idea of "filling the gap": If a defender broke for goal, a midfielder would drop in behind to retain the shape of the side. The attacks could come from anywhere and be launched by anybody at anytime.

All armies need marshaling, and the field general for Holland was Johan Cruyff, whose prodigious talents redefined the sport as Pelé's aura faded. With Cruyff leading the way, the Brilliant Oranje brought Total Football to the masses and it was like seeing the game in high definition for the first time.

The Dutch have a long soccer history of spite and rivalry. In 1974, coach Rinus Michels managed to combine the best players from arch enemies Ajax and Feyenoord, and convert them to his radical vision. The Dutch goals—15 in seven games—were scored from all parts of the field, including several gems by Cruyff, high-octane winger Rob Rensenbrink, and the "lesser Johan," midfielder Johan Neeskens. Wingback Ruud Krol was a constant attacking threat—Exhibit A was his 25-yard screamer against Argentina—and the bone-rattling Willem van Hanegem anchored the midfield.

The Dutch were unstoppable, breathtaking, invincible. Almost.

In the 1974 final against West Germany, Holland's swashbuckling confidence met its match in the well-rested, well-organized hosts. Once the Germans worked out how to neutralize Cruyff—if pit-bullish defender Berti Vogts had marked him any closer, he could have been arrested on a morals charge—they totaled Total Football.

The Dutch had cruised through the tournament, winning disciples for their cult. Yet it was their unwavering belief in their ability to overwhelm opponents that doomed them, for the Germans had too much mental fortitude to be cowed. After the final, some even had the temerity to suggest that Total Football was not a wise strategy in the first place. The victorious German captain Franz Beckenbauer danced on its grave: "Total Football owed more to the element of surprise than to any magic formula. It never dawned on them, certainly not until it was too late, that there were no tactics at all . . . just brilliant players with a ball."

JOHAN CRUYFF
Holland: 1974

Johan Cruyff was so indispensible to the great Dutch "Clockwork Orange" side of the 1970s that he had his own customized uniform. Because Cruyff was sponsored by Puma and the jerseys were made by Adidas, the team provided him with a tailor-made shirt featuring Puma's logo instead of the stripes worn by the other players. Gifted with balletic grace, and a Jedi-like ability to switch direction and leave everyone behind, this gaunt, long-nosed, rakish Amsterdammer was one of the greatest players never to win the tournament.

It took only seven games during his one and only tournament in 1974 to establish his legend. His enormously gifted Dutch team pioneered "Total Football," the versatile system in which all 10 outfield players could play in any position, confusing their opponents by consistently switching roles to take advantage of open space. Cruyff, nominally the striker, was almost always the fulcrum, finding a way to drop off to the flanks and attack from the wings. All 15 of the Dutch goals seemed to start or end with him and his flowing style and revolutionary thinking. The fact that his team fell short in the final against West Germany made him even more compelling and beloved, although his reputation wasn't helped by unproven allegations that the squad spent the night before big games luring innocent German *mädchens* into the hot tub (CRUYFF, CHAMPAGNE, AND NAKED GIRLS! screamed the German tabloids).

By the next World Cup he was gone. His controversial retirement from international soccer at his peak, on the eve of the 1978 Argentina World Cup has never fully been understood, although not for want of theories. It has been explained as a statement against the Argentinian junta, his wife's effort to keep him away from the hot tub, or, as he himself has claimed more recently, an attempt to protect his family's welfare after a botched kidnapping attempt at gunpoint. Whatever the reason, Cruyff, like Édith Piaf, claims to regret nothing: "I don't go through life cursing the fact that I did not win a World Cup.

I played on a fantastic team that gave millions of people watching a great time. That is what football is all about. There is no medal better than being acclaimed for your style." Although Cruyff's international scoring record was sensational (33 goals in 48 games), he is best remembered not for a goal, but for a move against Sweden that became known as the "Cruyff Turn." Trapped on the right-hand side of the penalty area and being marshaled into a harmless position by a Swedish defender, Cruyff somehow turned his upper and lower torso in two different directions while flicking the ball in a third. Watching the move in slow motion, you can almost see the defender's brain freeze as he struggles to stay upright, while the Dutchman breaks free to deliver a lethal cross.

Jan Olsson, the poor Swede victimized by the move, generously claimed that the moment was "the proudest memory of my career. I thought I'd win the football for sure, but he tricked me. I was not humiliated. I had no chance. Cruyff was a genius."

1978
Argentina

TAKING NO PRISONERS

Host Argentina salutes the junta with a "by all means necessary" victory over the wilting Dutch.

WHEN FIFA AWARDED the World Cup to Argentina in 1964, it had no way of foreseeing that by 1978 the country's two recent presidents, Juan Perón and his third wife, Isabel, would have been overthrown by a brutal military regime that proceeded to wage a barbaric war against its own people. Once more the World Cup had unwittingly become a corrupt government's golden life raft of

international legitimacy. Mussolini had provided the blueprint for the Argentinian generals, known as the junta. For a true public relations coup, the team had to win it all.

They set about the task with sinister abandon. Admiral Carlos Alberto Lacoste was selected to prepare the nation for the tournament, inheriting the role after his predecessor was mysteriously assassinated on his way to his very first press conference. Roads were built across the country.

Massive stadia were constructed whose seating capacities were larger than the populations of the towns where they were located. Slums were swept of their inhabitants, thousands of whom conveniently disappeared. Color television was suddenly introduced to the country. The American PR company Burson-Marsteller was hired to place its spin on the event, contributing a branding memo strangely titled "What Is True for Products Is Also True for Countries." Henry Kissinger was cajoled,

no doubt by his love of soccer alone, to publicly proclaim, "Now the world would see the true face of Argentina." Freed from checks and balances, Lacoste spent $700 million—over seven times what had been budgeted—while critics, including the treasury secretary, fell victim to a spate of car bombings. The Argentinian slogan "25 million Argentinians will play in the World Cup" was instantly bastardized by graffiti artists to read "25 million Argentinians will pay for the World Cup."

There were murmurs of political protest across the soccer world, but little materialized in the way of action. Amnesty International managed to persuade German goalie Sepp Maier and Italian striker Paolo Rossi to sign a petition against the torture of prisoners. The Dutch threatened to pull out. Indeed, Johan Cruyff did not participate, but that was probably because his wife grounded him after hearing rumors of his high jinks in the Jacuzzi back in 1974. But most of the reactions were pragmatic. The English Union of Journalists provided its members with a Spanish language handbook that included such phrases as "Stop torturing me!"

Once the tournament began, the soccer took over. Adidas unveiled a new ball named the Tango. Tunisia quickly tangoed all over the Mexicans, 3–1,

achieving the first ever World Cup victory by an African nation. The hapless Scots arrived with their manager, Ally MacLeod, boldly claiming they could win it all. Cheered on by its Tartan Army, some of whom were rumored to have requisitioned a submarine to make the trip, the team played in true Scottish style, getting thrashed by Peru and drawing with Iran, then beating the Dutch 3–2 in an unforgettable classic. It was the one game they were least likely to win, and it was good for a moment in the spotlight, but not good enough to prevent them from being on a plane home before the second round kicked off.

The star of the tournament was the host team, coached by the gaunt César Menotti, a walking cigarette advertisement. Between drags, he had con-

troversially omitted the nation's rising star, 17-year-old Diego Maradona, from his squad, preferring to build his team around the more experienced Mario Kempes, nicknamed "El Matador," and the guileful midfielder Osvaldo Ardiles. Ardiles played with a craftiness revered in Argentina as *La Nuestra* or Our Way—a style of play that was physical yet skillful, combining movement, energy, and passion.

From the outset, rumors of biased referees and steroid use dogged the Argentinians. To qualify for the final, they had to beat Peru by four goals to edge rival Brazil on goal differential. Historians may never know for sure whether the ease of their 6–0 win was connected to the 35,000 tons of free grain Argentina shipped to Peru, the $50 million in interest-free loans, or the erratic play of the Argen-

1978
RESULTS

(Group play until the semifinals)
THIRD PLACE
Brazil 2 Italy 1

FINAL
Argentina 3 Holland 1

(right) Scottish manager Ally MacLeod's efforts to blend in with the locals were no more successful than his team's efforts to qualify for the second round; (far right) Argentina 3, Holland 1.

tinian-born Peruvian goalkeeper, Ramón Quiroga. Already known as the Crazy One, Quiroga played like a psychotic. The Brazilians had no doubts there had been quid pro quos, awarding themselves the title of "moral victor" and leaving. They had been eliminated despite being unbeaten. Their coach, Claudio Coutinho, predicted, "The Peruvians will not feel proud when they hear their national anthem at the next World Cup."

Regardless, the Argentinians had demonstrated a surprisingly deft soccer style for a team that had a player named "Killer" among its ranks. Unfortunately for the Dutch, their dark side resurfaced before the final against Holland, which picked up where it left off in 1974, despite the absence of Cruyff. First, the Dutch bus was taken on a circuitous route to the stadium, then kept on the field for 10 minutes in front of a hostile crowd before Argentina emerged, only to protest a plaster cast on René van de Kerkhof's hand, a move intended to further rattle the Dutch. Having won the mind games, Argentina went on to take the trophy in extra time on the strength of two goals from dashing forward Kempes. The Dutch were despondent, having lost two consecutive World Cup finals to host countries, no less. Their team was inconsolable, unable to find the energy even to collect their medals. They limped out of town, claiming that Argentina would not have won anywhere but on home soil, which was perhaps true, and hinted at an impending radical transformation of the domestic game. It was about to go global. In 1978, Kempes was the only Argentinian squad member playing abroad. By 1990, all of them were.

ARIE HAAN
Holland vs. Italy, Second Round

For all the precision and artistry involved in an exquisitely worked team goal, there is something to be said for one player taking it on himself to settle matters with a single swing of his leg from 40 yards out. Certainly, Arie Haan was the only person in Buenos Aires on June 21, 1978, who thought, upon finding the ball at his feet and the goal guarded by the best keeper in the world, Dino Zoff, that it would be a good idea to attempt to score.

Think about it—too many things can go wrong from so great a distance. A defender can get a leg or body in the ball's flight path, or the player mis-kicks so badly that the ball sails closer to the corner flag than the net, unleashing a torrent of derisive whistles from the crowd and recriminatory glances from teammates, coach, and maybe even his mother.

But self-doubt was not part of Haan's DNA. After all, the converted midfielder turned sweeper wasn't known as Arie Mayhem for nothing. "That lad has suspenders in his shoes," said Johan Cruyff. Haan had already blitzed West Germany earlier in the tournament with a 30-yard blast that almost ripped the net off the post, but the notion that he'd pull the trigger from near midfield was a stretch even for him.

From such a lack of prescience are great goals made. With the game tied at 1–1 (and Dutch defender Ernie Brandts making history earlier as the only player to score for both teams in the same match), Holland was awarded a free kick so far out that the Italians didn't even bother to construct a defensive wall. The ball was tapped forward to Haan, who thundered a swerving drive that zipped off the turf and caromed in off the post with a *ding* that sounded like the tolling of a funeral bell in an Italian church. What at first must have appeared to be a desperate prayer turned into Zoff's worst nightmare as the ball kept lurching and bending from left to right. By the time he recognized his impending doom, flinging himself at full stretch toward the swooping comet, it was too late. Coming just 15 minutes from time, Haan's hammer blow proved to be the difference in a tough, evenly matched 2–1 win for the Oranje.

More than thirty years later, Haan is still at a loss to explain his wonder goal. He says he gets goose bumps when he sees the replay even now, suggesting that divine intervention just might have played a part. Alas, the soccer gods didn't stick around long enough to prevent the Dutch from losing their second World Cup final in a row.

ARCHIE GEMMILL
Scotland vs. Holland, First Round

There are certain words that don't belong together. "Germany" and "comedy" come to mind. "England" and "dental hygiene" is another odd pairing. But the strangest combination of all could very well be "Scotland" and "great soccer goals." The Scots do Scotch whiskey well, kilts superbly, and make a sublime dish from a sheep's stomach, but as a soccer nation, Scotland is best known for its assembly line of ginger-haired, doughty, put-a-nasty-set-of-bruises-on-you defenders. "Scottish" and "flair"—an oxymoron of the highest caliber.

So it's hard to believe a Scotsman scored one of the most exhilarating World Cup goals of all time. After a typically dour and disappointing performance in the first two matches of the preliminary round of the World Cup, including a 3–1 defeat to Peru and a 1–1 draw with Iran, the Scots entered their final group game needing to win by three goals

in order to move on to the next round. It was a tall order, given that many felt Scotland couldn't score three goals against Mary Ignatius of the Holy Blind, let alone in a single match against eventual 1978 finalist Holland. In the end, the Scots fell short of advancing, but they somehow pulled off a goal for the World Cup ages.

Its architect, dribbler, and finisher was all one man: Archie Gemmill, a squat, red-headed winger from English champions Nottingham Forest. With Scotland leading 2–1 and more than 20 minutes left, his jinking, miraculous hop-skip-and-jump through a Dutch defense, previously thought to be impregnable, was arguably the highlight of the tournament.

Playing a swift one-two with forward Kenny Dalglish, Gemmill picked up the ball on the right of the penalty area and danced past three heavy Dutch tackles, nutmegging the last defender before curl-

ing his shot into the net over onrushing goalkeeper Jan Jongbloed. His manager, Ally MacLeod, remembers it this way: "My abiding memory of that game was shouting at Archie: 'Pass the ball! Pass the ball!' . . . After that he [Gemmill] ran right over to the dugout and said to me: 'I did pass it, boss, right into the back of the net!' "

While the Dutch scotched the Scottish dream in scoring their second goal barely three minutes later in the 3–2 defeat, Gemmill's masterpiece remains the zenith of Scottish soccer, perhaps of all of post-*Braveheart* society. The goal inspired a song by the Tartan Specials ("I love sex and drugs and sausage rolls/But nothing compares to Archie Gemmill's goal") and was memorialized in the movie *Train-spotting* when Ewan McGregor, recovering his wits postcoitus, says, "I haven't felt that good since Archie Gemmill scored against Holland in 1978!"

Brazil, in unfamiliar blue
shirts, boots Argentina.

BRAZIL VS. ARGENTINA

There's never any shame in losing to Brazil. You lost? Well, not really. C'mon, it's Brazil. They're not like the rest of us. For Pelé's sake, even their yellow jerseys radiate sunshine and goodwill.

That may be the prevailing wisdom in the rest of the world, where Brazil brings out the just-glad-to-be-on-the-same-field-with-these-golden-soccer-gods in their opponents, but not in Argentina. "Brazil have sold the world this idea that they're the only ones capable of playing beautifully . . . bollocks!" Maradona wrote in his autobiography. "We can also do the *joga bonito,* we just don't know how to sell it."

And there you have the crux of this rivalry: the perceived goodness of Brazil and her people set against the seething masses of Argentina. "We play football for fun, for entertainment's sake, for the spectacle, for the beauty," says the bearded Brazilian legend Socrates, "The Argentinians play to win."

Brazil and Argentina face each other more than they would like in non-tournament years. In the regional qualifying phase for the World Cup, they are required to play twice, and they frequently clash in the Copa América, but those skirmishes pale next to their World Cup battles. It's gotten pretty nasty over the years in spite of the transcendent skills on display. For all of Brazil's mystique, it is a statistically balanced rivalry—33-33, with Argentina leading in goals scored (143–137). Yet almost everybody will tell you that Brazil is a far better team. Part of it, of course, is that Brazil has three more championships, but it's also true that Argentina is prone to acts of self-sabotage on the world stage.

Their first Cup showdown was a tense 0–0 draw in 1978, when Argentina was the host. After Brazil pummeled Poland, it was through to the final unless Argentina scored more than three goals against a decent Peruvian side. Instead of playing all of the last matches at the same time, FIFA permitted Argentina to kickoff later, and Peru (with its Argentinian-born keeper, Ramón Quiroga, between the posts) laid down like beaten dogs, 6–0. The World Cup rematch came four years later when Brazil sambaed to a 3–1 win that saw Maradona ejected for his spiteful kick to Batista's southern hemisphere. Maradona, being Maradona, showed a twisted sense of remorse afterward, saying, "It ended badly, I lashed out. . . . But it was meant for Falcão. . . . I turned round and hit out at the first guy I saw, I was so pissed off. . . . Poor guy, it was Batista."

Maradona and Argentina got a measure of revenge in a 1990 World Cup qualifier amid reports— Maradona all but admitted the skullduggery years later—that the men in baby blue had spiked a Brazilian water bottle with tranquilizers. But there was nothing he could do to escape the hurt that Brazil put on Argentina's 2010 World Cup hopes in their critical qualifying match in September 2009. Anointed with great fanfare to rescue his country's flailing campaign, Maradona was shocked to find that his presence on the sidelines didn't have the same galvanizing effect it did on the field. Two unexpected debacles—a 6–1 thrashing by Bolivia and a 2–0 loss to Ecuador—left the Argentinians needing a victory over Brazil to ensure they weren't in danger of the unthinkable: not qualifying for the World Cup for the first time since 1970. Desperate for any advantage, they moved the game to Rosario, where the Brazilians would be up against not just Messi and company but the ferocious partisanship of 37,000 home fans.

A hostile environment notwithstanding, beating Brazil also requires a game plan and Maradona had none beyond urging his players forward. As admirable as it is to instill an attacking mindset in your team, you also have to remind them to defend. By ignoring that strategic imperative and deploying two centerbacks with a whopping total of four international caps between them, Maradona invited Brazil to cut his team to sorry little pieces on the counterattack en route to a 3–1 thumping. "Never before have Brazil given Argentina such a lesson in class, effort, and teamwork," pronounced the Argentinian sports daily *Diario Olé.*

What grates on the Argentines is not so much Brazil's five World Cup titles but that each one, with the possible exception of their stolid display at U.S.A. '94, has been accompanied by global adulation, and even its most painful periods are strangely revered. Meanwhile, the world revels in Argentina's losses, and even its glorious two World Cup victories seem as tainted as that Brazilian water bottle. Its first, as the host nation in 1978, featured not only the highly suspect Peruvian surrender, but a laughable attempt at gamesmanship in the final, where the Dutch were forced to cool their heels on the field while the Argentinians deliberately delayed their entrance for 10 minutes. And then there was 1986 in Mexico, where Maradona dazzled the world with his feet, only to be stigmatized as a cheat for using his hand (*see Greatest Goals: Diego Maradona, page 131*).

And so it goes. When a team plays attractive, free-flowing soccer, a commentator will inevitably remark that it's Brazilian in nature.

A brazen illegal goal? That's Argentina.

A rivalry of two implacable foes forever locked in mortal combat? That would be Brazil and Argentina.

WANTED:

MULTILINGUAL MARATHONER WITH ENCYCLOPEDIC MEMORY

Blowing the whistles on referees

Soccer is a game in which 22 athletes compete on the field of play, yet many of the critical incidents take place in another venue altogether: the mind of the referee. In the final minute of a crucial game, when the ball ricochets amidst a cluster of players in the penalty area and an attacker tumbles to the turf as if he has been shot, the referee will be surrounded by screaming advocates from both teams. As the crowd goes berserk, the official has a split second to make a decision, aware that it will instantly be judged from all angles via instant replay in television studios around the world. A wrong verdict can end a career, even determine the fate of a nation.

Officiating a World Cup soccer match is a thankless task. If you do the job well, few notice. But if you make a mistake—for instance, allowing a certain Frenchman to palm the ball and set up a game-winning goal—you will be crucified for your unconscionable favoritism and general lack of omniscience. FIFA has resisted making refs lives easier by adopting technologies such as goal-line sensors, instant replay, or adding two assistants behind the goals, oddly preferring the position that "the perfect referee does not exist. It's one man against 90,000 people and 22 actors, and a percentage of calls will always be wrong." And so it has enshrined the human error as an inevitable factor in the tournament and exposed its referees to a verbal battering at the hands of players, fans, and the media. But before you join the masses in casting stones, take a moment to consider the breathtakingly eclectic set of conditions required to be a modern referee:

ENCYCLOPEDIC MEMORY: Their command of the written laws of the game must be absolute, yet their interpretation must be flexible enough to account for the spirit of any particular game.

SUPERIOR FITNESS: A referee must be in top-tier physical condition, arguably more so than even the players. They have to keep up with the flow of the game for the full 90 minutes, without the luxury of grabbing a quick breather.

SPLIT-SECOND DECISION MAKING: In every match there is a game within the game as the players probe and test the official, and the referee walks a tightrope between asserting his authority and stifling the free flow of the game. Aided only by two assistants running the line and two sideline assistants, a referee must make numerous, instant judgment calls in one highly charged situation after another, including repeated offside decisions, which are among the hardest to call in all of professional sport.

MULTILINGUALISM: To command respect from players in highly agitated emotional states, a referee requires the finely honed skills of an ambassador, able to be understood by people of different cultures, races, and education levels. It is not uncommon for a World Cup official to speak three or four languages.

NERVES OF STEEL: The World Cup is a crucible that can make a referee's name synonymous with incompetence. Jack Taylor, the English official who oversaw the 1974 final (in which he had the confidence to issue the first-ever penalty awarded at that stage, and quickly followed it with the second) admitted that "few toilets were used more than those in the referee's changing room."

This all suggests a cross between Ruth Bader Ginsburg and Lance Armstrong, but the closest the World Cup has come to perfection was the Italian Pierluigi Collina, who refereed the 2002 final. Collina turned the savage alopecia he contracted at age 24 into an extra tool of authority and intimidation. Collina claimed his secret lay in research—watching hours of game tape before critical matches to gain a sense of every player's moves, positions, and tricks. "It is important . . . to know what is going to happen," he said. "Reacting is too late." But his signature crazed, bulging eye sockets may also have something to do with his ability to control a match and its players. He remains the only referee beloved enough to launch a line of watches and sportswear, to say nothing of once being voted the Sexiest Man in Italy. He retired in 2005, possibly the last of his breed.

Who in his right mind would step up to be the arbiter for World Cup games that amount to global warfare by other means? Few do it for the money. Although the pay is decent, each receiving $40,000 in 2006, most referees have solid careers in other industries—finance and education are especially common. Many profess they do it "for the love of the game," although in *Men in Black*, a history of the modern referee, author Gordon Thompson determined in the words of one reviewer that the majority are "anal-retentive control freaks with no personality who are prone to childish sulking fits if they don't get their own way and who become worse the more attention they get."

Exhibit A for Thompson's theory would be Graham Poll, the English referee whose career is a morality tale for all those who follow. Poll was a smug official who had spent 26 years making his way from the minor leagues of English soccer to become one of the most prominent referees in the world. By the time the 2006 tournament rolled around, he was widely tipped to be the man in the middle for the final itself. But thanks to an uncharacteristically inept display during the group stage—he managed to award Croatian Josip Simunic three yellow cards when two should have been sufficient to send him to the showers—his career disintegrated overnight. Instead of trotting out for the final, Poll found himself disgraced and sent home early. A FIFA spokesman was a master of understatement as he announced, "We had a first in the history of the World Cup yesterday when one player was booked three times in the same match. That is a little too much." Poll was a shattered man and the vitriolic abuse English fans heaped on contributed to his decision to retire within a year.

THE SIX DEADLY PERILS OF REFEREEING

Because referees are human, every World Cup includes at least one horror show. Here are seven legendary decisions in six categories that have affected the outcome of matches, and in some instances, ended the official's career in the process:

1. CONTROVERSY
Gottfried Dienst (Switzerland)
England vs. Germany, Final, 1966

The World Cup final was tied at two goals apiece as the game entered extra time. In the 101st minute, England's striker Geoff Hurst thumped the ball against the crossbar and it rebounded straight down to land in the vicinity of the goal line. As the English players celebrated, Dienst, the Swiss referee, was befuddled, consulting immediately with his Soviet linesman, Tofik Bakhramov, who assured him that the ball had crossed the line, but the Germans have always maintained that the call was incorrect. In 1996, two Oxford University professors used "projective geometry" techniques to determine that the ball landed *on* the line, not over it, and so was "at least three inches from being a goal." FIFA resists using goal-line technology to this day.

(below) Welsh referee Clive Thomas deprived the Brazilians of a last-second goal against a relieved Sweden; (right) Card trick: Graham Poll, who mistakenly gave Croatia's Josip Simunic three yellow cards in 2006.

---

2. INEXPERIENCE
Ali Bennaceur (Tunisia), England vs. Argentina, Quarterfinal, 1986

England faced Argentina in this quarterfinal grudge match—the first time the two rivals met after fighting a real war over the Falkland Islands. Logic would dictate that an experienced referee would be handed the duty. Instead, the Tunisian representative, Ali Bennaceur, was awarded the honor. In the 51st minute, Maradona used the "Hand of God" to punch the ball past a stunned English goalkeeper into the back of the net. Everyone in the world saw the illegal use of a fist, apart from the one guy who mattered. Bennaceur awarded the goal, and later blamed his error on a hemorrhoid treatment he was taking that affected his sight. He never refereed a World Cup game again.

3. CONSPIRACY
Byron Moreno (Ecuador), South Korea vs. Italy, Second Round, & Gamal Ghandour (Egypt), South Korea vs. Spain, Quarterfinal, 2002

Just because you are paranoid does not mean they aren't out to get you. When host the Korean Republic bounced Italy from the 2002 tournament, Italian manager Giovanni Trapattoni cried conspiracy. The referee, Byron Moreno, seemed hell-bent on ensuring the Koreans progressed, disallowing a perfectly fine Italian goal and controversially sending off their star, Francesco Totti. The Spanish newspapers belittled the Italian claims, but when Spain lost to Korea in the very next round, they soon changed their tune, with *Marca*'s headline screaming *Italia tenía razón* (Italy was right!). Gamal Ghandour disallowed two seemingly legal Spanish goals and his linesmen—one Ugandan, the other Trinidadi-

an—enthusiastically judged attack after attack to be offsides. Moreno returned to a hero's welcome in Ecuador, but was out of the game within a year after receiving not one but two domestic bans for incompetent refereeing. Ghandour retired shortly after Spanish newspapers accused him of accepting a Hyundai car as a "gift" from a Korean FIFA representative who was the Hyundai scion.

4. LOSING THE PLOT
Valentin Ivanov (Russia), Holland vs. Portugal, Second Round, 2006

In what has become known as the "Battle of Nuremberg," the Russian referee entered the record books after handing out more cards than a croupier. In an orgy of card waving, 12 yellows were raised, along with four reds. Both teams ended the game with nine men on the field and FIFA president Sepp Blatter suggested that "there could have been a yellow card for the referee."

5. COMPULSIVENESS
Clive Thomas (Wales), Brazil vs. Sweden, Group Round, 1978

The Welshman was nicknamed "The Book" and he certainly went by it in the opening round match-up, which was tied 1–1 in injury time. Thomas looked at his watch as he awarded Brazil a corner, but then proceeded to blow the full-time whistle the very second Brazilian legend Zico headed the corner past Ronnie Hellstrom into the Swedish goal. Although Thomas was technically correct to disallow the goal (the laws state the amount of time is "at the discretion of the referee"), his reputation was battered for the rest of his career.

6. INEPTITUDE
Charles Corver (Holland), France vs. West Germany, Semifinal, 1982

German goalkeeper Harald Schumacher's demolition of French defender Patrick Battiston as he advanced one-on-one on goal has been heralded as the worst foul in World Cup history. Schumacher never touched the ball, launching his hip into the Frenchman's head. Battiston was stretchered off with a concussion, among other injuries, and hospitalized, yet Corver assessed Schumacher neither a red nor yellow card. Corver also deprived the French of a free kick, determining instead that the game should restart with a German goal-kick. *The Times* of London was particularly incensed by his performance, facetiously postulating that, as one of Corver's linesmen, Robert Valentine, was Scottish, he may have "turned a blind eye because it was the kind of thing you'd see outside any Glasgow pub on a Saturday night."

CULT FIGURES

OSVALDO "OSSIE" ARDILES, ARGENTINA

When Ardiles was a boy playing street soccer in Argentina, his older brother noticed that he undulated like a snake when the ball was at his feet, and stuck Ossie with the nickname *"Piton"*—python. The irony was that pythons are among the largest snakes, while Ardiles was invariably the smallest player on the field. Though 5'6", he squeezed the life out of Argentina's World Cup opponents with his lethal dribbling skills, and then swallowed English soccer whole as the first Argentine to ply his trade for a British club.

Long before the traditional #10 was awarded to Argentina's reigning midfield maestros (Maradona, Riquelme, and now Messi), Ardiles, who wore #2 in an era when the Albicelestes assigned team numbers in alphabetical order, was the fulcrum of an unheralded squad (only Mario Kempes, among the starters, played for a foreign club) that won its first World Cup in 1978.

He was blessedly free of the arrogance typical of ball wizards. Though Ardiles scored only a single goal in his 11 World Cup matches, no less a narcissist than Maradona called him "a phenomenon"—one who "always worried more about the team than himself." This was never more evident than in the final against Holland, when Ardiles sublimated his attacking instincts to focus on neutralizing the dynamic Dutch mid-fielder Johan Neeskens for 65 minutes. And he still found time to set up Kempes's first goal with a nifty pass delivered just as he was being upended from behind.

His skill and conditioning withstood a two-pack-a-day cigarette habit, and though celebrated in Argentina, he was possibly even more beloved in London, where, after the tournament, he and his countryman Ricky Villa not only adapted to the hurly-burly of the English game, but thrived in it. As they lifted their club, the chronically mediocre Tottenham Hotspur, into the upper echelon of the English league, they planted the flag for the subsequent invasion of foreign talent. Over nearly 11 years, Ardiles played more than 200 times for Tottenham, blazing the trail to England for Klinsmann, Henry, and Cristiano Ronaldo.

By 1981, his popularity peaking, Ardiles appeared in the soccer movie *Victory*, where he performed the "Ardiles flick," stealing the show from Pelé, Bobby Moore, and Sylvester Stallone. Without breaking stride—and more Houdini now than python—Ardiles rolled the ball up the back of his right leg with his left foot before propelling it over his head with his right heel so that it dropped directly into his serpentine path. Even Pelé shook his head in wonder.

Paolo Rossi opens the scoring for Italy against Germany in the final.

1982
Spain

MAMMA MIA!

After being written off, Italy doctors the entire script in a World Cup of epic matches.

THIS WAS THE YEAR the World Cup became a global gravy train. In 1970, a Carnaby Street men's outfitter, John Stephen, had purchased a quarter of the prime advertising space around the ground for England's showdown with Brazil. By 1982, only the largest global multinationals like Coca-Cola and Kodak could afford to compete for the space. The tournament's television audience was soaring. Millions of people tuned in to watch the 24 teams that qualified from the field of 97, with every region represented for the first time. By accepting micro-states and islands like Solomon Islands, Vanuatu,

Samoa, and Tahiti into its powerful infrastructure, FIFA now represented even more countries than the United Nations.

For champion Argentina, the World Cup came two months after their military junta had invaded the Falkland Islands, a South-Atlantic vestige of the British Empire, in an ultimately futile effort to divert attention from their domestic economic woes. The soccer squad, this time with the 21-year-old Maradona, was confident of victory, emboldened by the state-run media's conviction that the Argentinian military was on the brink of winning a glorious victory. The team arrived in Spain to read the free press and discover the truth—the military was actually on the verge of surrender. With its morale shattered, the team limped out in the second round, only to have a frustrated Maradona sent off for kicking the Brazilian substitute, Batista; it was the coup de grâce in their 3–1 loss to their archrivals. The Spanish had no such geopolitical excuses for their desperately disappointing performance. They used the tournament to establish their impressive track record of flattering to deceive, opening as one of the favorites, scraping through the first round despite being schooled by tiny Northern Ireland, the equivalent of a pub team, before rolling over in the second round—an act they would repeat with some regularity.

ROSSI REDUX

The Italians started slowly and unconvincingly, as they so often do, playing as if planning only on a short stay. The World Cup came at the end of a period of disgrace for their domestic game. Serie A had been enmeshed in a betting and match-fixing scandal in which star striker, Paolo Rossi, was a central figure. When he was allowed to rejoin the team after a two-year ban, he was portly and unfit, and his lackluster performances in the early games made him raw meat for the Italian press. The pressure on him soon compounded when he and his roommate were photographed shirtless, popping their heads out of their hotel window. The Italian press seized on the scene as specious proof of their homosexuality, and a national scandal ensued. The team barely survived the opening round. In their final group game against Cameroon, the Italians hardly attacked, strangely settling for a draw when they needed a win, fueling rumors of match-fixing. The Italians managed to pull through on goal difference after drawing all of their games, the first team ever to proceed without winning a match.

The scheming was hardly limited to the Italians. After Algeria shocked West Germany 2–1, Austria and West Germany put their heads together and, knowing a 1–0 German victory would allow both teams to progress at Algeria's expense seemingly arranged for the Austrians to leak a goal inside 10 minutes. From that moment on, both teams conspired to ensure the ball rarely made it out of midfield for the remainder of the game, as outraged Algerian fans waved banknotes from the terraces, and one German fan set fire to his own flag in protest. West German coach Jupp Derwall only fanned the flames when he shrugged, saying, "We wanted to progress, not play football."

France played some of the most beautiful soccer in the tournament, led by the offensive creativity of the deceptive Michel Platini, of whom *L'Equipe* wrote, "You can find three million French people who run faster than him, who can jump higher than him, but you could not find a man who can play football better than him." In the opening rounds the fluid French were almost unstoppable. The Kuwaitis finally developed a unique strategy to keep them from scoring. A sheikh, Fahad Al-Ahmad Al-Sabah, left his seat, walked onto the field, and

Paolo Rossi (in blue) scored six times in the 1982 World Cup to win the Golden Shoe.

removed his players in protest of a French goal, to prove it had been scored after his defenders heard a whistle blown in the stands and relaxed. The hapless Soviet referee, Miroslav Stupar, wilted in the spotlight and reversed his original decision, making this the only time a World Cup goal was influenced by a royal member of the crowd. France still won 4–1.

The Brazilians were still fuming about the suspicious nature of their exit in 1978. Their team was led by the greatest soccer playing MD of all time, Socrates, a chain-smoking orthopedist; Zico, known as White Pelé; and the adventurous Falcão. Their midfield was loaded, and a good thing it was since they were uncharacteristically short of firepower up front, a quality that haunted them in their classic matchup with the Italians. Although the form book predicted a game in which the incisive play of the Brazilians would slice through the smothering defense of the Italians, Paolo Rossi came alive, scoring a magnificent hat trick that transformed his career, his countrymen's view of his sexuality, and Italy's World Cup fortune. The Brazilians, who needed only a draw to advance, tied the score at 2–2, but it wasn't in their nature to settle. Naively, they continued to play open football, pressing for a victory they did not need, leaving themselves vulnerable to Rossi's opportunism. In the end, Brazil joined a category previously headed by the 1974 Dutch—the finest teams not to win it all.

The semifinal also provided a World Cup classic as plucky France lined up against one of its greatest foes, the West Germans. The game had all the plotlines of a great daytime soap opera, alternating moments of breathtaking play with ones of thuggish brutality, as when West German goalkeeper Harald Schumacher seemed to use kung fu to demolish naive French defender Patrick Battiston as he advanced one-on-one (*see Rogues, Part I, page 118*). The French recovered to go two goals ahead in extra time, a situation in which, as England fans will remember, Germany is at its most dangerous. They predictably slotted home two goals in six minutes to send a World Cup game to penalties for the first time. It was a format in which the West Germans were virtually unbeatable, prevailing this time 5–4. The French had been mugged.

Schumacher later beat Adolf Hitler in a French newspaper's poll of the nation's most-hated man, but the French could draw solace from the fact that they had exhausted the West Germans, who were picked off by Italy, 3–1, in the final.

Paolo Rossi predictably scored the opening goal, leading his team to a most unexpected victory—one that became a symbol of national rebirth, triggering the commercial rise of the Serie A and of the country's economy in general, and establishing a pattern that would repeat itself. Italy is never more dangerous than when it has been written off.

WEST GERMANY 3, FRANCE 3

Semifinal (West Germany wins 5–4 on penalties)

In 1982, the French finally had a team good enough to beat the hated West Germans and the perfect stage for payback—the teeming, raucous Sánchez Pizjuán stadium in Seville, Spain. Even the fates had nodded their beret in France's direction, as West Germany's star player, Karl-Heinz Rummenigge, was injured and forced to the bench. Rummenigge, who inherited the übermensch mantle from Franz Beckenbauer after Der Kaiser retired, had matured into Europe's Player of the Year. His absence put more pressure on West Germany's mobile backline, led by Afro-permed defender Paul Breitner.

The French, for their part, had come swaggering into the match behind their captain Michel Platini, one of soccer's transcendent players and the heart of a midfield—notably Alain Giresse and Jean Tigana—that bristled with creativity and speed. The question went begging: With so much world-class talent on both sides, would the teams cancel each other out and produce a cautious, defensive stand-off or would all that beguiling skill result in a game for the ages?

Despite temperatures in the mid-90s, both sides stuck to their strengths; France played with a *joie de vivre* more suited to a sandlot than to the crucible of a World Cup semifinal, while the West Germans countered with their trademark efficiency and indomitable will. Every great tale needs a potent antagonist and in the 60th minute of a pulsating 1–1 game, West German goalkeeper Harald Schumacher elected himself. France's Patrick Battiston had stormed down the middle of the field to latch on to a pass that had bisected the West German defense. What happened next is still being bitterly replayed in France almost 30 years later.

Simply put, Schumacher poleaxed Battiston. The thud was so sickening, and Battiston so lifeless, that for three long minutes Platini actually thought his teammate was dead—"He had no pulse," he said later, "he looked so pale." Medics ran out to administer oxygen to the unconscious Battiston, and when he was finally stretchered off—with spinal cord injuries, a massive concussion, and two missing teeth—everyone waited for the inevitable: Schumacher would be dismissed, and West Germany would be forced to play with ten men the rest of the way. Astonishingly, the Dutch referee not only didn't issue a red card, but declined even to

Klaus Fischer ties the score at 3–3 with a bicycle kick in extra time.

call an infraction on the play, suggesting that he was, at least for the afternoon, subscribing to the No Death, No Foul School of Officiating. Schumacher, playing his role of designated villain to the hilt (*see Achtung!, page 134*), further incited Gallic rage with his body language. According to one West German journalist, his posture during the entire stoppage was akin to his saying, "Please scrape this French vermin off the field so that I can take my goal-kick."

At the end of regulation, with the score still 1–1, the two teams moved into 30 minutes of extra time. When the French fired in two quick goals it looked as if karmic justice would prevail. Famed British announcer Martin Tyler proclaimed, "Germany is dissolving. I can't remember ever saying that about a German side."

NAIVE AND FATAL

But as its illustrious World Cup history testifies, Germany doesn't go gently into the *nacht*. In the 98th minute, after France had gone ahead 2–1 and all looked lost for the West Germans, Rummenigge could endure no more and entered the game. "It was much harder to watch the game from the sideline than to play in it," he would say later. "I died a thousand times before I decided to risk further injury by playing." West German hopes dimmed further when Giresse scored his goal in the 98th minute to put France up 3–1. Surely, France would now bunker in, pack their penalty area, and absorb West Germany's onslaught? But the French, like the Brazilians, know only one way to play. Behind Platini, their sublime conductor, the French kept willing themselves forward, inspired by their fallen teammate, Battiston, and seeking to heap further humiliation upon the West Germans.

As tactics go, it was naive . . . and fatal. With three minutes left before the overtime break, Uli Stielike, the West German sweeper, intercepted the ball and started a swift counterattack, a move that culminated with a goal by Rummenigge to cut France's lead to 3–2. Almost immediately after the restart, Rummenigge was again instrumental when West Germany leveled the score on an acrobatic bicycle kick by Klaus Fischer. The game was now tied and France barely held on through the remainder of the extra time.

In their infinite wisdom, the Lords of Soccer had decreed in the last decade that if a game is tied after overtime, it will then be decided by penalty kicks. So, after 120 breathtaking minutes, a game that had hurtled past epic into the realm of the mythical, would hinge on the outcome of that dreaded soccer crapshoot.

"It can't be fair to decide a match this important on penalties," the French coach, Michel Hidalgo, would say afterward. "Four years of hard work is ruined by one single save." Worse, now the French kickers would be facing the Spawn of Satan himself—Schumacher. Would France's *bête noire* end

up as the West German hero? France shot first, and after the teams each missed one penalty kick apiece through four rounds, the game moved into its version of sudden death. Maxime Bossis, the anchor of the French defense, drilled his shot toward the left corner, only to have Schumacher hurl himself across the goal to save it. When Horst Hrubesch scored, the Germans mobbed their goalkeeper, who by all rights shouldn't have been on the field.

"I can't accept we lost even to this day," Giresse said in 2009.

Twenty-eight years later, it remains the most heartbreakingly unlucky game in French history, even more so than Zidane's crackup in 2006. But, as much as it haunts him, Platini is grateful for having been a part of what he calls the most beautiful game he had ever played in.

"What happened in those two hours encapsulated all the sentiments of life itself," he said. "No film or play could ever recapture so many contradictions and emotions. It was complete. So strong. It was fabulous."

CULT FIGURES

ANTONIN PANENKA, CZECHOSLOVAKIA

The great players have always had their signature tricks, the deke that left a defender corkscrewed into the ground or haplessly flailing at the pocket of fresh air where the ball used to be. There was the Cruyff Turn, in which the Dutchman would fake a cross or pass to a teammate, then swivel sharply and drag the ball back behind his planted leg and into the open space. Or the Ronaldinho Flip-Flap, where the elastic-ankled Brazilian pushed the ball wide with the outside of his right foot, then suddenly cut it back with the instep and was gone.

And then there was the Panenka Chip. While the Czechoslovakian midfielder enjoyed an accomplished two-decade club career and was an integral part of the national team, Pelé didn't call him "a genius or a madman" because of his otherworldly ball skills or reckless tackling style. No, Panenka's speciality was the penalty kick—those 12 yards separating fame from ignominy.

To appreciate Panenka's greatness, you have to understand the pressure on the penalty taker. He is supposed to score. He knows it, as do his teammates, his coach, the fans, and the opponents. And the higher the stakes, the more suffocating the pressure. Ask Roberto Baggio, or any number of players from the English national team.

Panenka took 53 penalty kicks—and scored 53 times. It's a record as preposterous in its own way as DiMaggio's 56-game hitting streak. Panenka never shanked or skyed a kick; never put one where the goalkeeper had chosen to be. Part of it was due to Panenka's philosophy: "My credo and belief has always been to entertain the spectators." But it was a craft that he took pride in and practiced incessantly. His most remarkable kick, the one that he unveiled to the astonishment of the soccer world at the 1976 European Championships, took him more than two years to perfect at the team's training ground.

"I used to practice penalties after training with our goalkeeper," he said in an 2007 interview with Radio Prague. "To make it interesting, we used to wager a beer or a bar of chocolate on each penalty. Unfortunately, because he was such a good goalkeeper, I ended up losing money . . . as a result I ended up lying awake at night thinking about how I could get the upper hand. I eventually realized that the goalkeeper always waits until just before the last moment to try and anticipate where the ball is going and dives just before it's kicked. . . . I decided it was probably easier to score by feinting to shoot and then just gently tapping the ball into the middle of the goal. I tried it out on the training ground and it worked like a charm. The only problem was that I started getting a lot fatter because I won back all those beers and chocolates."

If this was a feature film, the ending would be deemed far too Hollywood. The largely anonymous Czechoslovakians had made a fairy-tale run through the Euro 1976 tournament to reach the final, where the dream-killers, West Germany, lurked. The teams battled to a 2–2 draw through extra time. After six straight successful penalty kicks, West Germany's fourth kicker sailed his attempt high. It all came down to the final kick—and Panenka.

He milked his moment before racing toward the ball as though he would crush it. Maier hurled himself sideways as Panenka slowed to a virtual stop, slid his foot under the ball, and chipped a lazy, arcing shot straight down the middle of the goal. As Maier crashed to the ground, he watched Panenka's kick finish its parabolic journey into the now-vacant net. The look on Maier's face was one of shock and awe as if to say, "What nuts of steel on that guy." Later, Panenka was asked about his confidence level as he approached the ball, "I was convinced—not 100% but 1,000%—that I would convert that penalty kick. I knew it would work."

In the 1982 World Cup, Panenka scored twice, both from the penalty spot, but it was another penalty kick 24 years later that made sure the Czechoslovakian's feat of derring-do would forever be enshrined in tournament lore. In the hysteria that followed what would sadly become known as his signature move, The Head Butt, people forget that earlier in the final, Zinedine Zidane scored one of the most audacious penalties in World Cup history, a delicate chip that barely reached the net after the Italian goalkeeper Gianluigi Buffon had dived to his right. Or as a French commentator with an institutional memory called it, *"La Panenka de Zidane."*

ITALY 3, BRAZIL 2
Second Round

When coach Enzo Bearzot named Paolo Rossi to spearhead his attack in this collision of soccer superpowers, all of Italy uncorked the vino and prepared to get blind drunk so it wouldn't have to witness the team's now-certain humilation at the whirring feet of mighty Brazil. Rossi was a man back from the dead. In fact, having been banned for two years on match-fixing charges, he was lucky just to be on the team, He was a *disgrazia* to Italian soccer—*and* he hadn't scored a goal in the Azzurri's four previous games in the tournament. But what choice did Bearzot have? For Italy to advance to the semis, they needed to score goals, and as out of shape and out of confidence as Rossi might have been, Bearzot had faith in his striker's clever opportunism.

"In the penalty area, he was extraordinary, always ready to pounce on the slightest mistake," said Bearzot. Which is why he positioned Rossi at the very tip of his attacking wedge, where he could best scrap for morsels. And sure enough, after only five minutes, Rossi gave Italy the lead, slipping unmarked to the back post to head in an inch-perfect cross from the left wing.

Brazil was shaken, but it had been behind twice before in the tournament and won both games. It didn't take them long to even the score. The Italians' notorious hatchet man Claudio "The Beast"

Gentile, who had locked up Maradona in Italy's win over Argentina with "something between defense and homicide," had Brazil's star striker Zico literally in his clutches from the opening whistle. But in the 12th minute, the "White Pelé," as Zico came to be known, broke free of his marker and threaded a sublime pass to Socrates. From a narrow angle, the good doctor smoked a low drive past Dino Zoff's outstretched fingers and it was 1–1.

Brazil started to find its rhythm, weaving hypnotic patterns as their rapturous fans chanted "*Braaaa-ziiiiiil*" with every sweet touch. It took another piece of inspired poaching from Rossi to silence them midway through the half. A sloppily hit crossfield pass by Brazilian defender Toninho Cerezo fell right at Rossi's feet at the edge of the penalty area and he needed only one touch to lash the ball into the net. Now the cries of "*Eeeeee-tal—yaaaaaa*" thundered around the stadium as Italy appeared on the verge of a monumental triumph. And who better to protect a 2–1 lead than the Azzurri with its ruthless defensive mentality? At one point, Zico, exasperated with Gentile's holding and shirt-pulling, stormed up to the Israeli referee Abraham Klein to show him the enormous hole that The Beast had ripped in his jersey. But Klein was unmoved and waved him away.

With the Italians bunkered in, Brazil laid siege to

their goal, only to have shot after shot repelled by the blindingly quick reflexes of Dino Zoff. But even Zoff was helpless when the strong and quick midfielder Falcão danced his way across the penalty area midway through the second half and threaded a left-footed screamer through a tiny chink in the Italian fortress. At 2–2, and with Brazil needing only a draw to reach the semis against Poland due to the round-robin format of the second round, conventional soccer wisdom dictated that Brazil take its foot off the pedal and drop its midfielders back to tighten the defense. But the unconventional Brazilians chose adventure over safety and kept on attacking remorselessly, leaving yawning spaces behind them.

Italy broke into one of those gaps, winning a corner—incredibly, it was its first of the game—and when Brazil failed to clear, "Paplito," as the Italians called Rossi, pounced on the loose ball. A flick of the ankle later, he had his astonishing hat trick, achieving not just redemption, but what Zico later called "a state of grace." The entire stadium seemed to lift off the ground in the final, thrilling minutes. Desperate for an equalizer, Brazil poured forward, and in the end it took one last acrobatic save from Zoff, their 40-year-old captain and wise old sage, to preserve Italy's memorable triumph over a team many consider the greatest in Brazilian history.

GREATEST TEAMS

BRAZIL, 1982

Just when the trend toward defensive soccer threatened to rob the game of its charm, along came Brazil with the gospel that soccer could be, and should be, beautiful. Their fanatical devotion to flair may have cost them the 1982 World Cup, but their skill and spontaneity were a joy to behold. No shot was too audacious to attempt, no defender too intimidating to humiliate, and no space too tight to wriggle out of.

Manager Telê Santana had at his disposal the greatest collection ever of show ponies, who supplied an endless highlight reel of flicks, feints, nutmegs, back-heels, and bicycle kicks, which has been since replicated only in video games.

Dressed in their bright, sunshine-colored uniforms, the Brazilians played with a carefree spirit that fell just short of reckless abandon—they scored 15 goals in five games, almost all of them jaw-dropping. Whether it was 40-yard turf-to-air missiles from the bearded Socrates (who was so wise he actually earned a degree in medicine while still playing for the national team), or Zico, "the white Pelé," gleefully volleying on the run against New Zealand, everything the Brazilians touched was in

turn met with reverence and awe by their adoring, drum-beating fans. It didn't seem to matter if they conceded a goal—and their comical keeper Waldir Peres frequently did—because they would score three in return.

Surely, it was a miscarriage of soccer justice that their wizardry was neutralized in the second round. There, Brazil's suddenly resistible force met Italy's immovable defensive monolith. The Italians' tendency to play for 1–0 wins had long been considered an insult to *joga bonito,* but they had added a surprise element to their repertoire—an attack led by mercurial forward Paulo Rossi, who returned from the purgatory of a cheating scandal to plunder all three goals in Italy's 3–2 victory.

Defeat shocked Brazil, whose fans were stunned to watch their heroes leave a tournament holding their heads rather than a trophy. But it's a tribute to this remarkable team that their exit from the World Cup practically upstaged Italy's eventual title. It was as if once the Brazilians departed, they took the wow factor with them. Or as Zico melodramatically put it, "This was the day soccer died."

MICHEL PLATINI
France: 1978, 1982, 1986

Scrawny, mop-topped, and heavily stubbled, Michel Platini looked more like a 1980s Madison Avenue account executive than a world-class athlete. He reinforced that impression by rarely seeming to run for the ball. Rather, it always appeared to come to him. When he had it, he blended the ingenuity of a midfielder with the goal-scoring instinct of a striker, controlling the pace of the game, and making free kicks as deadly as penalty shots. He was arguably the world's finest soccer player with a pack-a-day habit, notorious for sneaking a cigarette just before kickoff and at halftime.

Platini's confidence, flair, and ruthlessness characterized the French teams he captained. Playing alongside Alain Giresse and Jean Tigana as the "Three Musketeers," he transformed them into one of the most elegant and potent attacking forces of the 1980s. Their system gave him the freedom to initiate every move his team made, and he used his vision and ability to place a pass where few others could, dismantling defenses with the practiced ease of Warren Beatty in his prime.

Platini became a legend in 1982. After signing for the Italian powerhouse Juventus shortly before the tournament, he led an inexperienced French team into the semifinals against West Germany in what became one of the great matches of World Cup history (*see Greatest Games, page 108*), billed as a battle between the "artistes" and the "automatons." The game ended 3–3 after extra time and the match went to a penalty shoot-out won by West

Germany 5–4, during which Platini became a hero for holding the hand of his unconscious teammate, Patrick Battiston, as he was taken off the field after being flattened by West German goalkeeper Harald Schumacher. In defeat, France had become the world's darlings and Platini was left to spend the night racing through what he termed a "scaled down version of a lifetime's worth of emotions."

Although hampered by knee and ankle injuries, in 1986 he inspired his team, now known as the "Brazilians of Europe," to victory against the genuine article, in a sumptuous quarterfinal game in the heat of Guadalajara. During the postgame locker room celebrations, Platini somehow managed to remain the epitome of cool while sporting only a pair of flowery boxer shorts and an oversize baseball cap, but his team was exhausted by the win over Brazil and was eliminated for the second tournament in a row by West Germany in the semifinals. Though he led them to Euro triumph in 1984 (scoring an amazing nine goals in just five matches), the World Cup was beyond him. France had to wait until 1998 to win the trophy, by which time Platini had begun his second career as a sports executive (he is currently president of UEFA). But he was very much on the field in spirit. Zinedine Zidane, who inherited his mantle as sublime playmaker, said it best: "When I was a kid and played with my friends, I always chose to be Platini. I let my friends share the names of my other idols between themselves."

Platini invades, but doesn't conquer, Germany's defense in the 1986 semifinal loss.

ROGUES, PART I:

THUGS AND HARD MEN

THUGS

Soccer players don't have the armored advantages of their counterparts in other physical sports, like football and hockey. Their only protection is two small, plastic, token shin guards. As a result, every soccer player's résumé includes fractured ankles, shredded metatarsals, knee ligaments twisted like shoelaces, and heads cracked open like soft-boiled eggs.

But thugs are a dying breed now that flagrant violence—once the default strategy for overmatched teams throughout the World Cup eras of Pelé and Maradona—means almost certain banishment. Modern soccer etiquette has of necessity spawned two new creatures: the Thug's descendant, the Hard Man, who seeks and gives no quarter, but stops short of maiming opponents, and The Diver (*see Rogues, Part II, page 218, for more on that diva*).

Herewith, a studs-up tribute to the notorious hit men of the past and their more discreet heirs.

ANDONI GOIKOETXEA, SPAIN

If Goikoetxea were a fan of *The Simpsons*, his favorite episode would be "Lisa on Ice," where Lisa exhorts her team to "hack the bone, hack the bone."

The "Butcher of Bilbao" never encountered a leg he didn't want to chop, but he took special pride in slicing open opposing stars. Of his many victims, two stand out: Bernd Schuster and Maradona. Schuster, West Germany's golden boy of the early '80s, was just 21 and starring for his club team, Barcelona, when Goikoetxea slid into him and all but carved his initials in his knee. Two years on, in another Spanish league match against Barcelona, Maradona gathered the ball just inside the Bilbao half. Almost immediately, he was scythed down

Aptly named English defender Terry Butcher donated blood to ensure his team qualified for the 1990 tournament.

Massing's Indomitable Lions after making a Maradona kill in the 1990 World Cup.

gia was stumbling, fully exposed, when Massing ended a 30-yard sprint by launching himself into the stringy-haired striker with such brute force that Massing's boot flew off on impact. Caniggia crumpled in a heap. Massing was ejected from the game, but even with only nine men left on the field, Cameroon held on for a historic 1–0 upset.

While Massing's flying leg whip was deservedly chosen as one of the five worst tackles in the tournament's history by *The Guardian,* his entire World Cup career consisted of only two matches, in which he managed to collect two yellow cards and one red. No one can say Massing didn't make the most of his opportunities.

LEONARDO, BRAZIL

For *joga bonito,* it was an unthinkable act of ugliness, but there it was. The Brazilian midfielder Leonardo threw an ice pick of an elbow at the head of U.S. midfielder Tab Ramos in their round of 16 match at U.S.A. '94. It had been a chippy, hard-fought game featuring seven yellow and two red cards, and Leonardo was clearly frustrated with Brazil's inability to assert their authority over the upstart Americans. In the 43rd minute, he got tangled up with Ramos on the touchline as the two players battled for possession. Attempting to separate himself from the U.S. playmaker, Leonardo suddenly crashed his arm into the left side of Ramos's face, spinning him around before Ramos fell to the ground and briefly lost consciousness.

"I was just acting on instinct," Leonardo said afterward. "I didn't mean any harm." But the blow fractured Ramos's skull, sidelined him for months, and earned Leonardo a four-match suspension. Ramos, ever gracious, later said, "I don't think he meant to hurt me." Leonardo went to Ramos's hospital room to apologize. However, for virtually every one of the 84,000 people in Stanford Stadium, it was chilling proof that even

by Goiko. "I hadn't seen him coming on the pitch or I would have dodged him as I had on so many other occasions with so many other kicks," the Argentinian star wrote in his autobiography. "But I just felt the impact, heard the sound, like a piece of wood cracking, and realized immediately what had happened."

The assault broke Diego's ankle and severely damaged the ligaments, and was such an ostentatious display of goonish behavior that Goiko was hammered with an unprecedented 18-match ban (remarkably, he did not receive a red card for the foul itself, only a yellow). Did Goiko feel remorse? You be the judge: He placed the boot that did the damage in a glass case on his mantelpiece.

While Goikoetxea eschewed such blatant thuggery in his four World Cup games for Spain—he collected only two yellow cards—it was due mostly to the effect of his reputation on opponents, and not to any concerted effort on his part to behave.

As *The Times* of London famously put it: "The Butcher of Bilbao was plainly a prawn short of a paella."

BENJAMIN MASSING, CAMEROON

There are many ways for a plucky no-name underdog to show its heavily favored opponent that it will not be cowed. Cameroon's approach was simply to try to kick the stuffing out of more illustrious foes. Drawn against defending champion Argentina in the opening game of World Cup '90, the Indomitable Lions committed 30 fouls, more than half of them on Maradona, whom they mistook for a human piñata. At least Diego escaped with his limbs intact.

His strike partner, Claudio Caniggia, wasn't as lucky, thanks to Benjamin Massing, a bruising, thick-thighed defender who set the tone only 10 minutes into the game by picking up the first yellow card of the tournament. As it turned out, he was just getting warmed up. After Cameroon's André Kana-Biyik was sent off for mauling Caniggia in the 61st minute, the Indomitable Lions improbably forged ahead six minutes later. Desperately searching for the equalizer, Caniggia again ran at the heart of the Cameroon backline, eluding two defenders as they tried to cut him down. The second sliding tackle partially clipped him, though, and Canig-

the most stylish of soccer teams could commit acts of mayhem.

As further evidence of soccer fans' proclivity to forgive all things Brazilian, Leonardo did not suffer any lasting recriminations for his moment of ignominy. Fifteen years later, he would be named the head coach of the Italian powerhouse club AC Milan, even though he had no previous managerial experience.

LEONEL SÁNCHEZ, CHILE

Anytime you need to call in the police to assist the referee in keeping the players from killing one another, the fuse has usually been lit long before kickoff. That, at least, was the case with the 1962 World Cup group match between host Chile and Italy, dubbed "the Battle of Santiago." Passions had been running high in the days before the match as the Chileans were manipulated into believing that the Italians had made derogatory and insensitive remarks in the aftermath of the devastating 1960 Chilean earthquake. The enmity became so intense that two offending Italian journalists were forced to flee the country. The contest itself deteriorated quickly into one of the World Cup's most shameful displays of soccer.

It began with what appeared to be a fairly innocuous foul on high-scoring Chilean winger Leonel Sánchez by Italian defender Mario David near the left corner flag. Sánchez, the son of a boxer, bounded to his feet and coldcocked David with a haymaker that the announcer described as "the neatest left hook" that he had ever seen. Astonishingly, Sánchez's pugilistic gifts went unpunished. David, not surprisingly, retaliated a few minutes later, with a two-footed flying kick to Sánchez's neck that led to his immediate ejection and a full-blown melee between the teams. Amid the bedlam, Sánchez broke striker Umberto Maschio's nose with another textbook blow. There were now two Italians down, only nine to go.

Sánchez escaped punishment again, and the Chileans scored two late goals to secure the victory that vaulted them into the quarterfinals.

The national motto of Chile translates to "by reason or by force." Leonel Sánchez's motto was punchier.

JOSÉ BATISTA, URUGUAY

Prior to the '86 World Cup, Scottish striker Ally McCoist said, "I've heard of a group of death, but this has to be the group of certain death." McCoist's quote was prophetic. Needing a tie to advance to the knockout round, the Uruguayans—with a long, proud history of being South America's most infamous hatchetmen—were instructed by coach Omar Borrás in his pregame exhortation to show their "commitment" against Scotland.

Defender Batista committed himself to kicking lumps out of the Scots, waiting less than a minute to barge into the back of pint-sized Scottish playmaker Gordon Strachan without ever coming near the ball. And just like that, at 56 seconds, Batista earned the fastest red card in World Cup history. For the remaining 89 minutes, the South Americans fouled and hacked their way to a 0–0 draw, so enraging the Scots that a member of their delegation later called them "scum of the earth." FIFA was more diplomatic; they simply levied a fine and a threat of expulsion from the tournament.

HARD MEN

"Off the pitch I was always an ordinary, mild-mannered bloke," English defender Terry Butcher once said, "but it was tin hats and fixed bayonets the moment I pulled on a football shirt."

Despite his surname, the serrated-edged Butcher was the embodiment of a hard player rather than a dirty one. Since soccer teams no longer had the freedom to park a goon on the field, protecting superstars meant send-a-message tackles that would

make an opponent think twice about venturing into the defenders' zip code again. If you had Anglo-Saxon blood, Hard Men brought back fond, ancestral memories of tattooed faces, lusty battle cries, and the pillaging of coastal towns; the fans of the British Isles, Ireland, and Germany took to these players like a Scotsman to a discount store.

This is not to suggest that Anglo-Saxons have a monopoly on these rough-hewn warriors—Hard Men are also revered in Argentina and Italy—just that they hold them in higher esteem than the Brazils and Spains of the world who reserve their love for the step-over, the back-heel, and the beautifully curled free kick.

STUART PEARCE, ENGLAND

What do you call a guy who gets his leg snapped like a twig, waves off medical attention, and refuses to come out of the game? Brave. What do you call him if he breaks his leg in a second match and again insists on staying in? You call him "Psycho"—the nickname that English defender Stuart Pearce answered to in his 25-year career as a consummate Hard Man who left body parts—sometimes his own—scattered in his wake.

In the tradition of English working-class soccer heroes such as Nobby Stiles, Bobby Moore, and Bryan Robson, Pearce put muscle and bone on the line for 90 unrelenting minutes. "We are in a results business," he once explained, "so Stuart Pearce being a jolly old boy won't keep me in a job." Pearce helped lead England to the semifinals in World Cup 1990, where his reputation was mitigated when he missed a critical penalty against Germany. After the game, Psycho, normally the picture of stoicism, collapsed in a welter of tears.

All told, the rugged defender played in 18 World Cup qualifying and final round matches. Much like Italy's Claudio Gentile, Pearce was clever at masking his soccer crimes—he was never ejected and

Angel of Death Claudio Gentile puts the squeeze on Brazil's Zico.

accumulated only two yellow cards. Pearce has no regrets about his legacy, although, he once noted, "It can be a bit of a hindrance when you walk into a restaurant for a quiet meal and one or two launch into 'Psycho! Psycho!' "

CLAUDIO GENTILE, ITALY

Some soccer stars can only be controlled, not contained. By Spain '82, Maradona was clearly one of them. Or at least he was until he ran into Gentile, Italy's fearsome terminator whose job description was simple: Mark the opponent's most dangerous player into oblivion and don't get caught.

"A defender needs to find a way to let his presence be known," Gentile has said, and he went about his business with the subtlety of the Angel of Death. In pursuit of his prey, he spared no knee to the back, kick to the ankle, or elbow to the neck. In Italy's second-round upset of defending champion Argentina in 1982, Gentile reduced Maradona to a state of such whimpering petulance that he received a yellow card for excessive whining. "Football," Gentile once explained, "is not for ballerinas."

Born in Libya and endowed with the unfortunate nickname "Qaddafi," Gentile epitomized the fierce tackling and pugnacity that defined the '80s edition of the Azzurri, but his extraordinary skill lay in his ability to get away with tackles that would otherwise be cited for human rights violations. In Gentile's 71 games for Italy, he was never red-carded, though all eyes were upon him. He was the master of the stealth attack, cagily timing his assaults to avoid the referee's gaze. But it wasn't just well-disguised fouls that set Gentile apart. He was also adept at mind games, although he didn't always use his mind. Italian journalists still talk about how early in that Italy-Argentina match, Gentile attempted to provoke Maradona by sidling up to him from behind and administering the soccer equivalent of a colonoscopy.

For all his macho posturing, Gentile viewed his Hard Man reputation with a healthy dose of humor. The story is told of the black-tie awards dinner for European Player of the Year in 1978: As England's Kevin Keegan walked toward the stage to collect the trophy, Gentile stuck out a foot and tripped him. Picking himself off the floor, Keegan glanced up at the Italian who was smiling mischievously.

"You wouldn't have won any award," Gentile said, "if I had been marking you."

EL SALVADOR, 1982

WHY THEY MADE THE LIST: Every four years, the Confederation of North, Central American and Caribbean Association Football (CONCACAF) has to send somebody to be cannon fodder from its qualifying region. In '82, that fodder was named El Salvador.

THE HIGH POINT: Getting off the plane in Spain.

THE NADIR: A 10–1 annihilation by Hungary, featuring the fastest hat trick in World Cup history, by Laszlo Kiss, who came on as a sub and planted three big ones in under eight minutes.

ONLY IN THE WORLD CUP: The '82 team was so ill-prepared for the World Cup that nobody knew about the exchange of gifts before the start of the match. Goalkeeper Luis Guevara Mora spotted a pine tree, cut off a chunk of wood, carved "El Salvador" into it, and gave it to the Hungarians. It appears to have been the only thing he saved that day.

THE FALLOUT: It took Salvadoreans a mere 25 years to get over the humiliation. On June 16, 2007, a "rematch" was played in San Salvador between the same sides with the same players, just grayer, slower, and fatter. The teams drew 2–2, a result that applied some salve to wounded Salvadorean pride.

MEXICO 86

ITALIA 90

WORLD CUP '94

© 1991 WC'94 TM

'86 '90 '94

COMMERCIALISM HITS ITS STRIDE

Maradona is the master of all he surveys at the Azteca.

1986
Mexico

SINGLE-HANDED VICTORY

France stumbles and England grumbles as the hand of God touches Maradona.

AT 7:19 A.M. ON September 19, 1985, Mexico City was rocked by a brutal earthquake with the equivalent power of over a thousand atomic bombs, leaving more than 10,000 dead, a quarter of a million homeless, and $4 billion worth of damage. Miraculously, the quake left the city's soccer stadia intact, and with the World Cup just eight months away, FIFA's President João Havelange self-interestedly announced that "the earthquake respected football." And so, on May 31, 1986, Mexico became the first country to host the World Cup twice. This time, they inherited the duties from the original choice, Colombia, whose own efforts had collapsed under financial weight.

By 1986, there were nearly a billion television sets around the world—the vast majority tuned to the World Cup.

Mexico was hardly the most obvious option. The Mexican economy was far from robust and the altitude was the same challenge it had been in 1970, but Mexican broadcaster Televisa put together a remarkable financial bid that beat out even that of the United States. The bidding elicited complaints from many of the players that the sale of the tournament was becoming more important than the tournament itself—a point that was arguably correct. When the World Cup was first televised in 1954 there had been fewer than 50 million television sets in the world, the vast majority of which were in the soccer-averse United States. In 1970 the entire continent of Africa boasted barely a million sets. By 1986, however, there were nearly a billion sets around the world—the vast majority of them tuned to the World Cup. As David Goldblatt has written, "Every four years in early July, television provided the single greatest simultaneous human collective experience—the World Cup final. Even global eclipses must travel slowly across the earth's surface. Television transmission was effectively instantaneous." The World Cup logo, *El Mundo Unido por Un Balon*—The World United by a Ball—rang true at the cash register.

This was the tournament that saw Morocco become the first African team to emerge from the first round, after holding England and Poland to goalless draws and then feasting on a Portuguese team threatening to strike over shoddy training facilities. It also witnessed a cameo coaching role from the now-legendary Manchester United manager Alex Ferguson, who used his genius as a stand-in manager to lead the Scots to their usual first-round exit, this time failing in a must-win group match against Uruguay despite the fact that one of the Uruguayans received the fastest red card in World Cup history, after only 56 seconds (*see Thugs and Hard Men, page 118*). A more impressive coaching debut was made by the German icon Franz Beckenbauer, who overcame his lack of technical qualifications for the job by assuming the role of "team supervisor" instead of "national coach." But he was still Der Kaiser, and give or take a blowup or two with the media, he managed to instill his team with enough discipline to churn out unspectacular soccer relying at times on their determination to prevail.

Among the pretournament favorites, Italy offered a halfhearted title defense, falling to the Platini-inspired French, who also ousted a strangely sluggish Brazil on penalties in the quarterfinals. The penalty-shot format (*see Shoot-out at the PK Corral, page 178*) was needed to decide the winner in three of the four quarterfinals, before France fell to the West Germans in the semis for the second successive World Cup. "I knew we were in trouble when I went out for the coin toss and one of the officials wished me good luck in German," Platini would recall.

TURNING LIKE A LITTLE EEL

But from start to finish this was Diego Maradona's World Cup. Not even Pelé had dominated a tournament to this extent. Surprisingly, his coach, Carlos Bilardo, made the often-undisciplined El Diego his captain, emphasizing that this was his World Cup to win or lose. Maradona, who now revealed that he had collected over 200 captains' armbands from around the world, waiting for this very moment, responded. He led with his vocal cords (denouncing the conditions in Mexico by telling the media that the noon kickoffs were "ravioli time, not soccer time") and with his play. The Argentinean side had underperformed as they prepared for the tournament, only to play bravely and with joy once the

competition began for real, using a 3-5-2 formation built around Maradona. An Argentinean journalist described them as combining a "European rhythm with a Creole swagger."

In the quarterfinals, Maradona turned in one of his finest matches against an English team whose coach sent them into battle with a blunt game plan: "The nearest man to Maradona kills him. And if he doesn't, the next one does. It is as simple as that." The "Golden Boy," *El Pibe de Oro*, proceeded to score two of the most celebrated goals ever. One illegitimate, in which he punched the ball home with his hand, and one legal, in which he single-handedly beat half the English team, while, in the words of an English commentator, "turning like a little eel." Both were breathtaking. Steve Hodge, the man charged with covering him, admitted it was all

he could do not to clap as he watched the ball go over the line. Maradona modestly claimed he could only score such a goal against the English because they were "the only players noble enough not to knock me down," but then he promptly repeated his magic act against Belgium in the semifinals. In the final, the West Germans spent so much time worrying about Maradona that his teammates were left alone to score three goals to West Germany's two and claim the Cup. They returned to Argentina and were received at the presidential residence by Raúl Alfonsín, who had restored democracy to the country and freed it from the tyranny of the military junta. Standing on the balcony alongside Alfonsín with thousands cheering his name was the highlight of Maradona's turbulent career. With the trophy in his arms, he felt "like he was the president."

1986 RESULTS

QUARTERFINALS
France 1 Brazil 1 (4–3 PKs)
West Germany 0 Mexico 0 (4–1 PKs)
Argentina 2 England 1
Belgium 1 Spain 1 (5–4 PKs)

SEMIFINALS
West Germany 2 France 0
Argentina 2 Belgium 0

THIRD PLACE
France 4 Belgium 2

FINAL
Argentina 3 West Germany 2

"It was, and still is, the best goal ever scored," said England's striker Gary Lineker. "I just stood there on the halfway line and thought, *Wow*."

DIEGO MARADONA
Argentina vs. England, Quarterfinal

It was perhaps the most confusing four minutes in World Cup history. Tens of millions of viewers around the world had barely begun to digest Diego Maradona's "Hand of God" goal, an act so egregious that he shortly become the devil incarnate to decent and law-abiding people everywhere outside of Argentina, when the same man ran from 10 yards inside his own half, undressed five England players along the way, rounded the keeper, and scored what is indisputably one of the greatest goals ever.

British subjects and other soccer purists may be forgiven for devaluing Maradona's masterpiece, since there are reasons beyond moral ones for questioning its mythic status. The English, some point out, have traditionally ground to a halt when the temperature breaks 60 degrees Fahrenheit. In the Korea/Japan World Cup, they couldn't get near the ball for much of the second half against a 10-man Brazilian team; it was too clammy in Shizuoka for England to play at its usual frenetic tempo. And on that historic day in Mexico City, the mercury was running high and the noon kickoff meant that the playing surface in Azteca Stadium would be furnacelike.

England had kept pace—barely—with Argentina, when the Hand of God goal sent them reeling, only to have Maradona bury them four minutes later. As Maradona first controlled the ball in his own half, the English players deferred to the little man—like the Argentine military junta, he was going nowhere. Then, with his back to goal, he pirouetted around a couple of Peters—Reid and Beardsley—leaving them corkscrewed into the ground as he took flight up the right touchline. Terry Butcher closed on him and swung out the threshing machine that passed for his right leg but all it hit was air. Maradona had already accelerated past him to the edge of the penalty area. Now it was Terry Fenwick's turn to be humiliated. Earlier in the game, Fenwick had tried to dismember Maradona with a flying scissor tackle that had earned him a yellow card, and the Englishman was determined to get the job done this time. But Maradona's bewildering array of swerves and body feints left him sprawled on the turf. That left only England's ageless goalkeeper, Peter Shilton, between Maradona and the goal. One more shimmy and Shilton was on his ass, too, but Butcher came lumbering up from behind to take a second swipe at Maradona. This one succeeded in upending him, but Maradona had already bundled the ball past Shilton into the net.

So how good was it? Even allowing for England's slapstick defending, it was an incomparable display of speed, guile, balance, and stones of granite. But let's leave it to the victims to put in perspective.

"The second goal was, and still is, the best goal ever scored," said England's Gary Lineker. "To do what he did was just extraordinary. I have to say I just stood there on the halfway line and thought, *Wow*." But Lineker was a striker, too, and there's a mutual admiration society at work. Surely Butcher himself would cast the moment in a different light? "I did not like conceding any goals, but grudgingly, I have to say, it was a wonderful second goal against us that day." This astonishing concession from the same man who also said, "If he [Maradona] had come in and said, 'It was my hand and I apologize,' then I would probably have hit him four or five times rather than the twenty I felt like." Watching helplessly from the sidelines, Manager Bobby Robson had as clear a view as anyone. "The second goal was fantastic," he said. "I didn't like it, but I admired it."

And there you have it. Almost a quarter century later, Maradona's brilliant, swerving, pulsating run stands the test of time. You have to hand it to him.

DIEGO MARADONA
Argentina: 1982, 1986, 1990, 1994

If Diego Maradona's story was turned into a Hollywood movie, it would be eerily similar to *Scarface*. Both he and Al Pacino's Tony Montana were swaggering, self-made figures who rose from humble origins to dominate the world, only to flame out in a blaze of glory. While Montana's weapon of choice was his M16 ("Say hello to my little friend"), Maradona's was his legs in a career of extreme excess, during which the World Cup was the stage for both his greatest glory and humiliation. In 1986 he provided one of the singular virtuoso performances in World Cup. Just eight years later, he was sent home in disgrace for either ephedrine doping or enjoying an innocent energy supplement called Ripped Fuel, depending on whether you asked FIFA or Maradona himself.

Squat and impudent, Maradona was part urchin, part prince. At just 5'5", his career was proof that one need not be a titan to be a world-class soccer player. His low center of gravity was his best asset and he became one of the greatest dribblers in the game, almost impossible to knock off the ball. When another player managed to kick him off the field, he would quickly dust himself off

and demand the ball again, drawing strength as he drained defenders of their energy. In 1986 he single-handedly willed his team to victory, collecting the Golden Ball as the tournament's best player along the way. He scored both goals in the 2–1 victory over England in the quarterfinal, a game played in the shadows of the 1982 Falklands conflict. The first goal, when he used his left fist to reach over a 6'1" goalkeeper and punch the ball into the net, became known as the "Hand of God" around the world, as it was scored "a little with the head of Maradona and a little with the hand of God." (In England, it was referred to as the "Hand of the Devil.") Four minutes later, while the English were still reeling, he scored a goal that even God would have had difficulty replicating. He made a spectacular 60-yard dash, a brilliant display of the *Gambetta*, the Argentinian art of dribbling, weaving delicately past five English players, the last two of whom desperately tried to take out the man rather than the ball. Both goals reflect different sides of Maradona's persona: the first required the stealth and pluck of the pickpocket, the second, the daring and polish of Thomas Crown.

Maradona's retirement has been marred by cocaine addiction, organized crime ties, and idiosyncratic foreign policy pronouncements on behalf of Cuba, Venezuela, and Iran, all of which, perversely, have combined to make him more beloved than ever in Latin America. His left leg features a tattoo of Fidel Castro while the image of Che Guevara dominates his right bicep. Rumors that he was about to get a Hugo Chavez tattoo were international news. Perhaps not surprisingly, his talk show on Argentine television, *La Noche Del 10* (*The Night of the Number 10*) was one of the most watched in the nation's history. In and out of rehab, cynics suggested he scheduled his occasional television appearances to prove he is still alive. His recent erratic performance as Argentina's coach, which saw them struggle to qualify for 2010's World Cup, made many wish he had stuck with a career as a talk show host. Despite this blemish, he will always be remembered as he is in the classic image from the semifinal against Belgium in 1986. About to launch an attack. Never mind double- or triple-teamed. Six defenders surround him. You can smell their fear. And you know he likes the odds.

Clockwise from
upper left: goofball; god;
watching as the Belgian
defense prepares to soil
itself; as a teenager.

ACHTUNG!
Will the following five Germans please report to the pantheon of World Cup villains. . . .

Along with knockwurst and Werner Herzog, Germany's great postwar gift has been to churn out soccer players the world could despise. English author David Winner claimed that "in the narrative that is the World Cup, Germany plays the role of villain: the bad guy who kills the good guys, the beautiful teams. A World Cup without Germany would be like *Star Wars* without Darth Vader." The World Cup has a rich tradition of Teutonic heels who have managed to incorporate in a single individual everything that is despised about their entire team.

HARALD "TONI" SCHUMACHER (1982, 1986):
A blacksmith and apprentice boiler-maker turned World Cup goalkeeper, Schumacher is remembered for the brown-blond mullet-and-moustache combo he sported and the violence he inflicted in the name of keeping the ball at bay. Most famously, in 1982 he stopped a breakaway by Frenchman Patrick Battiston by employing a flying hockey-style hip check that shattered the defender's vertebrae and left him bloodied and unconscious—an act that transformed him into a despised figure overnight, and a recipient of death threats from around the world, even from compatriots. His autobiography, *Anpfiff* (*Blowing the Whistle*), a José Canseco–style tome rife with widespread allegations of substance abuse in his national team, cemented his position as the most reviled man in German soccer.

RUDI VÖLLER (1986, 1990, 1994):
His hair and moustache combination screamed porn star, but Völler was a world-class striker who appeared in two consecutive championship match-

Stefan and
Frau Effenberg

es and had an annoying knack for scoring critical goals. Despite this achievement, he is best remembered for being on the receiving end of two of Dutch midfielder Frank Rijkaard's greatest shots, volleys of spittle that landed and lodged in his curls as both men were sent off in 1990, a feat that earned Rijkaard an award for most popular sportsman in Israel.

JÜRGEN KLINSMANN (1990, 1994, 1998):
With his flaxen, shaggy mane and slight build, Klinsmann was known as the "Golden Bomber" and looked like Siegfried without Roy. Blessed with terrifying speed, Klinsi used it to run at defenders, often flinging himself to the ground and writhing in agony as soon as they entered his general vicinity, even though—and replays proved it—there had been no actual physical contact. He was one of the great divers of all time (*see Rogues, Part II, page 218*). Referees never saw through his histrionics, even in the 1990 World Cup final itself, where he used them to con the referee into sending off a hapless Argentinian defender. When Klinsmann moved to play in the English league, he publicly acknowledged his own thespian trickery by flinging himself to the floor to celebrate his first goal. This became his trademark celebration, demonstrating at the very least that not all Germans lacked a sense of humor.

OLIVER KAHN (1998, 2002, 2006):
He was a brilliant goalkeeper, known as "The Gorilla," whose fans delighted in

pelting him with bunches of bananas thrown from the stands. His outspoken conservative political beliefs already made him a controversial figure, but it was his intensity and competitiveness on the field that made him so utterly detestable and led his own teammate Mehmet Scholl to declare, "I am afraid of just two things in life: war and Oliver Kahn." It is said of him that, at a charity event where a number of small children lined up for the honor of shooting penalty kicks at him, he still could not stand to let anyone score.

STEFAN EFFENBERG (1994):
Few players have managed to alienate as many fans, teammates, coaches, and German FA bureaucrats in a single career as this midfielder, whose brilliance was matched only by his sheer arrogance. His World Cup experience ended abruptly when, while being substituted, he gave the bird to a whistling crowd of German supporters booing his mediocre performance. His career at German powerhouse Bayern Munich ended shortly after he launched a unilateral political attack on the nation's unemployed, who, in his view, were "too lazy to look for work." But he managed to top all that by stealing his teammate's wife, and then posing with her in a series of erotic photographs to promote his tell-all autobiography, *I Showed Them All,* which became infamous for its mix of sexual content and butchery of the German language. In one of the promotional photographs, he and his new girlfriend show off their fresh tattoos, testaments to their newfound love. They, too, had spelling mistakes.

Rudi Völler

Brown, the moment after he became one of the most unlikely goal scorers in World Cup final history.

CULT FIGURES

JOSÉ LUIS BROWN, ARGENTINA

If Diego Maradona didn't own Mexico '86, then he borrowed it for three weeks and graffitied his name all over it. In leading Argentina to its only World Cup title of the Maradona Era, he arguably put together the greatest string of seven soccer games ever played by one man. He dominated the tournament like nobody before or since, scoring or assisting on 10 of his team's 14 goals. But there would have been no trophy for the Argentines without the blink-and-you-missed-it heroics of José Luis Brown.

I'm sorry—who?

Exactly. Brown was a steady, hardworking central defender who enjoyed an utterly unremarkable career as a club player mostly in South America. He had proven his dedication when he used to hitchhike to practice with his first team, Estudiantes, as he had no other way to get there. Eventually, he was able to crowbar his way into the big time with Boca Juniors, the same club where a young Maradona had flourished three years earlier. Unfortunately, Brown was out of his league in every sense and was soon exiled to the hinterlands of Colombian

soccer. Even at that level, he struggled, failing to crack the starting lineup of his new club. Imagine if you had turned to the *hombre* next to you at a Buenos Aires *parillas* and said, "How much you wanna bet that José Luis Brown is not only going to start for Argentina in the World Cup, but lead them to the championship?"

With no club to call his own, Brown devoted everything to making the national team. When the rest of the players jetted off to their various clubs, Brown stayed behind with the architect of the Argentinian squad, the man known as El Professor, Ricardo Echevarría, and trained alone and without pay. His intensity and commitment earned him a place on the 22-man squad, but the odds that he would see serious playing time, let alone start, remained slim to none. If Brown needed reminding where he stood in the sweeper pecking order, all he had to do was glance at his roommate, the great central defender Daniel Passarella, who was the closest thing Argentina had to a star next to Maradona.

Cue the Broadway musical cliché. Brown got his big break when Passarella fell suddenly ill and his

understudy took center stage. He played every minute of every match, and anchored a defense that conceded only three goals in Argentina's first six games. But his Rocky-like rise to World Cup glory still needed a denouement and it fell to West Germany to play the unscripted antagonists.

For the '86 final, the Germans had decided to shadow Maradona with their best player, the domineering Lothar Matthäus. However, in nullifying the Argentinian superstar, Matthäus, the creative hub of the German attack, essentially took himself out of the game as well. The stage was set for a most unlikely hero.

When Matthäus chopped down Maradona after yet another sleight-of-foot, Argentina's Jorge Burruchaga lofted the resulting free kick into the box. Brown made the run that he had practiced alone hundreds of times and as Burruchaga's cross split the air, he ghosted toward the far post, rose perfectly to meet the ball, and thumped it into the net at the 23rd minute mark, before collapsing in a joyous, sweaty heap on top of Maradona.

It was the only international goal that José Luis Brown would ever score, and he understood what it meant. "Scoring in the World Cup is something that goes through my mind every day of my life," he said years afterward.

Later in the match, Brown was badly injured when he separated his shoulder. He had the trainer strap the offending arm to his body and gutted out the entirety of Argentina's eventual 3–2 win. Whatever pain he felt faded away in the euphoria of the moment, one that José Luis Brown had envisioned more than two months before the World Cup, when he had said to his ex-wife, "Phone me only if something serious happens to the kids. Otherwise I am not there for anybody."

When the match ended, an exhausted Brown spotted his mentor, Echevarría, embraced him, and took El Professor with him on his victory lap, lifting his one good arm into the air in triumph.

MANUEL NEGRETE
Mexico vs. Bulgaria, Round of 16

To leave your feet and launch your body parallel to the ground as you wrap your leg around the ball and direct it at a target requires perfect timing, a high degree of spatial awareness, and acrobatic coordination. It should come as no surprise then that 99 times out of 100, these trick shots end in the same, embarrassing way—with an absurdly scuffed shot and a sore tailbone.

But not in Estadio Azteca (Mexico's home stadium) in 1986, when an otherwise solid but little-noticed Mexican midfielder pulled off one of the most outrageous goals in World Cup history. Sadly for Negrete, it came in the tournament that will be forever remembered for Diego Maradona's twin strikes against England. Yet a case can be made that even Maradona's celebrated slalom through the English defense did not require the technical skill and supreme athleticism of Negrete's masterpiece.

The spectacular goal began in humdrum fashion just over half an hour into a 0–0 game. Mexico's Hugo Sanchez took possession along the top of the Bulgarian penalty box but was met by a lunging slide tackle that knocked the ball 40 yards out, where it was floated lazily back toward the top of the area. Negrete glanced up and collected the pass, knee high, with his left foot, juggling the ball once, before letting it bounce. He then lofted a quick lob to Javier Aguirre (now the manager of Mexico), who side-footed the return back to open space, about four yards in front of Negrete. Instinctively, Negrete had begun to move into the anticipated area, but the ball was beyond the reach of a normal run, so he catapulted himself off the ground, laid out his body sideways, and lashed a left-footed volley into the net. From the start of the sequence to its finish, the ball hit the ground exactly twice. The first was Negrete's deliberate piece of control and the second was when the shot caromed off the twine to the turf in the back of the net. Estadio Azteca detonated with the mass euphoria of 114,580 fans as El Tri matched their best-ever result at a World Cup, reaching the quarterfinals.

Negrete had a long, if uneventful, career, mostly kicking around in the Mexican leagues for 17 years. But the visual history of the World Cup will honor his glorious, jaw-dropping five seconds forever.

ARGENTINA VS. ENGLAND

What does it say about the blood feud between these two soccer giants that the Hand of God might not even be its most outrageous moment? Maradona himself saw that 1986 goal as karmic payback for the Falklands War: a brief but costly battle over a tiny group of islands with a couple of hundred thousand sheep and hardly a living, breathing soul.

"We knew they had killed a lot of Argentine boys there, killed them like little birds," Maradona wrote in his autobiography. "And this was revenge."

The truth is, the Argentina-England rivalry had been running on a toxic mix of animosity and adrenaline for 20 years before Diego's brazen volleyball spike and Argentina was not the only side guilty of bending the rules. While the English delight in hiding behind their veneer of nobility and culture of imperialism, forever labeling the Argentines as amoral creatures, the Brits are hardly innocents in this tango of soccer hatred.

The fuse was lit on the eve of their ill-tempered quarterfinal in the 1966 World Cup when Wembley officials canceled Argentina's final training session at the stadium on the pretext that they were preparing for a greyhound racing event that evening. In the English pecking order, dogs were more important than Argentines.

Then came the game itself, which will be remembered for the West German referee's farcical dismissal of Argentina's captain Antonio Rattín for abusive language; the referee spoke no Spanish and Rattín didn't understand German. When Rattín finally consented to leave the field, he wiped his dirty hands on a Union Jack. (*See When God Was An Englishman, page 49.*) After the game, which England won 1–0 on a goal the Argentines claimed was offside, the English players wailed about being spat on and getting their ears pulled by their opponents. Never mind that England committed 33 fouls to Argentina's 19. England's reactionary manager, Alf Ramsey, and its jingoistic media clung to the moral high ground. Ramsey even refused to allow his players to exchange jerseys with the Argentines and infamously called them "animals," while *The Times* of London made no secret of who was to blame with its headline DESTRUCTIVE ATTITUDE OF SOUTH AMERICANS. Emotions were further inflamed when the Argentine press reported that a Wembley employee had deliberately kicked a pregnant Argentinian woman in the stomach.

BAD BLOOD AND INDENTED KNUCKLES

For their part, the Argentinians didn't exactly acquit themselves as the second coming of Emily Post. Reports swirled that the visiting players urinated in the tunnel and along the hallowed walls of Wembley, and there were tales of the blue-and-white storming the English dressing room. Is it any wonder that the city with the highest per capita count of psychoanalysts is Buenos Aires?

Despite the evident bad blood, someone had the bright idea of arranging exhibition matches for the two sides in the 1970s. Is there a bigger oxymoron in soccer than a "friendly" between England and Argentina? At Wembley in 1974, they scrapped to a 2–2 draw that left England captain Emlyn Hughes with a black eye in spite of an unofficial peace treaty brokered in the referee's dressing room at halftime. When England traveled in 1977 to the Bombonera, home of the powerhouse Boca Juniors, Argentina forward Daniel Bertoni delicately removed two of defender Trevor Cherry's teeth, and, to the amazement of the English, *both* players were sent off. More than 30 years later, Bertoni still proudly displays the two indentations on his right knuckle.

Their 1986 World Cup meeting, however, ranks among the greatest sports robberies of all time. "In 1986, winning that game against England was enough," the Argentine defender Roberto Perfumo told the writer John Carlin in a 2002 interview. "Winning the World Cup was secondary for us. Beating England was our real aim." Despite hacking and whacking at Maradona for 90 minutes, including a blatant elbow to his face from bumbling defender Terry Fenwick, the English could not prevent the Argentine from scoring two memorable goals, one that remains indelibly wretched and wondrously illegal, depending upon the nation of one's birth. Striker Jorge Valdano reveled in the moment, noting that the Argentines "have been brought up to celebrate cheekiness and cunning." While the British press were apoplectic after the loss—*The Sun* noted that England had been beaten by "a little cheat"—the players and manager begrudgingly

acquiesced. Squeaky-clean striker Gary Lineker, famous for rarely receiving so much as a stern word from the referee in his 16-year career, admitted he'd have probably done the same were he in Maradona's boots, while noble coach Bobby Robson noted, "I'm sure we wouldn't have complained if an English player had scored that way."

Still, those measured responses, as well as that breathtaking second goal (*see Greatest Goals, page 131*) were buried amid an avalanche of anger and fury from the masses that erupted, once again, 12 smack-talking years later with the rematch in the 1998 World Cup. The game had everything—a Michael Owen swan dive and Alan Shearer's ensuing penalty kick; accusations of Argentine cheating; a spectacular Owen solo goal (*see Greatest Goals,*

page 189); and a penalty shoot-out that saw the South Americans prevail once again.

BECKHAM BASHING

Above all, the match was sanctified as the game in which David Beckham got his Armani knickers in a twist and petulantly kicked out at Diego Simeone, thereby earning both a red card and the wrath of his home nation. For months afterward, any Englishman who burned Beckham's likeness in effigy needn't take out his wallet in a pub. Beckham bashing became a sport, almost as popular as darts or snooker.

But there was so much more to the story, not the least of which was that getting an English player kicked out of the game had been part of Argentina's

strategy all along. Ricardo Villa, who played in England for five years, explained it this way: "In Argentina you go to the pitch with a master plan in your mind. It is a destructive one instead of a creative one. It is better to destroy than to create." Which, according to Perfumo, was exactly what Simeone set out to do to Beckham. "Simeone did an act and got Beckham sent off," he said. "This is not the kind of thing that could have been done by one of your naive, honest English players."

At Korea/Japan '02, Beckham bent his way back into the hearts of his countrymen, though it was a minor medical miracle that he even made it to the tournament; a couple of months before the World Cup, Beckham broke his foot in a Champions League game for Manchester United. The injury was inflicted by Deportivo La Coruna midfielder Aldo Duscher, an Argentine, who was lauded back home as a national hero for his efforts. Argentina's bestselling sports paper, *Olé,* ran an op-ed with the incendiary line "The Empire, the Queen, London Bridge trembles.... Once it was the hand of Diego Armando Maradona, now it is the foot of Aldo Duscher."

Despite the skullduggery, Beckham recovered in time to join the squad and resume his captaincy. England and Argentina ended up drawn in the same group, and before their game, the *Mirror* quipped "How Foul Can They Get?" and invited their readership to place bets on when the first incident of foul play would occur. In the final minutes of the first half, Michael Owen won a penalty with yet another suspect tumble, this time over Mauricio Pochettino's outstretched leg, and Beckham belted in the ensuing spot kick for a dramatic 1–0 victory that gave some respite to the ghosts of '98.

It's been many years since these two bitter rivals stepped onto the same field in a game of consequence, but when they do, elbows will fly, controversy is guaranteed, reputations for the ages will be won and lost, and Argentina will get all of the blame.

SO YOU THINK YOU'RE A FAN?

Put down your vuvuzela and measure your mania

All soccer fans share certain traits: They chant, sing, wear scarves and replica jerseys, wave flags and banners, and have the capacity to endure unbelievable heartache. But subtle differences distinguish the casual fan—or as they're sometimes called, "Americans"—from the certifiable lunatics who demand that their ashes be sprinkled on the penalty spot of their beloved home team's turf.

Take our quiz and determine your level of World Cup madness.

1. HOW DO YOU TYPICALLY TRAVEL TO A GAME?

•you don't; you stay home and watch the matches on TV (-5)

•chauffeured luxury town car (-1, because at least you're going)

•via public transportation (+1)

•on a chartered bus or train full of inebriated supporters (+3)

•as part of a five-hour pub crawl through town en route to the stadium (+5)

•by pedaling 70 miles a day from Buenos Aires to Mexico City to watch your team participate in a World Cup, only to find no tickets and have your bike stolen (*see Argentine superfan Pedro Garita, 1986*) (+1 for every 10 miles biked)

2. WHEN YOU GO TO A GAME, WHAT DO YOU USE TO MAKE NOISE?

•your BlackBerry, by gently tapping your fingers on it (-5)

•your hands (-1 if you use them to clap; +2 if you use them to slap your giant, naked belly that's painted in your team's colors)

•a cowbell (+2; +4 if you're not actually Swiss)

•drums for beating out Brazilian samba rhythms (+3)

•thundersticks, the preferred method of rabble-rousing in South Korea (+5)

•South African vuvuzela, those plastic, trumpetlike instruments that sound like a hornets' nest on acid (-10)

3. WHAT DO YOU WEAR TO THE GAME?

•your LA Lakers shirt (-5)

•jersey of your favorite player (0; +1 if it's a retro jersey with a favorite player from the '70s)

•face paint in your national colors (+2)

•the blood of your enemies (+3)

•Viking helmet and lederhosen (+2; +4 if you're neither Scandanavian nor German)

4. WHERE DO YOU SIT?

•in an air-conditioned corporate box (-5)

•on a pub stool (0)

•in the Fan Zone outside the stadium, where you pay $9 for a small beer (+1)

•in the home fans section (and you're a home fan) (+3)

•in the away fans section (and you're a home fan) (+5)

•in the rafters of the stadium (*see England fans at Wembley, 1966*) (+1 for every $10 saved on tickets)

5. HOW WELL DO YOU KNOW YOUR NATIONAL TEAM?

•you can't tell Ronaldo from Ronaldo (-5)

•you don't know the chants (-2)

- you can name your country's most famous player (-1)
- you can recall the most famous goal in national team history (+2; +4 if you act it out)
- you can name the starting lineup from the last three World Cups (+5)
- you can name the entire squad, their dates of birth, their dietary preferences, what clubs they play for, and the roster of the U-20 team set to replace them in four years (+10)

6. HOW DOES YOUR FANDOM AFFECT YOUR FAMILY?

- you force your spouse to stay awake until 1 A.M. to watch your country play Cameroon in a group game, but end up getting stabbed (*see Swedish fan during World Cup 1994, fatally wounded by his girlfriend*) (-everything)
- you bring your wife to the games (-5)
- you bring your kid to the games (+1)
- you bring your mistress to the games, because she understands and can explain the offside trap (+3)
- immediately after the game, you make your kid practice ball skills in the hope he evolves into the next Messi (+3; +5 if you force him to play left-footed so he's more desirable in the transfer market)
- you're unaware that you have a family (+10)

7. YOU WANT TO NAME YOUR CHILD:

- Jim Rome, Jr. (-10)
- Landon (+1)
- Edson Arantes do Nascimento (+2)
- Brooklyn, Cruz, or Romeo (+5)
- Kaká (+7)
- Mia (+10 and therapy if your child is a boy)

8. HOW DO YOU GREET THE FANS OF THE OTHER TEAM?

- fistbumps (-2)
- fistfights (+1 if you fight before the game, +2 if you fight after, +3 if you fight during)
- with chants like "We have dentists!" and "Are you Scotland in disguise?" (*See Sam's Army, U.S. vs. England, 2010*)
- with highly creative song lyrics calling into question the purity of the opposing star's mother/sister/wife (+3)
- with a dartboard featuring the face of the other team's best player (+4; +7 if you put Beckham on it just for fun)
- throwing bags of urine (*see Mexican fans hurling them at U.S. players in World Cup qualifiers in Mexico City*) (+10)

9. HOW DO YOU REACT TO YOUR TEAM LOSING?

- "There's always the next game" (-4)
- binge drinking (-2)
- you cry conspiracy to anyone who will listen (*see the Algerians during the 1982 World Cup, having watched Germany beat Austria 1–0 in a suspiciously perfect result that saw both teams advance in the competition at the expense of the North Africans*) (-1)
- you write an angry blog (+2)
- you compile a book of original poems about the defeat (*see Holland, in the wake of losing to West Germany in the 1974 final*) (+4)
- you wait all day at the airport for the team to return home, only to discover that the team has sneakily redirected its flight to a different airport, to which you're tipped off, only to arrive just in time to pelt the players with eggs and rotten tomatoes (*see Italian fans after the Azzurri were eliminated from the 1966 World Cup by lowly North Korea*) (+8)

10. THE REFEREE MAKES A BAD CALL AGAINST YOUR TEAM. HOW DO YOU RESPOND?

- you ask the guy next to you to explain why everyone's booing (-5)
- you tell everybody around you that the ref is only human and it's part of the game (-3)
- you leap off your seat in outrage, spilling your beer in the process (-1)
- you loudly question the purity of the referee's wife/mother/sister (+2)
- you ignite an emergency flare in the stands and burn a voodoo effigy of the offending whistleblower (+5)
- you become so crazed that the ref has to be escorted quickly out of the country, never to referee in a major tournament again (*see Byron Moreno after his gaffe-ridden effort in 2002 that saw Italy eliminated by hosts South Korea*) (+10)

11. YOUR TEAM'S FATE COMES DOWN TO PENALTY KICKS AFTER EXTRA TIME. WHAT DO YOU DO?

- penalties? You left ages ago thinking, this one ended in a draw (-5)
- curl up into a fetal position and weep gently as your best friend holds you (-3)
- sit and watch impassionately (-1)
- take out your flask of absinthe and shotgun it (+1)
- pull out your Buddha, rosary beads, Star of David, and Koran, and pray that the other team will shank one (+3)
- leave the stadium right away because you know your team will lose anyway (+4; +6 if you're an England fan . . . *see 1990, 1998, 2006*)

COMPUTE YOUR SCORE

Less than 0: Congratulations, you're still a baseball fan.

0–9: You are a casual fan who follows the World Cup, watches an occasional MLS game, and only sings when you're winning.

10–19: You are a passionate fan who supports a team in the English Premier League, Serie A, or La Liga (and you probably picked one of the front-runners, too).

20–29: You are a hooligan and your parole officer would like a word with you.

30 and above: You're the real deal, a hard-core fan who follows his national team to major tournaments and would happily sell your nephew—or someone else's—for a ticket to the World Cup.

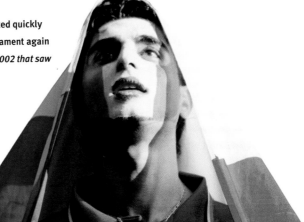

WANTED:
CHARISMATIC MASOCHIST WITH EXPERIENCE MANAGING EGOMANIACS

"There are 180 million people in Brazil ... and all of them are coaches."

Few jobs ask so much of a single individual under conditions of hysterical stress. An international soccer coach must be a tactical genius, psychologist, sports scientist, negotiator, data analyst, master motivator, and charismatic PR figurehead, able to carry the hopes of a nation on his shoulders, while the tabloid press mine the recesses of his private life for dirt.

All of these skills will be placed in the crucible in the run-up to the World Cup as every manager squares up to the central dilemma they all face—should they select the players who best match the most strategic system or select a system that plays to the strengths of their greatest players? Managers at club teams like Manchester United or Barcelona have the luxury of being able to wheel and deal, transferring players to develop the finest squad to fit their system, but national coaches are in a more Rumsfeld-ian position of having to "go to war with the Army you have, not the Army you want or wish to have." If they lack a quality player in a particular position (England, for instance, has struggled to fill the left side of its midfield for much of the last decade), they have no option but to play with the hand they are dealt, defining a style of play and then harnessing the personalities and raging egos of their players around that common mission, persuading them to set aside their conflicting agendas and domestic rivalries, while being undermined by the second-guessing of the media, sponsors, agents, and assorted flunkies who swirl around the team camp.

Sometimes it works, sometimes it does not. In 2002 the Irish team was shattered after their star player, Roy Keane, left Japan and went home after publicly berating his manager, Mick McCarthy, during training: "Mick. I didn't rate you as a player, I don't rate you as a manager, and I don't rate you as a person. You're a fucking wanker and you can stick your World Cup up your arse. The only reason I have any dealings with you is that somehow you are the manager of my country! You can stick it up your bollocks."

McCarthy was left with his reputation in tatters. But when a coach retains his authority, his vision can reign supreme. Argentina's two World Cup victories, in 1978 and 1986, were achieved only eight years apart but by teams that played radically different styles of soccer due to the clashing visions of two coaches who were polar opposites: the tall, gaunt César Luis Menotti, known as *El Flaco* (The

Skinny One) and Carlos Bilardo, known as *El Narigon* (The Big Nose). Menotti was a cosmopolitan, left-wing intellectual who strived to transform his team from physical counterattackers into a free-flowing creative unit. He cut a chain-smoking Zen presence on the sideline, ruthlessly dropping players who didn't suit this vision—including the young wonder, Maradona. Bilardo was a bawdy, parochial rightist who ripped up his predecessor's game plan, harnessing the brilliance of Maradona and motivating the rest of the team to adopt a brutal soccer style known as *anti-futbol* in which only winning mattered. As a player, Bilardo was rumored on occasion to bring a needle onto the field with which he would subtly stab opposing players (fittingly, he had qualified as a doctor). As a manager he was not averse to supplying Deep Heat to his players to rub into their opponent's eyes. His team battered their way to victory by any means necessary.

The coach's role was not always so absolute. At the advent of the tournament, team managers were viewed as little more than cabana boys, charged with coordinating the logistics of practice and making sure the players arrived on time to take the field. Italy's Vittorio Pozzo was ahead of his time, becoming the tournament's first truly modern coach in 1934, but until 1947, even the English team was selected by a committee of bureaucrats who would also determine the formation the starting 11 would adopt. Once the game itself became more complex, the position rapidly evolved and coaches today can often become bigger than the teams they manage, overshadowing even their nation's presidents and prime ministers. To prepare for the 2010 World Cup campaign, South Africa lured Brazilian coaching legend Carlos Alberto Parreira with an offer of $11 million, tax free, over four years. Then-President Thabo Mbeki made just $160,600 annually. Parreira lasted 16 months in the hot seat before resigning, only to be rehired in October 2009.

The demands on the modern coach remain constant, but the men themselves come from a variety of backgrounds. Most are former players. Some were once the world's greatest. Franz Beckenbauer used his legend to inspire the German team to victory in 1990, but others like France's Michel Platini were less effective. As players, the game came to

them so naturally that they are unable to empathize with the challenges faced by the mere mortal talents they manage. Others still had unremarkable careers or never played the game professionally. Arrigo Sacchi, who was once a shoe salesman before guiding Italy to the final in 1994, claimed, "You don't have to have been a horse to be a jockey."

Modern soccer has fostered a new breed of manager, the gun-for-hire. Mercenary managers who specialize in overcoming the language barriers

Guus Hiddink, posterized in Seoul.

inherent in the international game, hawking their World Cup pedigree to teams around the globe. The role was pioneered by a Serb, Bora Milutinovic, who became known as the "Miracle Worker" after a remarkable run coaching Mexico (1986), Costa Rica (1990), the United States (1994), Nigeria (1998), and China (2002) in the World Cup. Oddly enough, one of the few nations he did turn down was that of

his place of birth, Yugoslavia. The Dutch tactician Guus Hiddink perfected the wandering art, providing much-needed discipline for Holland (1998), and then overachieving with South Korea (2002) and Australia (2006).

The hired gun used to be solely the target of minnows eager for an instant upgrade, but it has recently and controversially been employed by more powerful yet desperate nations, most notably England, who swallowed their pride and hired a mild-mannered Swede, Sven-Göran Eriksson, to lead them at the last two World Cups. In 2010, they will be masterminded by a shrewd Italian, Fabio Capello, whose appointment was vocally criticized even by FIFA. President Sepp Blatter quipped, "I would say it is a little surprising that the motherland of football has ignored a sacrosanct law or belief that the national team manager should be from the same country as the players." But for the country, the competitive tactical advantage gained by "going foreign" outweighs the indignity. In the opinion of Italian legend Giovanni Trapattoni, who himself became the Irish coach, "A good manager, at best, can make a team 10 percent better; but a bad manager can make a team up to 50 percent worse."

Come the World Cup, the pressure of coaching can be crushing. Luiz Felipe Scolari, who led Brazil to victory in 2002, complained that every soccer fan believes they know better than the manager. "You know how many people there are in Brazil? . . . 180 million people. Pressure was when I was coach of the national team because everyone in Brazil is the coach." As the hapless Eriksson explained, the English press criticized him whatever move he made. "If we have only one system, you ask 'Where is Plan B?' and if we have two you say we don't know which to play." In such a situation, the end is never too far away, and as Sven experienced when his contract was not renewed after the 2006 World Cup, once it all falls apart, the manager plays his final and most excruciating role—that of national scapegoat.

The Germans smother Maradona, and
Argentina's chances, during the final.

1990
Italy

WORLD CUP MOST FOUL

Penalty kicks predominate, England tears up, and West Germany plods to another victory.

MUSSOLINI MAY HAVE BEEN dead and buried, but the Italian government channeled his spirit in preparing his country to host the World Cup for a second time. Tournament organizers oversaw a building boom that saw avant-garde stadia like the delle Alpi in Turin rise across the nation. As government investigators discovered after the tournament, this appetite for construction was stimulated by corruption and kickbacks rather than a true love of postmodern architecture. The findings were a

François Omam-Biyik and
Cameroon take African
soccer to new heights,
shocking Argentina in
the opening round.

Argentina forward Gustavo Dezotti gets up in the referee's grille.

The final was the worst ever. Argentina played for a draw from the start.

fitting coda for the most negative and cynical World Cup of all time. A global audience of 26 billion viewers tuned in to witness a bloated tournament, plagued by fouls, in which many of the big games were decided by penalty shoot-outs. The quality of the soccer was so poor in Italia '90 that FIFA spent the next year debating one radical rule change after another, from widening the goals to playing with 10 on a side, so desperate were they to pump up the action.

The physical tone of the tournament was set in the opening game when the Indomitable Lions of Cameroon, facing the reigning champions, Argentina, unleashed a barrage of brutal tackles, managing to have two men red-carded before the 90 minutes were up. But the end justified the means, as they held on to win 1–0, a victory that sparked a fairy-tale run

into the quarterfinals, the first African team to appear, the first to be truly feared. Costa Rica, another surprise package in their first World Cup, beat both the ever-hapless Scotland and Sweden on the way to the second round. Indeed, there would be few easy games in the tournament from this point on, unless you were playing the United States. In this, Costa Rica's first World Cup entry in 40 years, they surrendered a total of eight goals in three consecutive defeats. Their drab play was emblematic of the opening rounds of this tournament, which were so dull that perhaps the most replayed highlight was Holland's Frank Rijkaard spitting at the German Rudi Völler in the second round (*see Greatest Rivalries, page 150*).

Both of the semifinals were decided by penalty kicks. Maradona dragged his team into a semi-

final matchup with host Italy, which had found a folk hero in the relatively unknown Sicilian-born striker Totò Schillaci (*see Cult Figures, page 153*). He appeared out of nowhere to become a prolific goal scorer, only to skip back into obscurity after the tournament—soccer's equivalent of a one-hit wonder. Maradona dabbled in regional Italian politics in the days before the game, tapping into the fierce rivalry between the north and south. The tie was to be played in Naples, home of Napoli, his club team—a city that symbolized everything wealthy northerners despised about the south. He appealed to Neapolitans to turn on their own country and support Argentina. "For 364 days a year you are treated like dirt," he said, "and then they ask you to support them." It might have helped; Schillaci scored to put the Italians ahead, but once the Ar-

(left) Tears of a clown: England's Gazza strips in despair after being yellow-carded in the semifinal against West Germany; (right) Italian goalkeeper Walter Zenga in rush-hour Argentinian traffic.

1990 RESULTS

QUARTERFINALS
Argentina 0 Yugoslavia 0 (3–2 PKs)
Italy 1 Republic of Ireland 0
West Germany 1 Czechoslovakia 0
England 3 Cameroon 2

SEMIFINALS
Argentina 1 Italy 1 (4–3 PKs)
West Germany 1 England 1 (4–3 PKs)

THIRD PLACE
Italy 2 England 1

FINAL
West Germany 1 Argentina 0

gentinians equalized, the hosts lost their nerve and ran out of steam, eventually losing on penalties.

Maradona may have divided the crowd in the south, but he was punished in the final in Rome by spectators who drowned out the Argentinian national anthem (during which Maradona was seen to mouth *"Hijos de Puta"* twice in close-up on the stadium jumbotron) and jeered his every move.

English fans had spent the opening rounds watching their team on the isolated island of Sardinia—a deliberate ploy by FIFA to keep their hooligans off center stage. But once the English emerged on the mainland, their brittle confidence had been bolstered, and the already hyperbolic tabloid media coverage was at a jingoistic fever pitch by the time

they were drawn to face Coach Beckenbauer's West German team in the semifinal. Led by the flamboyantly brilliant Paul Gascoigne, they should have done better than a tie at the end of regulation. But his yellow card meant that, even if his team made the final, he would be unable to play, and his tears became iconic. But he need not have worried. His team did not let him down. The game went to a shoot-out, but soon the entire English nation wept, having dared to believe, only to have their hearts shattered by penalty kicks. It would be the team's equivalent of a poisoned chalice in both Euros and World Cups to come.

The final was the worst ever. Argentina, which had scored only five goals all tournament, played

for a draw from the start. They managed to be the first World Cup finalist to be shut out and they were also the first to have a player sent off in a World Cup final, only to have another follow him shortly before the end of the game. German professionalism won the day as the side scraped by, thanks to an 85th-minute penalty shot to claim their third title.

Giddy after becoming the first man to lift the Cup as both captain and coach, Beckenbauer capped the tournament by proclaiming, "I'm sorry for the other countries. But now we will be able to incorporate all the great players from the East. The German team will be unbeatable for a long time."

It was one of the worst predictions of all time. They have yet to win again.

WORST TEAMS

BRAZIL, 1990

WHY THEY MADE THE LIST: When your country has won the most World Cups, the law of averages dictates that eventually you'll give birth to a stinker. This was that team.

THE HIGH POINT: Winning their three group games, but they scored only a very un-Brazil-like four goals against lightweights Sweden, Scotland, and Costa Rica.

THE NADIR: In addition to playing prosaic soccer, the Brazilians were greedy. They demanded money and prizes should they bring home the Cup, and even posed for a photo with their hands covering their sponsor's logo, because they felt that the offer they had received was insulting.

ONLY IN THE WORLD CUP: In Brazil/Argentina second-round match, Brazilian defender Branco was given a water bottle by the Argentines that Maradona later revealed had been drugged. And Maradona would know.

THE FALLOUT: Coach Lazaroni was fired and pilloried by the Brazilian media. A newspaper in Rio de Janeiro reckoned that "never has Brazilian soccer been so far removed from its roots," while another called him "cowardly and stubborn." Less than half the squad were invited back to play on Brazil's team four years later—which won the World Cup.

GERMANY VS. HOLLAND

Journalist: "What's wrong with the Germans?"
Dutch midfielder Wim van Hanegem: "Well, they've got the wrong ancestors, of course."

Spit happens. At least when these two teams play each other.

For the Dutch, the animosity is deeply rooted in the Nazi invasion of Holland in 1940. "Every time I played against German players I had a problem because of the war," said van Hanegem, one of the Dutch stars of the brilliant '74 World Cup side. "Eighty percent of my family died in the war—my daddy, my sister, my two brothers. And every game against players from Germany makes me angry." It didn't help that van Hanegem's team lost in the '74 final . . . to the West Germans.

Four years later in Argentina, the teams played a relatively clean and incident-free second-round game that ended in a 2–2 tie—not that the players fell into one another's arms at the final whistle. "I think it's a true shame and pity that the Dutch regard football as an outlet for their hatred from the Second World War," said striker Karl-Heinz Rummenigge, in a typical German attempt to rise above the fray. Ten years later, the Dutch finally began to get under the German skin. In addition to eliminating the host nation in the semifinals (2–1) of the 1988 European Championship, Dutch defender Ronald Koeman added a whole new twist to the end-of-game jersey-swapping tradition. After collecting German midfielder Olaf Thon's #10, Koeman pretended to wipe his butt with the jersey. In front of thousands of German spectators. On international

TV. The outrage was instantaneous and massive, and made worse by Koeman's comments: "German reporters asked me if I made this gesture toward the German people. I said, no, no. . . . Only against the German team. But I know I shouldn't have done it. But to say I regret it . . . no . . . not really."

The tone was now set for a rematch; after an innocuous 0–0 draw in October '88, the two sides met in Rotterdam for a World Cup qualifier a year later that ranks among the ugliest of soccer nights. Roving gangs of Dutch and German thugs fought for hours on the streets of the city that had been almost completely destroyed by the *Luftwaffe* in 1940. By the time the game had ended in a 1–1 tie, dozens of people had been injured and more arrested. Fortunately, the game itself was relatively uneventful. That would change a year later.

As luck would have it, the two teams faced off again in a second-round match in Milan during Italia '90. This time, the tension in the stadium was palpable before a ball had even been kicked. The Dutch fans disrespectfully chanted *"Hup Holland Hup"* during the German national anthem, and the German faithful returned the favor by bellowing *"Deutschland Deutschland"* during Holland's anthem, drowning out the music. Germany won 2–1, but what everyone remembers is the saliva.

Just before halftime, German striker Rudi Völler went down softly after minimal contact with Hol-

land's Frank Rijkaard, who was booked for the foul. The yellow-carded Rijkaard, who now would be suspended for the next game, proceeded to launch a phlegm missile into Völler's perm. After Völler promptly showed the referee the evidence nestled in his mass of curly locks, Rijkaard pulled on Völler's mane, a gesture that, once escalated, led to the German also being booked. After another exchange of bodily fluids, the two combatants were ejected, upon which Rijkaard spit at Völler again as he ran past him toward the dressing room. The Dutchman still wasn't finished, reportedly grabbing the German by the throat in the tunnel as a brief fistfight broke out. Rijkaard was suspended for three games, Völler for one.

In the years since, the two nations have played only twice but the Dutch rarely miss an opportunity to mock their former occupiers. When Germany was dumped out of Euro 2004, Dutch supporters snuck into the German fan zone and hung a banner saying *ZIMMER FREI* (German for "open vacancy"). Said Franz Beckenbauer, the German legend: "Matches against Holland have cost me years of my life. But I wouldn't have missed them for anything. Those matches always breathed soccer of class, emotion, and unprecedented tension. Soccer in its pure form."

And who wouldn't salivate over that?

Spit takes: Völler
crumples, Rijkaard
moisturizes Völler's
locks, Völler prepares
to retaliate, and
nobody's to blame.

ROBERTO BAGGIO
Italy vs. Czechoslovakia, Group Stage

Italia '90 wasn't pretty. Cagey 1–0 wins, a slew of penalty shoot-outs . . . it was enough to make the hardcore fan turn to a higher power in search of deliverance. Those who prayed for relief received an answer in the form of Italy's *divin codino* (Divine Ponytail): Roberto Baggio.

Ask any casual soccer fan what the name Baggio conjures up and invariably he mentions the same image. It's the one that shows him despairingly on his knees, his head and famous mane in his hands, mere seconds after he sent his team's last penalty kick blazing into the Pasadena sun, thus handing the 1994 World Cup trophy to Brazil. But it's like memorializing Joe DiMaggio with a photo of him striking out. Small and wiry, Baggio was the little prince of Italian soccer, a mesmerizing player with a repertoire of sublime skills, many of which he displayed in his electrifying goal against Czechoslovakia.

Italy was up 1–0 in their final group game against the feisty Czechoslovakians, a talented team that had recently weathered a revolution at home. Since both countries had already qualified for the knockout stage, they were able to take the brakes off their cautious play. Enter Baggio, a man who three years earlier had shocked Italian fans by converting to Buddhism and letting his hair grow down to his shoulder blades. The 23-year-old striker was coming off a breakthrough season at Fiorentina, where his manager said that "angels sing in his legs." But Baggio was still struggling to get a foothold on the national team, where his Buddhist beliefs were looked upon skeptically.

Used sparingly for most of the tournament, Baggio provided only glimpses of his talent, but with 12 minutes left at Rome's Stadio Olimpico he casually collected the ball on the halfway line, worked a quick give-and-go with Giuseppe Giannini, and set off into the heart of the Czechoslovakian defense.

Fully 40 yards from goal, he skipped past the lunging tackle of Ivan Hašek (cousin of Dominik, the legendary hockey goalie), glided to the edge of the penalty area, and spun defender Miroslav Kadlec with a shimmy of his hips. The Czech goalkeeper dove early to his left, expecting a far post shot, but even if he had held his ground an instant longer, it wouldn't have mattered. Baggio had anticipated the keeper's move and had delicately lifted the ball over him, a finish so calm and controlled in its execution, it was positively Zen.

Later in the tournament semis, Italy fell to Maradona's Argentines in Naples on penalties (Baggio made his, for what it's worth), but Baggio and his partner in attack, Salvatore Schillaci (*see Cult Figures, page 153*), emerged from the tournament with enhanced reputations.

Though the ponytailed Buddhist is the only Italian player ever to score in three World Cups, Baggio may always be remembered for his agonizing penalty miss in the 1994 final, but the truly enlightened fan knows better.

SALVATORE "TOTÒ" SCHILLACI, ITALY

The eyes gave it all away. After every goal he scored during the glorious month of Italia '90, they bulged with disbelief, possibly at how quickly he was being transformed from trivia question—"Who is Italy's fourth striker behind Baggio, Vialli, and Carnevale?"—to national hero who inspired a baby-naming mania in his country.

No one outside of Schillaci's household could ever have imagined that Totò would become Italy's soccer savior, a position traditionally reserved for the more stylishly handsome Italians with glittering club résumés. Schillaci had neither the looks (with his bedraggled, thinning hair and heavily weathered face, he resembled a musty-smelling mutt) nor the pedigree—for most of his career he had toiled in the lower reaches of the Italian second division. He was, however, one of those dogged players who needed only to sniff a goal-scoring chance before burying the ball into the back of the net. Unlike Toto in *The Wizard of Oz,* Schillaci—and his feats—were real; he won the tournament's Golden Shoe with six goals while leading the Azzurri to third place.

A year before, in 1989, Schillaci's reputation as a prolific poacher induced Italy's powerhouse Juven-

tus to pay a hefty transfer fee for him. Although he scored a respectable 15 goals at Juve, his call-up to the national team was greeted with confusion and derision. Given Schillaci's upbringing as the son of a Sicilian bricklayer, the public wondered whether the *Cosa Nostra* had put pressure on the selection committee. Even his teammates largely ignored him. He was a journeyman, a squad player necessary to fill out a reserve team for the starters to train with on the practice field.

But when Italy's purebred attacking stars floundered against a lightly regarded Austrian side in the opening game of the World Cup, Coach Azeglio Vicini played a hunch in the 74th minute, and brought in Totò. Within four minutes, Schillaci had headed in the winner for a 1–0 victory. Even then, his teammates remained unimpressed, pointing out that anybody could "just stick out his head," and Schillaci himself downplayed the accomplishment in his postgame remarks, saying, "I'm a modest guy, and I hope that continues." By Italy's third game, Vicini realized that Totò and Italy's star striker Roberto Baggio had forged an instinctive understanding upfront, with Baggio playing the role of the pack-leading alpha dog, while Schillaci

pounced on the scraps like a crazed mongrel. In a tournament in which Italy won six of its seven games, Totò scored the winning goal a remarkable five times. During his scorching run, Schillaci was anointed the next coming of Paolo Rossi, Italy's 1982 World Cup deity, and serenaded by screams of "TO-TÒ Skee-LAH-chee! TO-TÒ Skee-LAH-chee!" He awoke to the following headline in one of Italy's tabloids: TOTÒ! WE DESIRE YOU PHYSICALLY! Schillaci, ever humble, dismissed the comparison, saying simply, "Rossi was a champion."

And then the World Cup ended and so, for all intents and purposes, did the *Notti Magiche* (magical nights) *di Totò Schillaci.* By 1991, Schillaci had been dropped from the national team. Within four years, he had left Italian soccer to earn his living playing in Japan. Rarely in the soccer universe had a player risen and fallen so dramatically. Two decades after setting Italia '90 aflame, he was once again the answer to another, albeit grander, trivia question: "What player went from virtual obscurity to Golden Shoe winner, only to never be heard from again?" This dog had had his day.

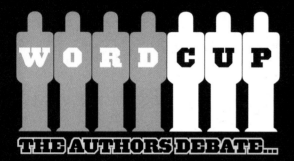

WORD CUP

THE AUTHORS DEBATE...

PELÉ VS. MARADONA— WHO'S BETTER?

HIRSHEY: This contest should be called before it begins. It's not a fair fight. Pelé has three championships to Maradona's one. And, like it or not, that's how we measure greatness.

BENNETT: Please—

HIRSHEY: Wait. I grant you that Maradona's close control was unsurpassed in the open field. His explosive acceleration and the unpredictability of his body swerves made him almost impossible to contain. Soccer, however, is about so much more than just skinning defenders at full throttle. It is about passing, heading, reading, recognizing, orchestrating, and extracting the best from the team assembled around you.

When Maradona had the ball, the thought of giving it up rarely entered his mind. It was as if the goals and glory were designed for him and him alone. By contrast, there was an imagination and selflessness to Pelé's game that Maradona never possessed.

BENNETT: Look, Pelé and Maradona were kings of extremely different eras. The debate traditionally breaks down by age. Older fans still marvel at Pelé. Younger ones idolize Maradona. But your opening fusillade is way wide of the mark: No single player has ever motivated a mediocre squad to win the tournament more than Maradona when he captained Argentina to glory in 1986.

The singular beauty of the goals he scored must have blinded you though, because Maradona dished the ball aplenty. He always knew the opposing team planned to shut him down with a double or triple team, so he specialized in making decoy runs to create space for his teammates to exploit. Witness the Argentinians' winning goal in the final. Maradona sucked four Germans into the midfield before slipping a perfect one-touch pass to spring Jorge Burruchaga for a solo run on goal. Maradona ended up with the trophy, five goals, and five assists.

HIRSHEY: It figures you'd go straight to the one moment in Maradona's career when he was sober. He was playing in Mexico against teams that were sapped by the searing heat, his most famous moment involved cheating, and in two other World Cups that he entered, he left in utter disgrace. Maradona was red-carded in his final match in Spain '82 and sent home as a drug cheat in 1994. Pelé, I will remind you, won the Jules Rimet trophy in three of his four World Cups, which included a remarkable strike in the final against Sweden in 1958 when he was only 17 years old. Trapping the ball with his thigh in the Swedish penalty area, he let it fall to the crook of his ankle and in one seamless motion looped it over his own head and that of a slack-jawed defender before cracking a volley into the net. The ball never touched the ground.

BENNETT: Going spectacular goal-for-goal against Maradona is a no-win proposition—

HIRSHEY: You have finally written truth. Pelé never punched the ball into the back of his opponent's net. Instead he scored 77 times in 92 matches for his country, while Maradona managed a mere 34 in 91. Don't forget the blind layoff to Jairzinho in 1970 that froze an entire English backline with a single swivel of his right hip.

BENNETT: Are you seriously putting that up against the 1986 Cup, when Maradona eviscerated the entire English team, evading all pursuers with a poetic run hailed instantly as the greatest goal ever scored? He then repeated the feat in the very next game, lacerating the Belgians.

But your mention of the brilliant Jairzinho leads us to a critical point. Maradona's play transformed an average team, turning them into world beaters. Pelé was always privileged to be the jewel in the crown on a team stuffed with talent.

HIRSHEY: I already conceded that Diego was spec-

actual in that Cup, although I am forced to remind you that the so-called magical goal against England might well be one of the most overrated in soccer history. And saying that Pelé should be dismissed because he was surrounded by greatness is like saying that Larry Bird, Magic Johnson, and Wayne Gretzky were overrated because they had a strong supporting cast.

BENNETT: David! In 1958, he won the World Cup with legends Nilton Santos, Garrincha, Didi, and Vava. In 1970, Brazil's victorious dream team included the dazzling skills of Carlos Alberto, Jairzinho, Tostão, Gérson, and Rivelino. In fact, the true strength and depth of Brazilian soccer in this era was proven beyond doubt in 1962 when the team lost Pelé to injury in the second game of the tournament but *still* managed to cruise to victory without him. I defy you to name three teammates of Maradona's 1986 team without the aid of Wikipedia.

HIRSHEY: You mean besides Doc Gooden and Mookie Wilson. Let's get real. If you want to take the measure of the men, look at how they spent their twilight and post-playing years. Pelé's love for soccer was so great that he came to the nascent NASL to spread the gospel for the game that he loved. What did your guy do with his later years?

BENNETT: Rose-tinted naïveté. What Pelé says and what he does are two very different things. His decision to abandon his retirement and join the NASL was less because of a humble urge to "spread the gospel" and more about a desperate need to pay off creditors after his business interests had gone belly-up.

HIRSHEY: Pelé's trademark mantra "to remember the children" was a bit cloying, I'll admit, but, he was no scattershot genius like Maradona. He prided himself on his fitness, consistency, and durability. Pelé was blessed with the perfect body for a soccer player, 5'8" inches of tensile strength with thighs so massive that only a landmine could knock him off the ball.

BENNETT: I'll give that to you, Pelé was the more physical player. But if you want to debate endurance, Maradona wins hands down. It did not take

a landmine to knock Pelé out of the World Cup in 1962, and it must have slipped your mind that in 1966 Pelé cried, *"Nâo mais!"* once Brazil was eliminated, threatening to retire unless referees shielded him from the rough stuff. Maradona never com-

plained, and he dominated an era when defenses were tactically tighter and against stronger, fitter, faster opponents who spent the entire game hell-bent on breaking his legs.

HIRSHEY: In Pelé's era, the entire strategy of the opposing team was to field two or three goons and encourage them to perform open knee surgery on Pelé.

BENNETT: Anyway, David, debating the players' personalities is almost impossible because we never really knew the real Pelé. His genius was to become the sport's first human billboard, shilling for global brands from Pepsi to Viagra. Maradona was always human, flaws and all. He remains revered among his fellow players for the way he used his fame throughout his career to fight for their rights. On the other hand, Pelé is less beloved, renowned for being predominantly motivated by monetary gain. Remembering the poor children may have been his mantra, but as Brazil's minister for sport, he managed to campaign against "corruption" while lining his own pockets and

was forced to resign after $700,000 of UNICEF money disappeared in connection to an unplayed benefit match he had promised to organize for free. The money was never seen again.

HIRSHEY: Since when has using one's fame to generate post-career earnings been anything other than capitalism at its finest? In any case, Pelé's supreme athleticism and uncanny grasp of the flow of the game would make him the most marked man on the field 100 years from now. Pelé was the complete soccer player—not just a fat bastard who could dribble.

BENNETT: A fat bastard who could dribble? That's beneath even you! When FIFA launched an Internet-based vote to determine the greatest player of the 20th century, Maradona pummeled Pelé, receiving three times the votes from soccer fans around the world. To keep Pelé's myth intact FIFA quickly changed the rules, awarding him a second award as voted by their officials, but by now even some of Brazil's greatest modern-day players have tired of the man. The great striker Ronaldo captured his essence with a quote that could easily be applied to your efforts to advocate on his behalf: "Pelé is well known for the shit he talks. Nobody should take him seriously. I don't want to end up a bitter old man like him who talks only bollocks."

HIRSHEY: Roger, I have only one thing to say to that: bollocks.

ENGLAND 3, CAMEROON 2
Quarterfinal

500 to 1. Those were the odds British bookmakers were giving anyone foolish enough to bet on Cameroon winning the World Cup.

For starters, no African country had ever made it further than the second round of the tournament, let alone squeezed past the velvet ropes to soccer's VIP room, where Brazil, Argentina, Germany, and Italy were not inclined to entertain outsiders.

But after Cameroon's Indomitable Lions giant-killed defending champion Argentina, and dispatched Romania and Colombia, they had made a strong case for African inclusion in that elite club. Of course, first they had to get by the oldest of the old guard, England, a team with plenty of skill and muscle of their own.

In proud underdog tradition, Cameroon had other handicaps. Four players had been suspended—two for leaving their cleat marks all over Maradona in the Argentina game and two more for accumulating too many yellow cards. Fortunately, they still had Roger Milla, the Methusalah of African Soccer, whom a presidential decree had forced out of retirement at age 38. He had already spiced up the tournament with four goals off the bench and his trademark corner-flag hip-shaking celebrations. Milla, who in 1994 would become the oldest player

ever in a World Cup, lacked the legs to start games from the beginning. However, in the second half, when the outcome hung in the balance, the ebullient Cameroon fans in their colorful flowing robes would chant his name, beckoning Old Man Milla off the bench to conjure his magic. This game would be no different.

Up against an England team that featured such battle-hardened stars as the midfield virtuoso Paul Gascoigne and the cold-blooded finisher Gary Lineker, Cameroon dominated much of the first half, forcing goalkeeper Peter Shilton into several lunging saves. Yet the Indomitable Lions found themselves behind 1–0 on a goal by England's David Platt just before the intermission. Cue Milla Time.

Within fifteen minutes of stepping on the field, he had transformed a 1–0 deficit into a 2–1 lead. Although no longer able to beat defenders off the dribble, he still had velvety control of the ball in tight spaces. First he won a penalty when Gascoigne upended him in the box. Then he set up the second goal by feinting and shimmying his way past three English players and slipping the ball to fellow sub Eugene Ekeke, who lobbed it over Shilton into the net. England was shaken. "They tore us to pieces,"

said the English defender Terry Butcher, while manager Bobby Robson thought, "We were on the next plane home."

Cameroon was eight minutes away from securing the most improbable semifinal slot in World Cup history when they were undone by their own recklessness. The thuggish defender Benjamin Massing, who had been hacking at Lineker's legs all game, finally went too far, mowing down the English forward in the box. Lineker dusted himself off and calmly converted the penalty kick to send the game into overtime. Twenty-two minutes later he was back at the same spot. Gascoigne had laid the ball in his striker's path and Lineker was bearing down on Cameroon's goal when Massing and another defender crunched him again. His second penalty kick was as nerveless as the first.

The Indomitable Lions would go home with their heads high, knowing that they had heralded a new era in African soccer, paving the way for the Nigerias, Senegals, Ivory Coasts, and Ghanas to one day enter the World Cup's inner sanctum.

"What we did was for the continent as a whole, not for ourselves or even for our countries," Milla said. "We wanted Africa to be respected around the world."

WORLD COIFFURE CUP

By a hair, it's . . .

There are two ways to be noticed at the World Cup: how you play on the field and what you do off it—especially at the hair salon. Every four years, a few players step onto the world stage and dazzle an audience of billions with Technicolor perms, blond dreads, and reverse mohawks. After all, this is a game where using your head matters, and these 32 did it better than anyone. Hats on to the winners.

GROUP B

GROUP A

CURL POWER
René Higuita, Colombia 1990
Graeme Souness, Scotland 1978
Dominique Rocheteau, France 1986
Ronaldinho, Brazil 2002

GROUP A WINNER:
Graeme Souness, Scotland 1978

GROUP A RUNNER-UP:
Ronaldinho, Brazil 2002

Normally hard men in soccer don't spend much time in front of the mirror unless they're suturing up a cut, but the Scottish midfield enforcer was a breed apart. His teammate Archie Gemmill once commented, "If Graeme Souness was a chocolate drop, he'd eat himself."

The Brazilian show pony Ronaldinho was so tricky he could make his Jheri curls go one way and the ball the other.

LONGITUDE, LATITUDE, AND MULLET-UDE
Roberto Baggio, Italy 1994
Chris Waddle, England 1990
Tony Meola, U.S.A. 1990
Marco Etcheverry, Bolivia 1994

GROUP B WINNER:
Chris Waddle, England 1990

GROUP B RUNNER-UP:
Marco Etcheverry, Bolivia 1994

Waddle may be best known for missing a crucial penalty in England's semifinal defeat to West Germany in 1990 but his perfect mullet scored consistently with the ladies. Etcheverry was nicknamed El Diablo and his mop of jet-black hair was as devilish as he was in the midfield.

GROUP C

THE DYE HARDS

Abel Xavier, Portugal 2002
Romania, 1998
Carlos Valderrama, Colombia 1990
Djibril Cissé, France 2002

GROUP C WINNER:

Carlos Valderrama, Colombia 1990

GROUP C RUNNER-UP:

Abel Xavier, Portugal, 2002

Only a single peroxided strand of hair separates the winners from losers in this tight group—the Group of Dye, as it were. Cissé changed the color of his mohawk from red to green to yellow with the same speed he used to beat defenders in the open field.

Displaying extraordinary follicular chemistry, several Romanian players dyed their hair Gwen Stefani–blond. But neither the flamboyant French striker nor Romania made it out of the group because they were up against a couple of hirsute deities: Valderrama, who was as creative with his rich caramel tresses as he was with his passes, and Xavier, who used his brief appearance as a substitute in 2002 to showcase his puffy platinum flat-top, which held up a lot better than he did on the field.

THINKING OUTSIDE THE BOWL CUT

Alexi Lalas, U.S.A. 1994
Christian Ziege, Germany 2002
Ronaldo, Brazil 2002
Clint Mathis, U.S.A. 2002

GROUP D WINNER:

Alexi Lalas, U.S.A. 1994

GROUP D RUNNER-UP:

Clint Mathis, U.S.A. 2002

A sweep for the U.S.A., and not just on the barbershop floor. Lalas's flowing red mane was worthy of a rock star, which is what he aspired to be off the field.

Mathis's minimalist mohawk made him look like soccer's answer to Travis Bickle, and never more so than when he scored that killer goal against South Korea.

GROUP D

GROUP E

BLOW DRY IT LIKE BECKHAM

David Beckham, England 2002 (The mohawk with highlights)
David Beckham, England 2003 (Cornrows)
David Beckham, England 1998 (Modest long hair)
David Beckham, England 2001 (Shaved head)

GROUP E WINNER:

David Beckham, 2002

GROUP E RUNNER-UP:

David Beckham, 2001

Say what you want about the English midfielder's World Cup career, but his hair always brings it. The cornrow look was as eye-catching as his move to MLS while his shaved pate (with which he scored a sublime 93rd-minute free kick against Greece in 2001 to send England to the World Cup) proved he was equally adept with or without gel.

GROUP F

'FRO TIME
Teófilo Cubillas, Peru 1978
Jairzinho, Brazil 1974
Rudi Völler, West Germany 1990
Leonardo Cuéllar, Mexico 1978

GROUP F WINNER:
Leonardo Cuéllar, Mexico 1978

GROUP F RUNNER-UP:
Teófilo Cubillas, Peru 1978

It's rare when you get two epic coiffures going head-to-head in the same tournament, but 1978 featured Cuéllar's modified 'fro anchoring Mexico's midfield while Cubillas's measured flat-top soared both aesthetically and athletically for Peru. Despite Cubillas's five goals, it was Cuéllar's bushy 'do that stood tallest.

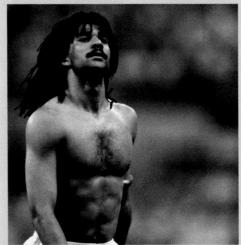

GROUP G

DRED HEADS
Clarence Seedorf, Holland 1998
Taribo West, Nigeria 1998
Ruud Gullit, Holland 1990
Steven Pienaar, South Africa 2006

GROUP G WINNER:
Taribo West, Nigeria 1998

GROUP G RUNNER-UP:
Ruud Gullit, Holland 1990

Go up against West's beaded green horns for a header and come down with one eye. Gullit's strong, uncompromising dreads reflected his dominance of the Dutch midfield.

GROUP H

(NEARLY) BALD AND BEAUTIFUL
Fabien Barthez, France 1998
Iordan Letchkov, Bulgaria 1994
Zinedine Zidane, France 2006
Juan Sebastián Verón, Argentina 2002

GROUP H WINNER:
Zinedine Zidane, France, 2006

GROUP H RUNNER-UP:
Fabien Barthez, France 1998

Barthez's kamikaze style of goalkeeping terrified both opponents and teammates alike but his gleaming pate had a pleasing consistency. After the 2006 World Cup final, are you going to tell Zidane's head it can't move on?

SECOND ROUND

ETCHEVERRY over **SOUNESS**
Bolivian Brylcreem bests the spit-polish Scot.

WADDLE over **RONALDINHO**
The Brazilian ball magician was as slick as they come, but a MacGyver mullet is a cut above.

VALDERRAMA over **MATHIS**
The Colombian maestro with the Technicolor 'fro easily manhandles a MLS mohawk.

LALAS over **XAVIER**
As with cards in soccer, yellow should be respected but red will send you off.

BECKHAM (2003) over **CUBILLAS**
The flat-top is overrun by Beck's orderly 4-4-2.

CUÉLLAR over **BECKHAM** (2001)
Size matters.

GULLIT over **ZIDANE**
Gullit's curls run rings around Zizou.

BARTHEZ over **WEST**
The Nigerian should never have locked horns with the Frenchman on this one.

QUARTERFINALS

WADDLE over **ETCHEVERRY**
The blond is all that separates these Kings of the Curling Iron.

VALDERRAMA over **LALAS**
Carlos's gold prevails over Alexi's copper.

BECKHAM (2003) over **CUÉLLAR**
Becks is just too metrosexy to be denied.

BARTHEZ over **GULLIT**
One dated Linda Evangelista. One didn't.

SEMIFINALS

VALDERRAMA over **WADDLE**
You could hide a team of mullets in Valderrama's hair and no one would notice.

BARTHEZ over **BECKHAM**
As with the real World Cup, England hasn't gotten past the semis since 1966.

FINAL

VALDERRAMA over **BARTHEZ**
In a battle of All or Nothing, the leonine midfielder puts one past the cue-balled keeper.

Arrivederci, World Cup: Roberto Baggio fails to bag the tying shoot-out goal against Brazil, handing them the title.

1994
U.S.A.

THE U.S. THROWS A PARTY

And in a battle of tiny terrors, the Italian Zen Buddhist Baggio is outfoxed by Romário, as Brazil finds nirvana.

SPACE MAY HAVE BEEN Captain Kirk's final frontier, but the United States was always soccer's. Fittingly, on July 4, 1988, FIFA announced its intention to seduce its largest and last untapped audience. The overture was not received with universal enthusiasm. Representative Jack Kemp, a former professional quarterback, defended America's honor on the floor of Congress: "I think it is important for all those young men out there who someday hope to play real football, where you throw it and

163

Jump if you're German: Bulgaria's Hristo Stoitchkov curls the ball around the wall in their quarterfinal match.

kick it and run with it and put it in your hands, that a distinction should be made that football is democratic capitalism whereas soccer is a European socialist sport." *New York Times* columnist George Vecsey had a more materialistic perspective: "The United States was chosen, by the way, because of all the money to be made here, not because of our soccer prowess. Our country has been rented as a giant stadium and hotel and television studio for the next thirty-one days."

Only three weeks before kickoff, national interest in the World Cup was so low that in one poll 71 percent of Americans didn't know it would be played in America. The ludicrous prediction grabbed the headlines and rattled World Cup organizers, but the tournament smashed the World Cup attendance record as teams played before full houses, even in the Pontiac Silverdome outside of Detroit, where the first-ever indoor game necessitated flying in giant squares of grass from California at great expense.

Much of the country, however, was too engrossed in the O. J. Simpson murder case to follow the action on TV. Outside the States, the tournament was broadcast throughout Latin and South America in color for the first time, and even rank-outsiders Bolivia sent a massive crew to capture wall-to-wall coverage. Viewers had only to wait till the opening ceremony for some headline-worthy action. Singer Jon Secada broke his collarbone when a trapdoor from which he was meant to emerge onto the stage misbehaved, forcing him to sing the national an-

them with just his head and shoulders protruding from a hole in the floor. Oprah then tripped and fell off a platform before Diana Ross capped off the action during her dance routine by slicing the ball wide of an open goal on a staged penalty shot.

There was malfunctioning on the field as well. The soccer was, in truth, mediocre. A slew of big teams—England, France, and Portugal—surprisingly failed to qualify, and the quality of play was reduced by overzealous referees who had been instructed by FIFA to punish the violent play that had marred the last tournament. Yellow and red cards were distributed freely and, as a result, most of the teams were unable to find their groove, In other words, the conditions were perfect for the dull, yet consistent Germans to prosper. They continued their tradition of overcoming the erratic behavior of their star players. Midfielder Stefan Effenberg flipped his own fans what they refer to as *"Der Stinkelfinger"* when being substituted and was immediately sent home in disgrace. The star-studded Dutch repeated their trick of arriving heavily favored, only to self-destruct from internal distractions.

ADRENALINE COCKTAIL

Maradona, the hero of 1986, was the villain of this one, banned after testing positive for ephedrine. In truth, he celebrated an opening round goal in such hopped-up style that a urine sample was almost unnecessary. Grabbing a sideline television camera and pressing his mug against it, Maradona, in

Ten days after Andrés Escobar scored this own goal in U.S.A.'s 2–1 victory, he was gunned down in Colombia.

1994 RESULTS

QUARTERFINALS
Italy 2 Spain 1
Brazil 3 Netherlands 2
Bulgaria 2 Germany 1
Sweden 2 Romania 2 (5–4 PKs)

SEMIFINALS
Italy 2 Bulgaria 1
Brazil 1 Sweden 0

THIRD PLACE
Sweden 4 Bulgaria 0

FINAL
Brazil 0 Italy 0 (3–2 PKs)

the words of *The Guardian*, "broadcast around the world, his contorted features made him look like a lunatic, flying on a cocktail of adrenaline and every recreational drug known to man."

Colombia began with high expectations after crushing Argentina 5–0 on the road to qualify, but Pelé picked them to win it all and this turned out to be the kiss of death. Quite literally. Colombia's campaign began when a local brewery offered players $300 for every goal celebration in which they imitated the company's trademark logo of a single pointed finger. However, after conceding an own goal during a loss to the plucky United States that eliminated them, defender Andrés Escobar, widely known as "The Gentleman of Football," returned home and was shot to death while leaving a nightclub in Medellín. The assassin fired a dozen times, yelling "Goal!" after every shot. It remains a mys-

tery as to why the highly touted Colombians lost so easily, and rumors abounded that Escobar's murder was connected to drug lords' gambling losses. Over 120,000 Colombians attended his funeral.

The goal-scoring in the rest of the tournament was dominated by a quartet of tiny but powerful attackers: Bulgaria's Hristo Stoitchkov, Romania's Gheorghe Hagi, Brazil's Romário, and Italy's Zen master, Roberto Baggio, a striker known as "The Divine Ponytail." Baggio played with guile and cunning to lead his team back from the brink of disaster—an early defeat against gritty little Ireland—into the final. Italy lined up against a functional, almost soulless, Brazilian team that had advanced on the strength of physicality (which peaked when Leonardo's elbow fractured the skull of U.S.A.'s Tab Ramos) more than its customary flair. Only the forward play of Romário seemed

truly Brazilian—he had a hand in 10 of the 11 goals his team scored in this tournament, and perhaps was the only person in the world not surprised by this achievement; he was so convinced of his talent from a young age that he taught himself to write so he could prepare for a life of autograph-signing.

The final itself was a spirit-crushing affair in which the Brazilians were negated by the Italians' smothering play. The crowd was so quiet you could almost hear the teeth-gnashing of everyone who had just invested in the soon-to-be-launched Major League Soccer, as the two teams conspired to provide every soccer cynic's worst nightmare: the first goal-less final, 120 minutes of dreary soccer followed by penalties. Tragically, the final penalty shot fell to Baggio, so exhausted and injured that he did his best impression of Diana Ross by blazing his shot over the bar.

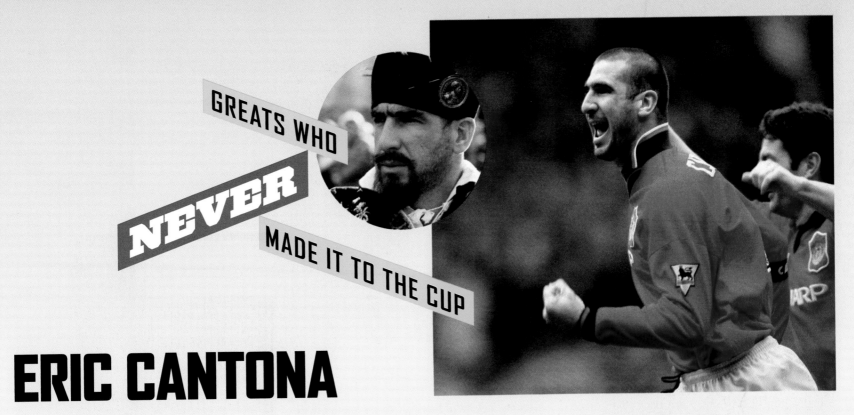

ERIC CANTONA

In his pomp at Manchester United, the fans simply called him God, and Eric Cantona didn't exactly discourage the comparison. With his popped collars and puffed-out chest, he bestrode the field as if it were his personal kingdom. There, he played by his own rules—whether stretching the realm of the possible by outwitting three defenders in the box before cheekily chipping the ball into the goal or meting out street justice to those unworthy of his genius by launching a kung fu kick at a fan in the crowd who had been heckling him.

As he himself pointed out in the eponymous movie *Looking for Eric,* "I am not a man, I am Cantona."

Part philosopher, part provocateur, and full-time soccer virtuoso, the mercurial Frenchman changed the history of Manchester United, a team whose massive support had heretofore not been matched by its trophy haul. With Cantona in the cockpit, United won four league titles and played the kind of creative, attacking soccer that would become its signature.

Yet when he pulled on the jersey of his country, Cantona's celestial talents seemed to desert him. Though he scored 20 goals in 45 appearances for France, he was never the game-changer he was at United, and in 1988 he was famously dropped from the national team for calling the manager "a bag of shit" on television. He was reinstated only after France failed to qualify for the 1990 World Cup.

Four years later, Cantona and Les Bleus fell short again, losing their final qualification match (a draw would have seen them through) and missing the tournament entirely. Cantona attended U.S.A. '94 anyway—as a commentator for French TV. But once again his legendary temper got the best of him and he was arrested on the eve of the semifinals for allegedly punching out a technician on the set. By 1997, he was still strutting his skills for Manchester United, albeit not as consistently, and hoped for one last chance to preen on soccer's grandest stage. But French manager Aimé Jacquet had found another temperamental artist to build his team around—Zinedine Zidane—and Cantona was forced to watch from the sidelines as France lifted the Cup on their home turf. Ignored by his country, and with his passion for the game ebbing, King Eric decided to abdicate his throne. "Retiring from football felt like a death," he told *The Guardian,* "but I prefer to live this kind of death than kill myself."

He's never forgiven his homeland for the World Cup snub and during the 2004 European Championship he bitterly announced he was supporting England in the tournament. Why? Because the English recognize talent. "The French have only negative things to say about everything and everyone," he said with characteristic hauteur.

Cantona finally made it to a World Cup, but it was the one where the game is played on sand in bare feet. He managed France to the 2005 Beach Soccer World Cup title and two top-four finishes in the following seasons before deciding to devote himself fully to his acting career. He got off to a shaky start, debuting in *Mookie,* a French comedy in which one reviewer said Cantona's performance was eclipsed by that of his pet monkey. But Cantona was serious about his new craft—"Football is a minor art; what interests me is major art"—and he has since won over the critics with bravura performances as a burly French inspector in a TV police drama, and, of course, in *Looking for Eric,* where he appears as himself—a superior being who can seemingly do anything in life except play in a World Cup.

BRAZIL 3, HOLLAND 2
Quarterfinal

Bringing the World Cup to the Land of the Free and the Home of the Soccer-Phobic was a decision roundly mocked by the other nations that had bid to host the tournament. For one thing, the United States didn't even have a legitimate professional league (the last attempt, the North American Soccer League, imploded way back in 1984) and was largely considered to be a country that held the sport in slightly less high esteem than tractor-pulling. What kind of atmosphere is that for the biggest soccer tournament on the planet? Would fans even show up? Would America have to import hooligans from across the pond to inject some passion into the event? For its success to be assured, the game would also have to be repackaged for the American audience: goals galore, colorful personalities, and scantily clad women in the stands.

So far in the tournament, the biggest media talking point had arguably been the murder of Colombian defender Andrés Escobar upon his return to the country. Escobar had made the tragic mistake of scoring an own goal against the U.S., of all teams, leading to a defeat on which the bookmakers made a killing, so to speak. A full week after the murder, Holland and Brazil took the field in front of—so much for fears of low attendance—63,500 spectators at the Cotton Bowl.

After an uneventful first half, Brazil scored twice in 11 minutes thanks to the tandem of Romário and Bebeto, the great Brazilian strike force of the 1990s, perfect in their contrast: Romário, the aloof womanizer who perpetually showed up late to training, and Bebeto, the clean-cut family man who quietly did his job. But Brazil's lead was not to last. A minute after Bebeto scored Brazil's second, Dennis Bergkamp, the blond heir to Johan Cruyff, flummoxed the Brazilian defense with some clever footwork and finished neatly from the left-hand side of the box. Twelve minutes later, Aron Winter tied it for the Dutch. Game on.

With barely 10 minutes left, the two sides were still deadlocked, setting the stage for the old Brazilian warhorse, Branco. He was seemingly an afterthought in Coach Carlos Alberto Parreira's squad because of his age (he turned 30 just before the tournament) and physical decline, but Parreira's decision was gloriously vindicated when Branco unleashed a 35-yard free kick of such torque and spin that it's still swerving even now.

Five goals in the last 37 minutes—just what the U.S. audience craved. Unfortunately, Americans came to expect similar pyrotechnics from *every* soccer game, regardless of who was playing.

Romário was flat-out brilliant against the Oranje.

Milla commits grand theft, stealing the ball from Colombian goalkeeper Rene Higuita in 1990.

ROGER MILLA
Cameroon: 1982, 1990, 1994

Some are born great, some achieve greatness, and some have greatness thrust upon them. Still others do it by walking onto the field of play as a substitute with 15 minutes to go in a World Cup game and scoring late and critical goals. Roger Milla is one such figure. In 1990, after being coaxed out of retirement, the 38-year-old became the oldest man to score a World Cup goal, leading Cameroon further into the tournament than any African team had ever ventured.

Such an act is quite a feat for any man, never mind one who was probably even older than his reported age, and who, until the World Cup, had been playing part-time football on the remote Indian Ocean island of Reunion, after retiring from an unspectacular career spent predominantly in the French leagues. It took a call from the Cameroonian president himself to persuade Milla to join the squad, whereupon his team shocked the world, despite being reduced to nine men by battering defending champions Argentina in the opening game.

From that point on, it was always Milla Time. Against Romania he powered through the defense and fired Cameroon into the lead with 14 minutes

remaining before striking again 10 minutes later. He then repeated his "supersub" feat, coming on in the 54th minute to score twice against Colombia, barreling through to drive the ball home for the first, and then humiliating the goalkeeper by grinning ear to ear as he sauntered past him and slotted the ball into the open goal for the second. Joy was a critical component of Milla's game. He had the foresight to brand all of his goals with a trademark celebration, first running along the goal line to dry-hump the corner flag, then gyrating with the exuberance of Barney the Dinosaur. The move became the signature highlight of the tournament as the Indomitable Lions, with their organized displays—physical at the back, and relying on Milla to score a goal or two up front—shattered every cliché previously attributed to African soccer.

In the quarterfinals, England was Cameroon's toughest test yet. By this point in the tournament, the mere sight of Milla preparing to enter the game was unsettling to opponents. Cameroon was one goal down when he came on at halftime and, true to form, set up two goals to put the Africans within a few minutes of what would have been one of the

greatest upsets in World Cup history. But England equalized with a penalty in the 83rd minute and then went ahead in extra time, ending Cameroon's adventure and, it appeared, Milla's international career along with it. But four years later, the Abe Vigoda of the World Cup was back. At 42, he repeated his supersub exploits, setting a new longevity record and scoring against Russia. The team was lackluster, though, and lost 6–1.

For all of his strengths—his anticipation in the box, and his clinical finishes—Milla is possibly best remembered for the unbridled joy of his goal-scoring celebrations, but he was far more than a curiosity. After Milla, African teams, who had previously been considered mere practice squads, were respected and feared. He was a game-changer who also altered the perception of an entire continent. As Milla watched his president being congratulated by other heads of state after his team surprised Argentina, he told the French press that "An African head of state who leaves as the victor and who greets with a smile the defeated heads of state . . . It's thanks to football that a small country could become great!"

WORD CUP

THE AUTHORS DEBATE...

WILL THE U.S. EVER WIN THE WORLD CUP?

BENNETT: America will win the World Cup in my lifetime. I have no doubt of that, even though I'm the co-author who's English. The country that won the Battle of Saratoga, put the first man on the moon, and persuaded the world to part with five dollars for a cup of coffee will find a way to win. It just has to turn its mind to the task. . . .

HIRSHEY: Much as I've been praying to the Landon Donovan shrine in my home—wait, you must be referring to the U.S. women's team. Sure, they'll win the World Cup again.

BENNETT: Careful—you sound like you've internalized the worst of American soccer low self-esteem. The collapse of the NASL in the eighties taught us one thing: American soccer success cannot be fabricated

overnight. Its growth will be slow and steady. I draw confidence from the way the game has evolved in this country. Not from Major League Soccer, but from the number of Americans with the skills to compete in the major leagues across Europe.

HIRSHEY: I'm sorry to be so unpatriotic, but name me one American player other than Donovan who possesses the speed and guile to carve open a world-class defense. You need game-breakers like Messi and Kaká to win the World Cup and the U.S. just doesn't have them despite all the promises over the last decade that we were creating a master soccer race in our youth academies. Remember good ol' Project 2010? It was U.S. Soccer's rose-tinted blueprint for the national team that they unveiled to great fanfare in 1998? Can you guess what the goal was? To win the World Cup in 2010! Project 2030, anyone?

BENNETT: How many Turks or South Koreans could you have named before they reached the semifinals in 2002? It was their organization and work ethic that took them so far. But, with or without a good American run deep into this

tournament, the sport's American profile will improve, courtesy of the unprecedented exposure the sport is receiving, thanks to ESPN's investment (in HD no less, and excuse the product placement). For the first time since Pelé's New York Cosmos—and for all the right reasons—soccer is no longer considered a dirty little secret to be buried in the back of the sports section. What impact do you think that will have on younger viewers watching at home?

HIRSHEY: Perhaps your job history at Best Buy has you a bit confused but raising a remote control, even if it's for HDTV, is not the same as raising the World Cup trophy. A good Cup showing by America and all that media coverage will spike soccer's popularity but, for the sake of American soccer, I sure hope that a good percentage of your imaginary kids watching the U.S. run riot on the small screen also possess a mean left foot.

BENNETT: And, I might add, a good dose of the old American profit motive. Soccer stars are now among the highest paid sportsmen in the world, and as the great American philosopher Gordon Gekko once said, "Greed captures the essence of the evolutionary spirit."

HIRSHEY: What salaries are you looking at—the hundreds of millions that Ronaldo and Kaká make? The last time I checked, some of the Americans who were playing alongside David Beckham when he came to the Galaxy were pulling in a whopping $12,500. The bottom line is flashing a wad of bills is not the answer to making the U.S. a World Cup contender. There are some goals, like saving the planet or marrying Gisele, that can take generations to achieve.

BENNETT: Mark my words ye of little faith: The United States will bring home the World Cup before they ever win the World Baseball Classic.

BECKHAM'S FIRST LAW OF MOTION
The Physics of the Free Kick

Every team has an elite free-kick master who's a threat from anywhere within 90 feet of the opposing team's goal. The likes of Alessandro Del Piero of Italy, Shunsuke Nakamura of Japan, or Cristiano Ronaldo of Portugal, smell blood as soon as the referee blows his whistle and the ritual choreography of the free kick commences. The goalkeeper frantically attempts to shield his goal, constructing a human wall with his defenders, placing them in the line of fire, a mere 10 yards from a ball about to be driven at speeds of up to 100 miles an hour. The defenders cover their family jewels while the goalkeeper works out how to cover 75 percent of

his goalface, protecting the far post while leaving himself a clear sight line on the shot.

All the while, the kicker stands Jedi-like under pressure while his brain computes a complex set of equations involving spin (impart too much and the ball won't clear the wall; too little and it will sail over the bar) and atmospheric drag (which accounts for the aerobatic dips and curves of the most spectacular blasts). The margin for error is infinitesimal. The striker is attempting to slot the ball through a letter box of extraordinarily small dimensions just above the wall. Physicist Ken Bray calculated that for a kick from 75 feet, the target is

a mere six ball widths across, causing physicists to marvel at the act, particularly because players, not typically known for their intellectual prowess, can process the information quicker than even the most powerful computer. Women around the world may adore more palpable aspects of David Beckham, but engineering professors like Keith Hanna lust after his mind. "The man can carry out a multivariable physics calculation in his head to compute the exact kick trajectory required, and then execute it perfectly. That is why the man is a football physics genius."

The Dream-On Team

Why America Is Forever the Next Soccer Superpower

There are just two things about the World Cup that prevent Americans from caring: It involves soccer and the rest of the world. When I hear that Tunisia is playing Belgium for the crucial Group H runner-up spot, all I want is a map. The only way Americans are going to learn another country's name is if it attacks us.
—Joel Stein, *Time* magazine, June 2002

America's winning mentality has made it the world's sole superpower. In the realm of sports, nothing said it quite like the original Dream Team's performance at the 1992 Barcelona Olympics, crushing the rest of the world without pausing for a single time-out. We tend to reclassify sports in which we don't excel as trivial, if not irrelevant. Noblesse oblige requires that we cede Ping-Pong to the Chinese or rugby to New Zealand's All Blacks.

When it comes to soccer, however, something is different. The emotional energy we spend on actively hating the game is nothing short of extraordinary. Surely, we doth protest far too much. Our feelings of inadequacy are no doubt compounded by the fact that while our men toil away unsuccessfully against the likes of the Czechs and Ghana, our women's team is perpetually ranked number one in the world.

Yet, the United States's relationship with the World Cup started out on somewhat of a high note. At the very first tournament in 1930, the Americans arrived as seeded favorites, thanks to many European countries who declined an invitation, but also thanks to the semiprofessional American Soccer League which had prospered since its creation in 1921 by British, German, and Scandinavian immigrants up and down the East Coast. Known affectionately as "The Shot Putters" on account of their stocky physiques, the team made it as far as final four, with striker Bert Patenaude notching the tournament's first hat trick in the opening round. The team was bounced by Argentina in the semifinals, and when their league fell victim to the Great Depression shortly afterward, it had dire consequences for the future of the sport in America. Because soccer had been established here solely as a professional game, lacking essential amateur roots at the collegiate level, the sport now had no chance to develop them, and began its history of decline.

In 1950, soccer was so insignificant that the United States World Cup victory against the mighty English barely registered in the national media. The United States fielded a ramshackle team, some of whom were not even citizens, and entered the game expecting to be cannon fodder, a 500-to-1 long shot after beating and then tying Cuba in qualifying—after losing their five previous games by the combined score of 41–3. Their 1–0 victory remains one of the greatest upsets in the history of the sport to this day—as great a shock as if the English trounced an American All-Star team on the baseball diamond.

The two heroes of the game were Haitian-born striker Joe Gaetjens, who scored a wonder goal against the run of play, flying in with his head to deflect a shot over the line in the 38th minute, and

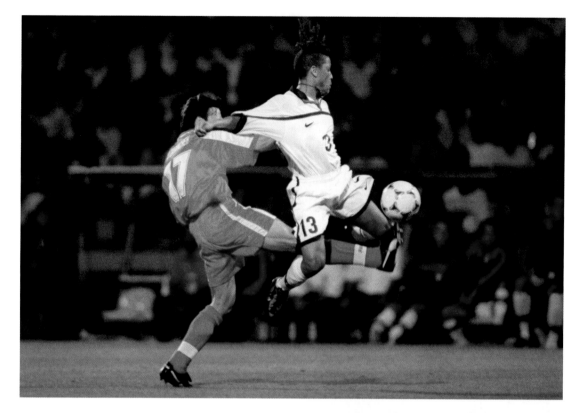

gal's Eusébio, Brazil's Carlos Alberto, Italy's Giorgio Chinaglia, and England's Gordon Banks. But Pelé remained the league's marquee name, soccer star by day, Studio 54 visitor by night, often seen in the odd fellow company of soccer lovers Henry Kissinger, Mick Jagger, and Elton John.

The league acquired glamour, big names, and buzz, but ABC could not sell it to the American people and the NASL went belly-up in 1984. In 1983, its penultimate season, the U.S. Soccer Federation had the brainstorm of entering the national squad into the league as "Team America" in an attempt to strengthen their play through regular competition. The effort backfired as the better players refused to leave their original clubs and the Team America experiment ended in embarrassment. The team finished dead last.

After the NASL's collapse, the American pro game retreated indoors, which turned out to be a blessing in disguise. To improve their technique, gifted American players now had to move to Europe and the national squad became more experienced as a result. Californian Paul Caligiuri was the trailblazer. He signed for SV Hamburg in 1987, and a goal he scored against Trinidad and Tobago qualified the United States for the 1990 World Cup in Italy, after a 40-year absence from the international stage. The team may have been smashed by Czechoslovakia and defeated by Italy and Austria, but they had accomplished enough to host the next tournament with a modicum of World Cup bona fides, and a sense that they belonged.

Team U.S.A. has been a World Cup fixture ever since, becoming a regional powerhouse in CONCACAF, FIFA's tongue-twisting name for the region covering North and Central America as well as the Caribbean. The group is a mixed bag of talent, including legitimate threats in Mexico, Costa Rica, Honduras, and lightweights like the lowly St. Kitts

goalkeeper Frank Borghi, a former minor league catcher, who parried every English shot—and there were many—as the Three Lions laid siege to his goal for the remaining 52 minutes of play. One English newspaper compared the enormity of the loss to that suffered at Dunkirk. Another ran black borders on every page as a sign of national mourning, but the American press virtually ignored the story. In today's media-saturated world, the team would be lionized and the requisite Disney version of their against-all-odds victory would hit movie screens around the same time Gaetjens and Borghi popped up on the front of a Wheaties box. But it was 1950 and soccer in America was a marginal activity, popular only among immigrant minorities and their kin. The team arrived home without fanfare, as anonymously as they had left.

The United States would not qualify for the World Cup for another 39 years, and few would care. In the late sixties, though, American soccer was revived after the 1966 World Cup final was televised on tape-delay by NBC—to surprisingly good ratings. A number of businessmen, pro football owners Lamar Hunt and Jack Kent Cooke among them, believed there might be a market for the game in an era of unprecedented prosperity; the expansion of leisure

coincided with the successful commercialization of both sports and television. Professional soccer rose from the dead in the guise of the North American Soccer League (NASL), which initially showcased a motley crew of homegrown players mixed in with a handful of low-grade foreign imports. All of this changed when Steve Ross of Warner Communications bestowed enough cash on the New York Cosmos to coax the great Pelé himself out of retirement. The Brazilian showered his celebrity on both the club and the sport at large, becoming the first of a cavalcade of former World Cup stars to parade into the league, including West Germany's Franz Beckenbauer, Holland's Johan Cruyff, Portu-

and Nevis. Team U.S.A. has prospered, qualifying for six straight World Cups, with mixed results, disappointing when expectations are high, but turning in workmanlike performances to surprise their opponents when prospects seem dim.

The U.S. qualified as tournament hosts in 1994 and the team played with understandable tightness, desperate to avoid the humiliation of becoming the first home team unable to emerge from the opening round. Sporting faux stonewashed denim uniforms, they managed to scrape through the group stage as one of the best third-placed teams. They departed in the second round after a hard-fought 1–0 loss to Brazil allowed them to slip away with their dignity intact, which is more than can be said for midfielder Tab Ramos's skull, fractured by an elbow from Brazilian defender Leonardo. The team's guitar-strumming defender, Alexi Lalas, who became the ginger-haired face of U.S. soccer, was plucked by Italian minnow Padova, to become the first American player to grace the Serie A in the modern era. His team proceeded to finish at the bottom of the table and Lalas soon returned to play in the new American league, Major League Soccer, which FIFA initially insisted be a precondition for hosting the 1994 World Cup, but turned out to be its legacy.

America's greatest humiliation was self-inflicted. In 1998, coach Steve Sampson sabotaged his own team, making wholesale changes to the lineup on the eve of the tournament. He cut veteran midfielder John Harkes, whom he had called his "Captain for Life," *(see Worst Teams, page 187)*. Sampson replaced them with a number of inexperienced players, including David Regis, a French-born defender who was promised a starting position if he agreed to become a U.S. citizen. The team ended dead last,

gaining no points and finding the net only once, during garbage time at the end of a mortifying 2–1 loss to the team from the country that often topped the CIA watchlist, Iran.

In 2002 a young, well-organized team played with vigor and enthusiasm during an exhilarating run in which they surprised both Portugal and Mexico on the way to face Germany in the quarterfinal. In a phone call before the Mexico match, President George W. Bush assured the team that "A lot of people that don't know anything about soccer, like me, are all excited and pulling for you"—perhaps helping to inspire the Americans to dominate the game, only to fall 1–0. Eliminated with heads held high, the team had proved for the first time they could compete at the highest level of world soccer. FIFA agreed as the U.S. rocketed up the official (though occasionally dubious) world rankings, peaking at number 4 a mere two months before the 2006 World Cup. Expectations were high as the tournament began—too high as it turned out. Stuck in the Group of Death, the U.S. nonetheless would have advanced had they not choked against Ghana. At any rate, the competition provided a brutal reality check, as the team was punished for relying on trusty warhorses Eddie Pope and Brian McBride for the third consecutive World Cup, limping out in the opening round. Despite the early exit, television ratings continued to rise as the competition progressed, an impressive sign that the game was at last finding an audience in the States.

American soccer's many false dawns prevent most intelligent people from proclaiming that 2010 will be America's year in terms of team performance on the field or the game's popularity off of it. But there is much to be positive about. Soccer is the sport most played by children up to the age of 13, even though passion for the game evaporates among adolescents as they turn to more indigenous pastimes—

In 2002, a young, well-organized team played with vigor and enthusiasm during an exhilarating run.

baseball, basketball, and football—that have contributed the highly evolved hand-eye coordination that helps explain America's remarkable strain of world-class goalkeepers, led by Kasey Keller, Brad Friedel, and Tim Howard. And while the world still waits for the first truly great American outfield player, weathering a number of false messiahs like Clint Mathis, Landon Donovan, Freddy Adu, and Jozy Altidore, American businessmen have quietly snapped up majority ownership of a number of the flagship teams in the English Premier League, such as Manchester United, Liverpool, and Aston Villa.

So just how will the team fare in 2010? In recent World Cups, a number of underdogs have shown that teams without marquee stars can go deep into the tournament precisely because they are highly organized, motivated, and egoless. Turkey, South Korea, and Senegal played that role at the 2002 World Cup, and it is a formula that the current American squad could well follow in South Africa.

And if the planets do align and the Red, White, and Blue play like magic, every Chinese Ping-Pong star and New Zealand rugby player should take note.

SHOOT·OUT
AT THE
PK CORRAL

★ **Five Men. Five Shots. One Sudden Death.** ★

On paper, penalty shoot-outs should go on all night. The best players in the world are given the simple task of hitting the equivalent of a barn door from a mere 12 yards away. Yet the fact that so many of the real greats have failed spectacularly at this task—Maradona, Baggio, Zico, and Platini among them—suggests the challenge is largely psychological, a test of soul rather than skill. The penalty shoot-out is the closest many of us will come to watching a game of Russian roulette unfold. It's a sudden death-defying spectacle only tangentially related to the previous 120 minutes of action, during which the team game morphs into an individual joust between two exhausted men, one trying to score, the other desperate to prevent that from happening, live, in front of an audience of millions.

One by one, like dead men walking, the players must leave the relative comfort of the team cocoon huddled together at the halfway line. Their rendezvous with destiny can end in only one of two ways—despair or delirium. The penalty taker addresses the ball, trying desperately to remember where he planned to place the ball while cleverly concealing his intentions. Zinedine Zidane was once seen to throw up from nerves before shooting. But the penalty shoot-out ups the ante as each kick is related to the last, and, as the competition is best of five, many shots are taken by players who are far from expert, under condition of stress that can never be adequately replicated in training.

Should you ever find yourself in goal during the two-person zero-sum melodrama known as a World Cup shoot-out, here are seven useful things to know.

1. WHAT YOU CAN DO DURING THE BREAK.

In the 2006 World Cup, Germany's Jens Lehmann famously stuffed a scrap of paper supplied by his goalkeeping coach into his sock—a cheat sheet on the go-to penalty moves of an all-too-predictable Argentinian side. Technology has rapidly evolved. In the 2010 World Cup, expect to see the stunt first executed by Manchester United's English international goalkeeper, Ben Foster, in the 2009 League Cup final in England. He calmly watched footage of all of the kickers he was about to face on an iPod and proceeded to block a critical attempt, helping his team to victory. Penalty shoot-outs? There's an app for that.

2. WHAT TO WATCH FOR AS THE SHOOTER WALKS TO THE PENALTY SPOT.

Some players stroll toward the goal with the confidence of a pool hustler. Others drag themselves forward, sphincter tightened, desperately signaling to the world that they would like to be anywhere but here. English players usually fall into this latter category, most famously, defender Stuart Pearce in the team's 1990 semifinal loss. By the time he had lumbered up to the spot his nerves had led him to

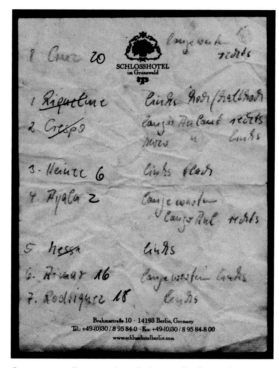

German goalkeeper Jens Lehmann's cheat sheet on Argentina's penalty kick techniques.

pull his shorts up so high it was, in the words of one journalist, "as if they had snagged on the hairs of his armpits." His penalty was saved.

3. WHY YOU SHOULD RELAX.

Before the kick is taken, the pressure is all on the shooter. The ball takes 0.3 seconds to hit the back of the net. No one expects the goalkeeper to save it. A fact that grants him a psychological edge, as the shooter steps up and the fight for control begins. Holland's Edwin van der Sar dries his hands for an eternity on a towel placed to the side of the goal, forcing the shooter to contemplate the vast noth-

ingness that is his target. France's Fabien Barthez preferred to stand between the posts but slightly to one side, daring the shooter to go for the larger void. Italy's Gianluigi Buffon employs game theory, diving unpredictably for each kick so the shooters can never determine his pattern.

4. ESPECIALLY WHEN THE SHOOTER STARES AT A SPOT.

Where are the strikers' eyes focused? Some shooters turn their back on the keeper to avoid being distracted by their mind games before the kick. This is rarely a good sign. Some focus obsessively on the spot they ultimately plan to shoot the ball; others stare intently at a spot far away from the spot they intend to aim for. This latter tactic rarely ends well. Soccer players are not renowned for having Mensa-quality IQ's, and this deception—the penalty shoot-out equivalent of trying to walk and chew gum at the same time—often means the only one they end up fooling is themselves. A confident player never takes his eyes off his nemesis.

5. WHY YOU SHOULD HOPE THAT THE KICKER CAN'T WAIT TO GET HIS SHOT OFF.

Once the referee blows his whistle, is the shooter in a rush? Some kickers run at the ball the instant the referee blows his whistle, desperate to end their stay in purgatory. Others putter around as if they are alone in their kitchen fixing a midnight snack. A University of Gröningen report suggests that unreasonable haste is the direct road to error. Those who take more than 2.8 seconds succeed 77 percent of the time. Those who take less than 1.7 seconds have a 58 percent success rate.

6. WHY YOU SHOULD WORRY ABOUT THE LEG THAT'S *NOT* GOING TO KICK THE BALL.

The relationship between the angle of the kicker's run-up and his point of ball contact becomes more predictable the closer he is to the kick, although the longer the keeper contemplates all of the above, the later he dives and the less time he has to react. The most reliable indicator is the position of the non-kicking foot as it plants before contact. Many keepers dive whichever way it points, as that's where the ball is going 80 percent of the time.

7. WHY YOUR BEST HOPE IS FOR YOUR OWN TEAM TO BE AHEAD.

If your team's up a goal and a missed kick means the kicker's team will lose, the shooter has a miserable 52 percent success rate. England's David Batty took and butchered the first penalty of his career, eliminating the hapless English against Argentina in 1998 and causing *The Guardian* to report, "David Batty juggled the ball as he approached the penalty spot like a man wanting to show an insouciance he didn't feel."

On the other hand, when success means the kicker's team will win, the ball finds the net 93 percent of the time.

And if you should happen to find yourself *kicking* a penalty instead of trying to stop one? Italy's Roberto Baggio, who ballooned a penalty over the bar to lose the 1994 World Cup final, maintained that there is only one guaranteed way to avoid missing a penalty, and that is not to take one.

But there are two conflicting "can't miss" approaches to converting a penalty kick. The first comes from England, official home of World Cup shoot-out disasters, and it is almost absurdly academic. A research team from Liverpool John Moores University in England, has analyzed hundreds of penalties to determine the perfect penalty kick. First, the shot should travel at 65 mph, after a run-up of four or five paces, with an approach angle of 20 to 30 degrees. Finally, the ball should cross the line both 50 centimeters (20 inches) below the crossbar and 50 centimeters in from either post. In other words, in the most unreachable locations for the goalkeeper. Du-uh. As Professor Tim Cable, director of sport and exercise sciences, said, "Many factors make up a 'perfect penalty.' But we've finally nailed the key elements."

England's archrivals, the Germans, have a different theory and, since they have a perfect World Cup shoot-out record, who are we to argue? Their last coach, Jürgen Klinsmann, inadvertently revealed their secret at the 2006 World Cup, when he was caught on film commanding his players to simply blast the ball as hard as they could, on the theory that if they didn't know where the ball was going, the keeper wouldn't have a clue either.

CULT FIGURES

GHEORGHE HAGI, ROMANIA

A rare and idiosyncratic breed, the great left-footed soccer players have always dribbled to the beat of their own drummer. From Ferenc Puskás to Maradona to Hristo Stoitchkov, they worked their magic on their own terms, knowing that they possessed an inherent advantage over their peers—that defenses are constructed to combat *right*-footed attackers.

From the moment that Hagi arrived on the international soccer scene as a precocious 18-year-old left-footed attacking midfielder playing for his native Romania, the glamour clubs of Europe were so anxious to recruit the man who would eventually become known as the "Maradona of the Carpathians," that they went to extraordinary lengths to liberate him from behind the Iron Curtain. Gianni Agnelli, the president of Fiat, reportedly offered to build a car factory in Romania if Hagi would agree to play for Agnelli's beloved Juventus. It was a far cry from Hagi's hardscrabble childhood, when his parents were so poor that even bread was a luxury. "I always wanted to be a waiter in a restaurant," he once said, "because I heard that they got good tips and free food."

He was a soccer anomaly, beyond his unusually cultured left foot. He played better for his country than he did for his club team. Every four years, Hagi would set the soccer world aflame with an incandescent display of shooting and passing. In 1994, he led an erratic Romanian team to its best-ever quarterfinal finish and scored a wonderfully cheeky goal when he spot-ted the Colombian goalkeeper Óscar Córdoba on a little walkabout in his penalty area, and lobbed a 40-yard shot straight into the net. "I still can't believe it went in after this many years," Córdoba said in 2008. "I was positive that he was planning to serve the ball into the box, that's why I came out of goal. When I met him years later, I said, 'I will never forget your goal against me, but thanks to you, I am famous, too.' I believe that Hagi and Maradona are equal in what they did on the field, sensational players who could win games by themselves."

Hagi scored more times for his country than any other player in Romanian history, but when the lights dimmed and he returned to club competition, his game would lose its luster. He underachieved at both Real Madrid and FC Barcelona, and it wasn't until he moved to Turkey that club success arrived. Even though he was older, slower, and heavier when he played for Galatasaray (where his nickname was the Hunk with a Chunk), Hagi won eight trophies in his five seasons. His finest year came in 2000 when, at 35, he led the Istanbul team to its first European title in the UEFA Cup.

While Hagi was annoyed about the public perception of his fading gifts—"Today, you seem to be considered good only if you can run fast, or are physically strong"—his countrymen gave a rousing testament to his magnificence when they elected him the Greatest Romanian Footballer of the 20th Century.

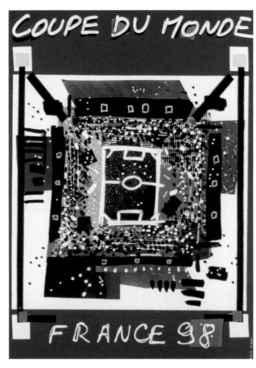

COUPE DU MONDE

FRANCE 98

2002 FIFA WORLD CUP
KOREA/JAPAN™
31 MAY – 30 JUNE

2002
FIFA WORLD CUP
KOREA JAPAN

FIFA WORLD CUP
GERMANY 2006

2006 FIFA World Cup Germany™
June 9 – July 9

'98 '02 '06

GLOBAL DOMINANCE

Zidane put his head to proper use in this final.

1998
France

FRENCH COOKING

France's melting pot of a team burns

Ronaldo and Brazil in the final.

THE STAR OF THE sixteenth World Cup was the French nation itself, which was just as well, since that other great sporting emblem of everything stereotypically Gallic, the Tour de France, was about to be immersed in a doping scandal that would leave Richard Virenque as the symbol of everything wrong with the sport. Politically, there could not have been a better time for a cup invented by a Frenchman to finally be won by the French. It took an ethnic

(above) Croatian players revolt against their hideous uniforms.

(left) Beckham revolts against a red card after he kicks out at Argentina's Diego Simeone.

(opposite) Ronaldo, blurred.

1998 RESULTS

QUARTERFINALS
France 0 Italy 0 (4–3 PKs)
Brazil 3 Denmark 2
Croatia 3 Germany 0
Netherlands 2 Argentina 1

SEMIFINALS
Brazil 1 Netherlands 1 (4–2 PKs)
France 2 Croatia 1

THIRD PLACE
Croatia 2 Netherlands 1

FINAL
France 3 Brazil 0

bouillabaisse of players to pull it off precisely at a time when the vitriolic far-right, anti-immigrant platform of Jean-Marie Le Pen was dominating the national scene. The French were represented by a team of "Rainbow Warriors," uniting players from French territories and former colonies of Algeria, Guadeloupe, and Senegal (as well as one from the former British colony of Ghana). Their coach, Aimé Jacquet, was able to weave together players who spoke four different languages into a single voice on the field and a potent political symbol off it.

This was a tournament marked by intrigue, mystery, controversy, and passion. The play on the field was often intoxicating, enhanced by the appearance of the sudden-death "Golden Goal" overtime format. The *drame* managed to overshadow even the relentless commerciality surrounding the tournament. Ricky Martin sang the official theme song, "La Copa de la Vida." Need we say more?

The story lines were manifold. The gleeful Nigerians emerged from a Group of Death, surprising Spain, which yet again failed to live up to the hype. The United States descended to a new level of humiliation with a loss against Iran in the opening round. Final score: Iran 2, Great Satan 1. The

American players were instructed to exchange shirts at the end of the game, but to leave the field clutching them in their hands rather than putting them on, depriving the Arab world of a great PR opportunity. David Beckham took early, faltering steps on his march to global domination, showing the world his more petulant side—and emulating the English hooligans who smashed up Marseille—as he kicked out at Argentinean midfielder Diego Simeone and was sent off. England departed after characteristically losing on penalty shots. The Germans were also booted, stunned 3–0 in the quarterfinals by the Croatians, with their coach, Berti Vogts, crying conspiracy and believing that his team had been penalized by referees as punishment for being too successful in the past.

TWO HEADERS BETTER THAN ONE

Once they had qualified for the semifinal stage, the French team was delirious, France itself hysterical. Unlikely hero defender Lilian Thuram was so overwhelmed after scoring the first of the two goals to fend off the courageous Croatians that he lost consciousness on the field. His team emerged victorious to meet the Brazilians. For the first time

ever, the final would feature the host nation and the defending champions, but what happened on the field was almost eclipsed by happenings off. In what amounted to a 30-minute mystery on the day of the game, Ronaldo, then the world's greatest player, was shockingly left off the Brazilian lineup. Rumor was that he had suffered a fit so severe that his roommate, the normally pugnacious Roberto Carlos, was reported to have run out of his room, screaming that his friend had died. Just before kickoff, Ronaldo took the field, some believed under the order of sponsor Nike, leaving the mystery to be unraveled someday, perhaps by Oliver Stone.

Ronaldo might as well have stayed home, as that magnificent icon for balding men around the world, Zinedine Zidane, used his pate to pop in two first-half headers from corner kicks, and Emmanuel Petit iced France's 3–0 victory just before the final whistle, sending an estimated one million people onto the Champs-Élysées to celebrate through the night. The nation was besotted. Even the chilly, urbane French president, Jacques Chirac, a man whose hatred of soccer had been on the public record, donned Zidane's number 10 shirt for a photo op.

"The Devil Makes Schnapps"
And Other Timeless World Cup Song Lyrics

After successfully navigating two years of highly competitive qualifying matches, what is the final step a squad must take before boarding the plane to embark on a monthlong World Cup odyssey? If the evidence is to be believed, it's nipping into the studio with a slightly over-the-hill recording star. Long before "The Super Bowl Shuffle" was even a twinkle in Jim McMahon's eye, soccer teams from around the world have made a tournament tradition of recording a crude yet infuriatingly catchy World Cup single, utilizing lyrics that poet Robert Frost obviously had in mind when he remarked that "Poetry is about the grief."

The English squad invented the medium in the '70s, arguably perfecting it with 1990's "World in Motion," in which they teamed with electro-dance pioneers New Order, who predictably packed as many nudge-nudge drug double entendres as is humanly possible into a four-and-a-half-minute track. The Germans boldly extended the genre in 1978, aiming for quantity over quality by recording an entire album with Austria's answer to Billy Joel, Mr. Udo Jürgens. The album, *Buenos Días, Argentina* covers a gamut of emotions, from the romantic "Think About Me, Young Girls" to the cautionary "The Devil Makes Schnapps."

"Sing when you are winning" is a traditional chant used by a victorious team's fans to mock the silence-stricken fans of the losing team. But it is perennial loser Scotland that has been the most musically prolific squad, leveraging the shock value of qualifying for the tournament to lure some of the nation's finest performers into the studio with them, including Lulu, the Bay City Rollers, and Rod Stewart (twice!). Our favorite is their 1998 smash "Don't Come Home Too Soon," written by Glasgow's pop philosophers Del Amitri. The lyrics lay out a country's low expectations for all to see:

So long, go on and do your best
Let all France have whisky on its breath
The world may not be shaking yet but you
    might prove them wrong
Even long shots make it.

HRISTO STOITCHKOV, BULGARIA

If soccer greatness were measured only in lunatic behavior, Stoitchkov would have been Pelé. As technically brilliant as the Bulgarian was, his genius for thuggish antics and outrageous pronouncements was unrivaled. After winning the 1994 European Footballer of the Year Award while playing in Spain, Stoitchkov came up with this gem: "There are only two Christs. One plays for Barcelona, the other is in heaven."

And yet somehow it all worked for Stoitchkov, a man who possessed divine skills, the ego of a messiah, and a five o'clock shadow that occurred at eight in the morning. Had he not been a soccer prodigy, the swarthy Bulgarian would have made an excellent *Sopranos* soldier. As a teen, he escalated a brawl of such brutality that he earned a season-long suspension and his team was disbanded by the Bulgarian authorities. But he could score, and how—38 goals in 30 games for CSKA Sofia. Barcelona, one of the top clubs in the world, swooped in and snatched him up for a hefty fee and a lifetime supply of razors. In his debut season, Stoitchkov, incensed at the referee, stomped on the man's foot and was suspended for two months. For an encore, he questioned the parentage of one of Barcelona's directors on live TV ... and also managed to score 20 times in limited duty. Not surprisingly, the Camp Nou faithful adored him. As his career inevitably wound down, he came to play in MLS, and broke a college student's leg in a 2003 scrimmage. His reckless style gave birth to a Sean Combs–level assortment of nicknames—The Mad Bulgarian, The Raging Bull, The Dagger, and *El Pistolero*, to cite but a few.

Stoitchkov was almost certainly the best player in the humdrum of U.S.A. '94. He won the Golden Shoe as co-leading scorer with six goals, but it was the nature of his strikes that made him a crowd favorite. He seemed to score all of his team's important goals as lightly regarded Bul-

CULT FIGURES

garia stormed past Greece and Argentina before stunning a heavily favored Germany in the quarterfinals. Trailing 1–0, Stoitchkov launched one of his left-footed missiles from a free kick 25 yards out. Bodo Illgner, the German goalkeeper, never moved a muscle. "When I saw the kick," he said, "it was pretty much in the goal."

The semifinal was a clash of styles as the attack-minded Bulgarians drew Italy, a nation that owned the copyright on defensive soccer. Italy won 2–1, but Stoitchkov, who scored Bulgaria's goal on a penalty kick, was furious at the referee's failure to grant a second penalty. In the postgame interview, the Mad Bulgarian put his team's heavenly run into perspective: "Yes, God was on our side—but the referee was French."

WORST TEAMS

Coach Steve Sampson

U.S.A., 1998

WHY THEY MADE THE LIST: In spite of the high hopes, and big-time smack talking by the players, Team U.S.A. finished dead last in the field of 32.

THE HIGH POINT: German-born team captain Thomas Dooley unintentionally predicting the score in U.S.A.'s opening loss to Germany, "I don't want to say the Germans are arrogant, but they're probably thinking, *It won't be easy, but in the end we will beat them, 2–0.*"

THE NADIR: In April of 1998, U.S. coach Steve Sampson dropped captain John Harkes, heart and soul of the midfield, for defensive liabilities. In 2010, in the wake of England's John Terry scandal (*see The WAGS That Tail the Dogs, page 232*), Harkes's teammate, star striker Eric Wynalda, revealed the real reason—that Harkes had slept with Wynalda's wife.

THE FALLOUT: Head coach Steve Sampson (above) "resigned," an event that served as excellent practice for his future terminations as coach of the Costa Rican national team and of the LA Galaxy.

MICHAEL OWEN
England vs. Argentina, Round of 16

The goal is immortal, though the goal scorer never quite lived up to the boundless promise he displayed as a teenager. Injuries, loss of form, and a dream move from Liverpool to Real Madrid that turned sour ultimately achieved what Argentina's defense couldn't.

But for one extraordinary moment in one epic match, Michael Owen was the Great English Hope. Out of nowhere, the slight, boyish striker, playing in only his ninth match for England and still looking forward to his first shave, controlled the ball with the outside of his right boot, and slipped past Argentine defender Jose Chamot. It was a crafty move, but trouble awaited the 18-year-old.

For one thing, he had half the field left to navigate, and for another, Roberto Ayala was stand-ing on the edge of his own box. Ayala played his soccer in the traditional mold of a South American dictator: What he couldn't understand, he brutally repressed. (He'd already plowed into Owen and given up an early penalty that allowed England to even the score at 1–1.) English fans everywhere had two thoughts: What in the world was Ayala doing standing on the edge of his own box, a full forty yards from the play—and would he kill Michael Owen?

It's called "magic" for a reason. Twenty-one other players simply disappeared from the match and Michael Owen began to live the fantasy of every soccer-playing schoolboy. He blew past Ayala as though he were a ghost and surged into the heart of the Argentine rear guard.

England's Paul Scholes was racing alongside, ready to steer a pass into the back of the net, but he, too, was invisible to Owen. The striker burst into the penalty box, and like a man oblivious to everything but completing the dream of running 60 yards with the ball at his feet and earning the adulation of a nation.

But Michael Owen's goal in the 16th minute actually happened and the 5,000 English fans in Saint-Étienne's Stade Geoffroy-Guichard really chanted, "There's only one Michael Owen!" And then, later in that game, it also really happened that Argentina leveled at 2–2, David Beckham got sent off, England lost on penalties, and everyone woke up.

GREATEST TEAMS

(below) The French rejoice after beating Croatia in the semifinal; (right above and below) French goalkeeper Fabien Barthez leapfrogs Ronaldo in the final, then employs a special technique to enhance the thrill of victory.

FRANCE
1998

There is what everybody else does and then there is the French way. Panache, after all, is a French word. For more than 40 years, the French tantalized the soccer world with their attacking flair and tortured flameouts, a style epitomized by their Belmondo-cool '82 side, which captivated the tournament before falling in a semifinal classic to Germany. 1982 represented the second of three times that France had reached the Final Four only to exit in a vale of Gallic tears.

By 1998, it had been 12 years since they'd even qualified for the World Cup and now they were hosting the damn thing. And no team in World Cup–winning history had ever moved further away from its soccer evolutionary tree than Les Bleus, although France still possessed the requisite midfield maestro around which everything revolved. The granite-featured Zinedine Zidane had inherited the baton from the great Michel Platini and waved it with breathtaking skill and a barely controlled fury. Zizou, born to immigrant parents from Algeria, was the rough-hewn hood ornament of the New France, a multiethnic, multiculti blend of homegrown players and those born in former colonies (17 of the 23 players were members of racial minorities and hailed from places like Guadeloupe, Martinique, and New Caledonia).

The makeup of the team became a hot-button topic in France, leading Jean-Marie Le Pen, the head of the country's right-wing National Front party, to rail that it was "artificial to bring players from abroad and call it the French team." The sustained derision and criticism of a small, but vocal, segment of the French population proved to be a minor distraction since the squad's diversity had maximized its talent. The front line, which included two of the top scorers in the French league, Stéphane Guivarc'h and David Trezeguet, as well as a silky marksman named Thierry Henry, would play *très jolie* soccer, the goals and the plaudits would flow, and they would lose gallantly, albeit with style. Astonishingly, France's

three forward musketeers would score not a single goal in the last five games of the Cup.

In lieu of an offense, France was forced to rely on its defensive fortress—a rear guard featuring West Indies–born Lilian Thuram, Ghanian-born Marcel Desailly, the mullet-haired enforcer Laurent Blanc who had played for clubs in Italy and Spain, and the pint-size Bixente Lizarazu, who plied his trade in Germany. It was the most polyglot, and perhaps the best, quartet in World Cup history. And in goal they had the chrome-domed daredevil Fabien Barthez, who threw himself at supermodels and opponents with equal zeal and wound up getting his arms around both Linda Evangelista and a World Cup.

There was no measure of adversity—not injuries and suspensions to key players, not the French media second-guessing manager Aimé Jacquet's tactics as "paleolithic"—that could disturb their sangfroid. France outlasted every favored team they came up against: the always obdurate Italians on penalties, the quicksilver Croatians in the semifinals, and then a Brazil side, still dangerous even with a zombielike Ronaldo, in the final, 3–0.

Fittingly, it was France's charismatic leader Zidane who leapt to the heavens to head home the winner on July 12, 1998. Forty-eight hours later, on July 14, Bastille Day, the French had another revolution to celebrate.

DENNIS BERGKAMP
Holland vs. Argentina, Quarterfinal

In art, it's a Picasso. In filmmaking, it's a Kurosawa. In World Cup soccer, it's Dennis Bergkamp's goal against Argentina. Has any player ever inspired such obedience from a ball, let alone one that was arcing 60 yards across the field and descending out of the sun in the 89th minute of a 1–1 World Cup quarterfinal death match?

This was the Dutch forward's challenge as he caught sight of the Hail Mary that Frank de Boer had launched from deep in midfield. It had been a relatively quiet tournament for Bergkamp, the angular Sting look-alike who had inherited the mantle of Dutch Master from the legendary Johan Cruyff, but Bergkamp had always been a player who saved himself for the big moments. And this would be Holland's last, best hope to win the game and advance to the World Cup semifinals

for the first time since 1978. So when he saw the pass leave de Boer's foot, Bergkamp sprinted into the Argentine penalty area and gauged the angle of the ball's flight. Nothing Bergkamp did obeyed convention—terrified of flying, he eventually refused to travel to matches by airplane—but his spatial intelligence set him apart on a soccer field. In this instance, he flung his body into midair like a man in an Olympic long jump trial, and caught the ball on his right foot as if it were an egg. An astonishing piece of soccer acumen—but Bergkamp had only just begun.

Stride for stride with Bergkamp was Argentina's magnificent thug, Roberto Ayala. In what was no less extraordinary a demonstration of skill than his first touch, Bergkamp, in a single motion, brought the ball down *and through* the legs of Ayala, who

was stunned to find both the ball, and the player, suddenly beyond him.

The Dutchman cut inside and, with only a sliver of goal to shoot at, flicked out his right foot. The shot came off his instep and flew over the goalkeeper's right shoulder and into the far corner. The entire sequence was preposterously brilliant.

Famed Dutch commentator Jack van Gelder all but spontaneously combusted. His screams of "DENNIS BERGKAMP! DEN-NIS BEEEERG-KAAAAMP!!!!!!" were followed by a sound previously emitted only by dolphins that went something like: "WWWWHH-HHOOOOAAAAAHHHH!!!!!"

From the time he first controlled de Boer's pass to his emphatic finish, perhaps two seconds had passed. Not even Picasso created a masterpiece in so little time.

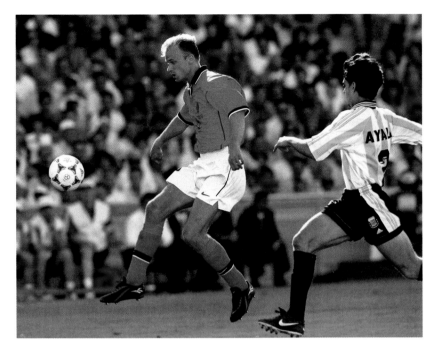

Anatomy of a masterpiece:
Bergkamp controls, finesses,
and finishes his work of art.

ZINEDINE ZIDANE
France

Few have used a World Cup final to unify a fractured nation, and fewer still have used it to tear one apart. Zinedine Zidane did both within the space of eight years, inspiring France to an unprecedented triumph on home soil in 1998 before infamously losing—and using—his head, in 2006 by burying it in an Italian defender's sternum, providing ESPN's *SportsCenter* with its all-time favorite soccer clip.

The son of poor Algerian immigrants, "Zizou" grew up in the notorious La Castellane ghetto of Marseille. On the soccer field, he was a preternaturally talented child who could, in the words of French teammate Thierry Henry, "do things with his feet that some people can't even do with their hands." He was shy on the surface but, like Bruce Banner, was cursed by a temper he could channel yet never fully curb. The two sides of his personality were perfectly captured in the documentary, *Zidane: A 21st Century Portrait*, which dazzled Cannes in 2006. In the movie, 17 synchronized cameras tracked the player in close-up over the course of a single game, following every balletic move as he dominated the proceedings from kickoff until—true to form—he was sent off toward the end of the match.

When France hosted the 1998 World Cup, Zidane was part of a multiracial team known as the "Black, Blanc, Beur" (Black, White, and Arab). It was dominated by stars from French territories or former colonies, such as Lilian Thuram (born in Guadeloupe), Christian Karembeu (New Caledonia), and Patrick Vieira (Senegal). The squad's skills were undebatable, but France was a country riven by deep ethnic tensions around the issue of immigration. When far-right parties vociferously questioned the mélange's ability to represent the true spirit of France, the ensuing political debates only increased the pressures traditionally faced by the World Cup host. The team started slowly and Zidane did little to help matters. He had barely sung "La Marseillaise" before he stomped on a Saudi opponent who had allegedly insulted him, and was sent off—a foreshadowing of things to come. But he returned in the semifinals, a man possessed, leading France into a final against Brazil in which his two first-half headers led the team to an improbably easy victory. The two headers shattered the mystique of Brazilian invincibility and silenced the French right wing. The victorious squad was proclaimed the face of a new France—a proudly multicultural nation that could be the best in the world. The streets of Paris had not seen such celebration since liberation. The slogan "Zidane for President" was graffitied all over the city and Zizou's face was beamed 100 feet wide against the side of the Arc de Triomphe.

That was then. Plagued by injury in the run-up to the 2006 World Cup, Zidane announced that he would retire from the sport at the tournament's end. He then proceeded, at 34, to prove that time had eroded few of his skills by leading his team on an unlikely and spectacular run into the final. His performances were imperious as the aging team eliminated first Spain and then Brazil, a game in which Zizou played with such guile and mastery that it was as if he were the only real Brazilian on the field. A win against Portugal placed them in the final against Italy. Zidane put his team ahead with a cheeky chip of a penalty shot, an event almost immediately eclipsed by his infamous assault on Italian defender Marco Materazzi (*see What Materazzi Said to Zidane, page 227*).

The violence of the attack was especially shocking in a sport known for simulated injuries and melodramatic overreactions. Zidane trooped off the field in disgrace, head down, a defeated gladiator, walking past the World Cup trophy without so much as a sideways glance. "With one blow, an icon is smashed!" proclaimed *Le Monde* as newspapers debated the incident, which fulfilled every violent far-right stereotype of Arab behavior as it reignited the national debate on immigration. Zidane slinked off into retirement, leaving the world to decipher the complicated legacy of a man who had roamed the field and dominated play with furious intensity while a cartoon angel and devil argued on his shoulders. Part Mother Teresa, part Hannibal Lecter, he was one of the most human performers to grace the World Cup and living proof that genius often has a dark side.

ITALY VS. FRANCE

For two nations that enjoy so much in common off the field—joie de vivre, la dolce vita, the Alps—they have certainly gone their separate ways on it. What the French live to create, the Italians seek to destroy. Les Bleus are fluid and effervescent like a new glass of champagne; the Azzurri, as heavy as a slab of lasagna bolognese.

It's often a difficult rivalry for the fans, torn between supporting many of their favorite players from their club teams who are now wearing the colors of the enemy. With the unrestricted movement of soccer talent worldwide, the best French players have often left their comparatively inferior domestic league for Serie A, where they have starred for several of Italy's powerhouse clubs. Of the 22 members of France's 1998 World Cup–winning side, seven of them made their living on the Italian side of the Alps.

When France and Italy meet in the World Cup, as they have a remarkable five times, three times the winner has gone on to hoist the trophy. Is it any wonder that when Zinedine Zidane, the greatest player of his era, lost his mind—and some would say the 2006 World Cup—he would do it in the cauldron of a France-Italy death struggle? After all, one of Italy's great strengths is its cunning—the ability to identify the flash point in an opponent and then work tirelessly to detonate it. For all his magical gifts, Zidane, with his surly demeanor and petite fuse, was an inviting mark, although it's unlikely the Italians foresaw the Def-Con 1 level of his response.

It wasn't, after all, the first time Italians had targeted a prominent Frenchman: At Mexico '86 they tried in vain to unsettle Michel Platini but the peerless midfielder kept his cool in the face of the Azzurri's provocations to score the goal that eliminated the defending world champions. The result marked France's first-ever World Cup triumph over Italy and was only its second victory over their silkily coiffed neighbors in 64 years. So dominant was Platini's performance that even the Italians couldn't muster any complaints. "In a class of his own," trumpeted one Italian newspaper, while another burbled, "Not so much in the match as above it."

It would be 12 years before the two sides met again in a major tournament. France was the host of the 1998 Cup and Zidane had replaced Platini as *Le Grand Fromage*. Only this was not the sweet-passing, debonair French team the world knew and loved, but one built surprisingly around a formidable defense. Italy, of course, hadn't changed their lockdown style since Julius Caesar invaded Gaul. The game was fraught with tension and the slow-burning dread, at least in Italy's case, that it would end 0–0 and go to penalties. When Roberto Baggio missed a golden goal by six inches in extra time, the Italians' fate was sealed. With the exception of England and Holland, the Italians have lost more shoot-outs than any other team in the world and have been eliminated from three World Cups because their knees turn to gelato on the penalty spot. And this time, France could trot out three of the deadliest penalty-kick marksmen in captivity—Zidane, Thierry Henry, and David Trezeguet—to put them out of their misery, which they did 4–3, on their way to claiming their one and only World Cup trophy.

By the time that Germany 2006 rolled around, French "champagne" soccer was going flat and Italy was, at long last, emerging from its mournful defensive shell. In the round of 16, the Italians were reduced to 10 men against an inspired Australian side, but advanced on a dubious penalty. For their part, France's graybeards found another keg of Ponce de Léon Gatorade to carry them through an inspired fight back against an excellent Spanish team and then a brilliant master class against Brazil. In the semis, Zidane's sorcery and Henry's speed were too much for Portugal, while the Italians attacked the Germans with unusual abandon to win 2–0 and set the stage for another memorable showdown.

Everyone knows what happened next. With the game tied 1–1 in extra time Zidane went beserk, and Italy exorcised its penalty-kick ghosts while Trezeguet, the man who scored the winning penalty in the '98 match, clanged one off the crossbar.

As shocking and abject as Zizou's fall from grace was, it should not take away from Italy's coronation. Into each game, the Azzurri had carried the taint of the match-fixing scandal back home, the sadness of their former teammate Gianluca Pessotto's suicide attempt, and the uncertainity of their own futures. At times, they whined and flopped and dove under the strain, but they never buckled. As Fabio Grosso's decisive penalty kick hit the back of the net, his scream was like a cry of redemption: *We are not criminals*, it seemed to say, *we are* campioni.

Luigi Di Biagio hangs his head after his shoot-out miss sends host France to the semifinals.

In 1978, emerging power France faced off against fading giant Hungary in the opening round before a meager 23,000 spectators in Mar del Plata, Argentina. When both teams arrived in their "away" white jerseys, the game had to be delayed half an hour while officials raided the locker room of a local club for colored shirts. Which explains why "Les Bleus" took the field that day wearing the green-and-white vertical stripes of CA Kimberley.

That wardrobe malfunction is a quaint little footnote, as unimaginable today as a crowd of only 23,000 for a World Cup game. The major sports apparel companies now carefully choreograph what teams wear and when they wear it. For the longest time, national kits were an afterthought; through the Dark Ages of marketing and into the 1970s, many around the world still watched the World Cup on black-and-white TVs. Uniforms were just clothing, not valuable marketing real estate. Now there are millions to be made adapting a country's flag for uniforms. France's blue shirt, white shorts, and red socks, for instance, derives from its famous tricolor. Argentina basically *wears* its flag as its jersey. Two notable exceptions are Italy and Holland, which forego their flags' colors to honor instead their royal pasts—the former using the blue of the House of Savoy (the "Azzurri"), and the latter the Royal House of Orange.

Uniforms, however, serve not just nationalism, but capitalism. Adidas has been providing shoes for the German national team since the 1950s, but it was another two decades before the unmistakable triple-stripe design and logo were slapped on team jerseys. Conflicts of interest ensued; Dutch captain Johan Cruyff—brilliant on the field, combative off—insisted on remaining loyal to his sponsor, Puma (owned by the brother of Adidas founder Adi Dassler), and refused to wear the Adidas logo on his uniform. Cruyff was allowed to tear off one of the three stripes; the first shot had just been fired in the sneaker wars.

By the 1978 World Cup, the Puma logo appeared on Austria's jersey, Umbro on Scotland's, and Adidas on France's. West Germany was outfitted not by Adidas but by a brand called Erima. Most team uniforms, though, were still bare, except for the national crest on the left breast and a large number on the back. By 1986, though, the majority of uniforms had manufacturers' logos on them. In 1994, when the World Cup came to Disney World—literally—two major design changes were made to make the tournament more America- and TV-friendly: A small number was placed on the front of the jersey and a last name was added to the back, just like the vast majority of uniforms in the United States. The improvements stuck. Then teams realized they could sell all that white space on road uniforms, and suddenly those jerseys started looking like Route 1 signage. By the mid-1990s, the advent of online shopping meant that, to acquire replica jerseys of their own, soccer fans no longer needed to rely on friends vacationing in Europe.

In the late 1980s and early '90s, national teams—or, rather, the sneaker companies that bid to win the outfitting rights for teams from a country's soccer federation—began altering the uniform every two years so fans would keep shelling out to look *exactly* like their heroes. But despite the tweaking, most national teams have always been instantly recognizable by their home jerseys. Brazil and Romania may both wear yellow, but true fans recognize the critical difference in the shades. And the classics have thus far remained classic: Brazil, Italy, Argentina.

In the United States, the national team, unfettered by long tradition, has struggled to find a distinctive uniform—or even stable shades of red, white, and blue. There's been some red, all white, mostly white, royal blue, navy blue, and, most shamefully, faux-faded blue with gigantic stars. There have been diagonal stripes, horizontal stripes, vertical ones, and squiggly ones.

One might ask how soccer can really catch on in a country whose national team changes outfits more often than Miley Cyrus.

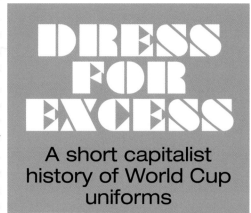

DRESS FOR EXCESS

A short capitalist history of World Cup uniforms

BEST

ARGENTINA (all years): Formal and tasteful. The soccer equivalent of Yankee pinstripes. Classy, even when they use their hands.

BRAZIL (1970): Best team ever, best uni ever. The perfect fusion of uniform and athletic function. Yellow jerseys, radiant play, sunny country—it all works perfectly. But who knows what we'd think of these unis if Uzbekistan wore them.

PERU (1970, 1978–82): This reductionist homage to the national flag makes players all look virtuous, no matter how poorly or dirty they may play. The U.S. prefigured these uniforms in 1950, the year they shocked England. With England looming again in 2010, the U.S. unveiled a fresh version of that diagonal design.

SENEGAL (2002): It's not easy to rock red, gold, and green without looking like a traffic light, but these stylish unis were a complete go when, in 2002's opener, the men wearing them ran over reigning champions—and erstwhile colonizers—France.

SOVIET UNION (all years): The Cold War is over, but that CCCP acronym lives on in our nuclear nightmares. Most of us still can't figure out what those letters stand for, which is part of their mystique and menace. A lot more menacing than the Russian team, which didn't even qualify for the 2010 World Cup.

WORST

UNITED STATES (1994): Faded, denim-colored star-spangled jerseys? How could the hosts come to the door wearing *that*? The team got to the second round, but the unis earned these ugly Americans a sartorial red card the minute they stepped onto the field.

DENMARK (1986): "Danish Dynamite"? Their uniforms, which mixed patches of red pinstripes with what looked like bloody chicken tracks up and down their sleeves, fizzled completely.

CROATIA (any year): Our specials tonight include veal saltimbocca and a lovely carbonara. Would you like to start with some Chianti?

GERMANY (1994): A nauseating orgy of argyle in black, red, and gold. *Nein!*

MEXICO (1994): Remember that psychedelic hallucination you had in 1972 after you ate your first 'shrooms? Guess what? It was just a premonition of Mexican goalkeeper Jorge Campos's 1994 bad trip.

Rivaldo and Ronaldo lock lips with the trophy.

2002
Korea/Japan

IN THE LAND OF THE RISING CUP

Fan hysteria, a new world order, and some dodgy refereeing all lead to a familiar result.

HOLDING THE FIRST World Cup outside of Europe and the Americas was not the gamble it looked like. The joint hosts, Japan and South Korea, were soccer crazy, thanks to the recent return from injury of the fashion-forward Manchester United midfielder David Beckham, who was more fetishized in the Far East even than homegrown sporting heartthrobs like Parma's Hidetoshi Nakata. Beckham obliged with more image changes than a runway model.

FIFA's experiment in cohosting could kindly be referred to as a marriage of convenience. South

Aerial view of human origami at opening ceremony in Seoul.

Korea and Japan's joint bid was fractious from the outset, as it was one of the first examples of the two regional rivals actually doing something together, or more accurately, alongside each other. The two countries had originally competed for sole hosting duties, and the rivalry continued in the form of a frenzied stadium construction competition. Both countries tossed state-of-the-art facilities around like giant roulette chips, some of them even landing on cities that were not actually home to soccer teams. South Korea built the World Cup Fountain on the Hangang River, at 633 feet high the world's tallest, and the Japanese countered by constructing a stadium that used a computer system to control the growth rate of the grass.

Things turned nasty during the opening ceremony,

held in Seoul, when the South Koreans neglected to mention their Japanese partners—payback perhaps, as the Japanese had erased the word "Korea" from the World Cup logo on the tickets for the matches they hosted. The result was a strangely bipolar competition, in which South Korea used the tournament to announce itself to the world while Japan was more relaxed, seemingly content to enjoy the sheer spectacle.

This was the first World Cup in which the traditional power base was challenged by the new world of Africa, Asia, and the U.S.A. Senegal kicked things off by beating their former colonizer, the defending champions, France, who, with Zinedine Zidane hobbled, seemed collectively comatose, exiting without scoring a single goal. In previous

World Cups, emerging nations with no tournament pedigree and few recognized stars expected to be slaughtered. However, in this new global era, their players knew that a stand-out performace or single dazzling goal could trigger a big money move to an Italian, English, or Spanish league club. In this tournament, the smaller nations were often more motivated, cohesive, and fearless than the superpowers, whose fat-cat players were preoccupied with sponsors obligations, book deals, and image rights.

BE THE REDS

England finally got the better of a disappointing Argentina in the group round. All it took was striker Michael Owen stealing a leaf from the South

Maniacal South Koreans watch their team on an outdoor television.

American playbook, as he threw himself to the turf in the penalty area as if he has been shot. The resulting penalty was coolly dispatched by David Beckham, who thereby redeemed himself after the shame of his dismissal four years earlier. Cue Beckham-mania, especially across England, where the very same tabloids that once buried their star now came to praise him. However, England rolled over meekly in the quarterfinals against Brazil, when Ronaldinho floated a long free kick just over the head of David Seaman, the off-guard English goalkeeper. Team U.S.A. also reached the quarters, playing with energy and distinction as they stunned both Portugal and themselves, winning 3–2 in their opener, then beating rival Mexico in the Round of 16, only to be dumped in the quarterfinals by Germany,

a team it outplayed. U.S. midfielder Claudio Reyna was selected for the All-Tournament team.

The semifinals featured two surprise teams— Turkey and host South Korea. Longshot Turkey's progress had been stealthy, as they shrugged off an opening game loss to pick off China and tie Costa Rica, then defeat Japan, and Senegal, using a physical style of play to reach the final four. Coached by a Dutchman, Guus Hiddink, South Korea prospered thanks to their organization and pluck and the fanatical support of their cultic followers who, in their red T-shirts branded with the ubiquitous phrase BE THE REDS!, provided some of the most amazing national fan spectacles ever. Outside of the stadia, up to a million fans at a time would gather to watch the games screened publicly

on a jumbotron, while inside, thousands more used precisely choreographed cheerleading to whip fans into a frenzy that made the NCAA college basketball tournament seem introverted. One misguided fan doused himself in paint thinner and set himself on fire, leaving a suicide note that explained his intention to "be a ghost, the 12th player on the pitch, and do my best for the team." When the fans could not pull the South Korean team through, the referees occasionally stepped in, most controversially in victories against Italy and Spain in the knockout stages (see WANTED, page 98).

The game against Italy had echoes of North Korea's 1–0 victory in the 1966 World Cup, although this time the poor Italians were victims of three dreadful refereeing decisions: They had a goal wrongly disallowed and their star striker, Francesco Totti, was controversially sent off, before the Koreans tied the game late as regulation was about to expire. In extra time, Jung-Hwan Ahn scored the sudden-death golden goal to seal the victory and instantly become a national hero, a position that entitled him to free life insurance, exemption from military service, and free flights on the national airline for life.

After a World Cup so far marked by talented in-terlopers and spectacular upsets, order was restored for the final, as serial winners Brazil and Germany emerged to face each other. Neither team had been its usual self. Brazil had been poor in qualifying for the final and demonstrated little of its traditional polish during a workmanlike campaign. Germany had limped into the tournament through the play-offs after suffering the ignominy of being crushed 5–1 by England in Munich. Strong performances by their Neanderthal goalkeeper captain, Oliver Kahn, and potent midfielder Michael Ballack helped them to one 1–0 victory after another. Ballack scored the only goal of the game against the U.S.A. in the quarterfinal and South Korea in the semis, a game in which he picked up his second yellow card of the knockout phase, sidelining him for the final and rendering him powerless to prevent Ronaldo, the mystery man in 1998, from gaining his redemption. Donning a pair of silver boots, the curiously coiffed striker scored both goals, one courtesy of an über-

Germany's Michael Ballack lost his head after scoring the winner against South Korea in the semifinal.

rare and uncharacteristic Kahn mistake, as Brazil won its fifth title. As Brazil claimed the cup, thousands of origami cranes, symbol of luck and long life, fell to the field, a stunning spectacle that surpassed almost everything that had taken place in the previous 90 minutes. It was a fitting end to a joyous, passionate World Cup, whose most moving aspect was fan fever in general, and in particular the 100,000 Koreans who registered to become "volunteer supporters" of *other* nations.

2002 RESULTS

QUARTERFINALS
Brazil 2 England 1
Germany 1 U.S.A. 0
Korea Republic 0 Spain 0 (5–3 PKs)
Turkey 1 Senegal 0

SEMIFINALS
Germany 1 Korea Republic 0
Brazil 1 Turkey 0

THIRD PLACE
Turkey 3 Korea Republic 2

FINAL
Brazil 2 Germany 0

It was a joyous, passionate World Cup full of fan fever.

France's Vieira and Senegal's Diop do a duet in the opener.

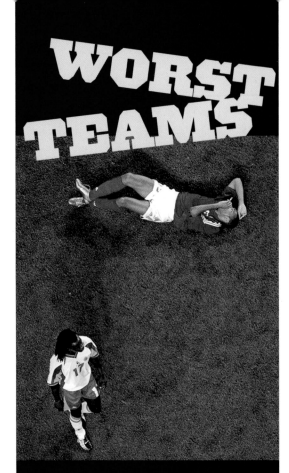

WORST TEAMS

FRANCE, 2002

WHY THEY MADE THE LIST: The worst performance by a defending champion in history. Winless, goal-less, and joie-less.

THE HIGH POINT: The team chef made excellent croissants.

THE NADIR: Scoring as many goals as they had notched military victories against the Germans in the 20th century.

ONLY IN THE WORLD CUP: French players hit the woodwork five different times, including at least once in every match.

THE FALLOUT: After France's ignominious ouster, the Gallic press feasted on its carcass. The sport daily *L'Equipe* trumpeted, "On the plane back to Paris first thing on Wednesday, the French players will still not have realized the almost unbelievable scale of their sporting failure." Others were not so kind: "Choose your own epithet: debacle, rout, collapse, fiasco, nightmare, trauma, humiliation," declared *Le Parisien*, "For Les Bleus, this is *Apocalypse Now*. No one imagined such a catastrophic scenario."

Border War: Clint Dempsey mistakes Gerardo Torrado's head for the ball during a 2009 qualifier in Mexico City.

MEXICO VS. U.S.

On May 24, 1934, the U.S. defeated Mexico 4–2 in Rome in a World Cup qualifying match. The Americans would put a man on the moon and celebrate their bicentennial before they managed to beat Mexico again—in 1980. In the interim, El Tri humiliated the red-white-and-blue; between 1937 and 1957 the teams played each other 10 times, with Mexico spanking them by a cumulative score of 56 to 11. It wasn't a rivalry—it was arena combat between a pit bull and a toy poodle.

Not that anyone should have been surprised. Soccer is Mexico's most popular sport. The game was hardwired into the nation's soul, while in soccer's global hierarchy, the U.S. was considered a third-world country. So how, then, did the yawning gap between these fractious neighbors narrow to the point that not only was a rivalry born, but soon became perhaps the most venomous one of its generation? If Brazil and Argentina is the classic South American rivalry, U.S. and Mexico is the newer, sexier North American model. It's the future of soccer hatred. The two countries share a border that spans 1,969 miles, but the bad blood flows a lot farther when it comes to soccer.

As always, it begins with history. Over the last two centuries, the U.S. has annexed more territory from its southern neighbor than did any of the marauding European powers, and the Americans haven't exactly been subtle about it. In California, they didn't even bother to change the names of the cities, and of course one state

was unimaginatively called *New* Mexico. Then there's the long and painful immigration conflict with Mexican laborers, who've been perennially treated like two-legged oxen.

But for 50 years, there was at least one arena in which Mexico didn't have to genuflect to the rich, self-satisfied gringos to the north. As the competition between the two countries intensified in the '80s, the U.S. soccer poobahs attempted to cash in on the fanaticism by scheduling matches in cities with large Hispanic populations. It didn't matter that the U.S. faced overwhelmingly hostile crowds at *home* games—the money was pouring into the national team's coffers. Take Landon Donovan's first senior international game in 2000, when he scored to lead the U.S. to a surprise 2–0 victory, presaging his reputation as Mexico's designated buzz-killer. As Donovan and his teammates streamed joyously off the field, they were pelted with rocks, batteries, and bags of urine. What else would you expect in Mexico City? Except the match was played at the Los Angeles Coliseum.

By the following year, the U.S. had grown wilier and not above resorting to gamesmanship. For a crucial 2001 World Cup qualifier, for example, the U.S. Soccer Federation chose to play its home leg in Columbus, Ohio—hoping it would be Mexico's chamber of horrors. Not only would Crew Stadium's intimate seating capacity leave only a few thousand tickets available to Mexican fans, but it was winter in the Midwest, and below freezing at kick-

off. Sure enough, the U.S. dominated the miserably cold Mexican team for a 2–0 victory.

The rivalry was growing, but still lacked the critical element that would elevate it to mythic status—the collective agony that only the most soul-destroying of defeats can visit upon a nation's psyche. As the French had Waterloo, Mexico had Jeonju, South Korea. It was June 17, 2002, and both teams had made it out of the first round. Mexico had been drawn into a difficult group, featuring both Italy and Croatia, but had played tough and resourceful soccer as Cuauhtémoc Blanco and Jared Borgetti led coach Javier Aguirre's men to a surprise first-place finish. The U.S., conversely, had followed its shocking opening win over group favorite Portugal with a hard-earned draw against South Korea and a lackluster 3–1 loss to last-place Poland. All of Mexico rejoiced upon realizing that there was just one piece of flotsam now standing between their beloved El Tri and a place in the quarterfinals: the overrated, overblown, Donovan-led Americans who don't even play *"futbol de verdad* (true soccer)." Sure enough, Mexico dominated the time of possession by a 2–1 margin, outshot the U.S., and enjoyed nine corners to the U.S.'s three. But when the final whistle blew, Brian McBride and Donovan had both scored—and the Mexicans hadn't. That albatross of a score would not go away; thus far, in the first decade of the 21st century, the Mexicans have lost five matches to the Americans by a 2–0 scoreline.

Can't we all just be *amigos*?
Mexico and the U.S.
tangle in 2002.

It was all too much for Mexico's regal captain, Rafael Márquez, who delivered a Zidane-worthy head butt to America's Cobi Jones and was red-carded for the assault in the 88th minute. As if his head butt weren't enough to stoke the enmity, striker Luis Hernandez had told Donovan during the game that he'd "find my mom and kill her." Two years later, Donovan responded by "watering the field" at one of Mexico's most revered stadiums, Estadio Jalisco. His defense? "You gotta go, you gotta go."

With that sign of disrespect, "El Landito" single-handedly turned the pissing match into a full-fledged border war. This time it was goalkeeper Oswaldo Sánchez who said some "extremely inappropriate" things about Donovan's *madre* in a magazine article. "It is flattering in a way," Donovan says earnestly about the howling wrath he provokes in Mexican players and fans. "I know why they are upset. It is because I have played a part in beating them a few times. That hurts them and makes them want to beat us so much more."

And finally, they did. For the first time since 1999, the Americans lost a match to El Tri on home soil — before 79,156 predominantly pro-Mexican fans in

New Jersey — when their inexperienced B-team was pummeled 5–0 in the 2009 Gold Cup final. Mexican players celebrated as if it had been the World Cup and not just the Gold. "We know that soccer doesn't matter that much to Americans," said Mexican journalist Alejandro Asmitia. "They didn't even care that they had a team in the World Cup. But in Mexico, it means everything. So to lose to the United States? I mean, for years, they didn't even have a professional soccer league."

Of course, the U.S. has never beaten Mexico south of the border; the Americans are 0-for-forever in the 7,300-foot altitude House of Pain called Azteca Stadium. Amazingly, they had never even taken so much as a one-goal lead in almost 40 years of playing there. So you can imagine the seismic shock that gripped Azteca last August when the U.S. scored the opening goal in their World Cup qualifier. Such was the gloom and doom that the Mexican fans were too numb to throw anything more than a few beers at the goal scorer, Charlie Davies, whose giddy celebration proved a bit premature — there were still 81 minutes left to play.

Stunned but not panicked, the Mexicans hauled

themselves off the canvas and dominated possession with their slick passing game. The catalyst was the 36-year-old warhorse Cuauhtémoc Blanco, named for the nephew of Montezuma, who would soon exact revenge. With a perfect pass in heavy traffic, he found his teammate Israel Castro, who fired an Exocet from 30 yards past the outstretched hand of American goalkeeper Tim Howard. When the ball caromed off the underside of the crossbar and over the line, Azteca looked to be in danger of combusting, leaving behind nothing but the charrred remains of the fans' green jerseys. Now, whenever the Mexicans passed the ball around and through the legs of the Americans, shouts of *"¡Olé!,"* instead of debris, rained down from the stands. With the will-sapping altitude and heat taking its expected toll on the U.S. players, Mexico ramped up its game. It was a surging run into the box past a weary Donovan that set up the winner in the 82nd minute and sent the oxygen-starved Americans home, grateful for the knowledge that the next time these implacable rivals could meet in World Cup competition would be in South Africa in 2010, where no one plays more than 5,100 feet above sea level.

GREATS WHO

NEVER

MADE IT TO THE CUP

GEORGE WEAH

Which would you rather do, lead your country to a World Cup or become its president? Weah tried to do both. Oh, how he tried.

Short of cloning himself, Weah did everything humanly possible to catapult Liberia onto soccer's biggest stage—first as a player, then as a coach, later as a technical director, and finally as the national team's financial angel. Never mind that he had a trophy case filled with virtually every major individual award—FIFA World Player of the Year, UEFA European Footballer of the Year, African Player of the Century—the World Cup offered Weah's beloved Liberia a chance to transform its image from a war-torn, poverty-ravaged country into a proud and joyful soccer nation. "He's been designated by God," Liberian striker Frank Seator told the journalist S. L. Price in 2001. "George has assisted millions of people, indirectly and directly. We have ministers here who have money, and they don't give anybody one cent. But he takes his time, his money, to go out to the people. I'm telling you: He's designated."

Unfortunately, there was one man in Liberia—its dictator, Charles Taylor—who didn't appreciate his messianic zeal and after Weah called for the United Nations to intervene in his country's civil war, Taylor had his house burned to the ground. But if Taylor thought that would stop Africa's greatest player from pursuing his mission, then he didn't know Weah's history. Born into a family of 13 siblings in a poor village outside Monrovia, Weah had been confounding the naysayers since the day the über talent spotter Arsene Wenger had plucked him from Liberian obscurity at the age of 22. "For me," said Wenger, who brought Weah to Monaco, the French club he coached at the time, "it was like a child discovering a chocolate bunny in his garden at Easter." From Monaco, Weah went on to play at several of the biggest clubs in Europe (including AC Milan and Chelsea) but it was to Liberia that he always returned to follow his World Cup dream. After Taylor's goons torched his house, Weah spent close to $2 million of his own money to fund the national team, paying for equipment, travel, and even the players' salaries. "If you lose in this country, they will kill you," said Francois Massaquoi, Liberia's minister of youth and sports, himself later murdered. "But I sleep; I snore in the night. Even if we lose, the fans know this team has done its best. They trust George."

In 2002, George came agonizingly close to World Cup nirvana, only for the Lone Stars to fall short by a single qualifying point. After such a crushing disappointment, you could have hardly blamed Weah if he had decided to take his millions and live the good life in one of his four homes on three continents. But that would be underestimating Weah's commitment to the cause. When Taylor's regime was finally toppled, Weah rode the wave of popular support in his 2005 run for the presidency, where he was narrowly defeated by Ellen Johnson Sirleaf, Africa's first democratically elected female leader. This time, Weah did leave Liberia to move to Florida, where he took political science classes at a local college, with an eye toward running again in the next election. Weah in 2012!

SOUTH KOREA 2, ITALY 1
Round of 16

In addition to wine, women, and song, there is nothing Italian fans like more than suffering for their soccer. Oh, how they wail operatically over every perceived injustice. *The game was fixed! The ref was crooked! The world is out to get us because we play boring, defensive soccer.* And that's when they *win*.

Imagine the nefarious plots at play when the Italians *lose,* as they did to South Korea in a game that oscillated between despair and delirium for 119 unbearably tense minutes. When South Korea dramatically tied the game in the 88th minute, the roof of Daejeon Stadium nearly lifted off from the sound of 40,000 people in matching red shirts all blowing their high-decibel horns and banging their gigantic drums. And yet that was a mere prelude to the bedlam that followed Jung-Hwan Ahn's golden goal one minute from the end of overtime as fans leapt from their seats into each other's arms and chanted, "Oh Korea, Oh Korea."

Italy's disbelief at their worst World Cup embarrassment since they were eliminated by North Korea in 1966 was as palpable as South Korea's joy. It was a game that the cagey Italians thought they had salted away after taking an early lead on a Christian Vieri header and then massing their defenders behind the ball. It almost worked.

With two minutes left in regulation, a long South Korea free kick pinballed around Italy's penalty area, ultimately bobbling off the thigh of defender Christian Panucci. Before Panucci could react, Ki-Hyeon Seol hooked the ball into the net and the Koreans were level.

There was still time for a response, and barely a minute later Vieri collected a perfect cross in stride about six yards from goal. With the net gaping, Vierri screwed his shot high and wide. The game would go to extra time, and not long after the Italian fans would go bonkers. Francesco Totti, the prodigal son of Italian soccer who had picked up a yellow card in the first half, was fouled in the penalty area. However, referee Byron Moreno saw it differently, and issued Totti a second yellow for diving, leaving the Italians not only demoralized but down a man. It was a call controversial enough to break many lesser teams, but the Italians weren't done. Within minutes of the foul, they had a goal disallowed for offside (even though replays show the player to be well onside), and again the Italian fans howled.

For all the pressure Italy put on South Korea's goal, you knew what was coming next: One minute from the end of extra time, Ahn outjumped Italy's most experienced defender, Paolo Maldini, and headed the ball beyond Gianluigi Buffon's desperate dive. Amid the insanity that followed, Ahn was mobbed by his countrymen but trashed by his employer. Luciano Gaucci, the president of Perugia in Italy's Serie A where Ahn played his club ball, immediately vowed that the Korean hero "will never set foot in Perugia again . . . I have no intention of paying a salary to someone who has ruined Italian football."

The ever-sporting Italian media chose to focus their bile on referee Moreno, calling him "a fat little toy with bulging eyes" who "has the appearance of a depressed cow." However, all the name-calling in the world couldn't mask the fact that the Italians had washed out of a tournament many had thought they could win. Yes, the officiating may have been dodgy, but so was the Italians' vaunted defense, which creaked with age and uncertainty. The South Koreans, meanwhile, continued their joyride all the way to the semifinals, beating Spain on penalties after the Spanish had, ahem, a perfectly good goal, which would have won the game in regulation disallowed by the referee. Okay, so it's good to be a World Cup host, but the South Koreans deserved their fairy-tale run through the tournament.

And if nothing else, they gave the Italians a chance to indulge in their favorite postgame pastime—making excuses for why they lost.

Francesco Totti was sent off for this alleged dive in the penalty area.

RYAN GIGGS

Perhaps we should be grateful that Giggs has never played in a World Cup. Though he has enjoyed a glittering 20-year career at Manchester United, where he has won 11 league championships and two Champions League titles, he will forever be remembered for doffing his jersey after scoring a brilliant goal against Arsenal in the 1999 FA Cup semifinal and revealing a hairy, sunken chest that looked like something PETA would take out ads to protect.

The world has been spared that unsettling sight because, for all his dead-eye swagger in a United jersey, the Welsh winger has underachieved internationally (in his defense, Giggs, like George Best, has been hamstrung by the fact that his country has a shallow pool of quality players from which to choose). During his career, Wales only came close to qualifying for the World Cup once, falling a single victory short for U.S.A. '94.

While consistent in his strike-rate for both club and country (averaging one goal every five games

from the wing), none of his goals for Wales came when the stakes were high enough to really warrant a topless celebration.

Giggs still calls failing to qualify for the World Cup his biggest career disappointment, but the truth is that he never displayed the passion and commitment playing for Wales in his prime that he does even today for United at age 36. With just 64 appearances for his country, he has missed almost a quarter of Wales's games over nearly two decades, due to injuries and scheduling conflicts with his club.

Many wonder if things might not have been different had Giggs been strutting his talents for England rather than Wales. He came to Manchester United as a schoolboy after dazzling Alex Ferguson in a tryout. "I shall always remember my first sight of him floating over the pitch . . . so effortlessly that you would have sworn his feet weren't touching the ground," the famously hard-bitten United manager

rhapsodized in his autobiography. "He carried his head high and he looked as relaxed and natural on the park as a dog chasing a piece of silver paper in the wind." Giggs was allowed to play for England at the youth level (once even at center-back), but FIFA's arcane rules about nationality (if you have a grandparent from a particular country you'd like to play for, you're in!) prevented him from continuing with the senior team—not that, as a proud Welshman, he ever wanted to.

Still, the vision of Giggs in an England shirt tearing past defenders on the flanks, the ball Velcroed to his feet, remains one of soccer's great what-ifs, especially given the dearth of good English left-wingers.

"I'm not going to grumble about my career," Giggs said upon announcing his retirement from international competition in 2007. And why should he? All he missed was a World Cup and a good wax.

SALIF DIAO
Senegal vs. Denmark, Group Stage

The 2002 World Cup began with the soccer equivalent of a war of independence. In the opening game, defending champions France swaggered onto the field against Senegal, a former French colony, as if about to impose martial law for the next 90 minutes. But the twin stereotypes of French invincibility and African naïveté were rendered obsolete when the Lions of Teranga shocked Les Bleus 1–0. The result so discombobulated the French that they failed to score a single goal the rest of the tournament, which they left in as much disarray as Napoleon's troops retreating from Russia. But it just wasn't hubris that undid the French. In their very next game, Senegal dispelled any doubts about their historic upset with a sweeping end-to-end counterattack that Pelé called "the best goal of the tournament."

Trailing Denmark 1–0 in the 52nd minute, the Africans went box-to-box, a distance of 70 yards in 13 seconds. Henri Camara stole the ball deep in the Senegal end and quickly passed to El-Hadji Diouf (who subsequently plied his unusual trade—that of spitting at opposing players and fans—in the English Premier League). Diouf advanced up the right flank before back-heeling to Salif Diao, who found Khalilou Fadiga rampaging down the left wing. Fadiga's return pass split the defense, and Diao, who had continued his lung-busting run into Denmark's penalty area, was there to meet it, spinning the ball off the outside of his right foot past the lunging goalkeeper, Thomas Sorensen. It was the kind of play that coaches diagram in their dreams, a marvel of angles, spaces, and speed. In Diao, it

also had the unlikeliest of finishers—a robust, lumbering defensive midfielder who managed only five goals in over 200 games for club and country.

While his World Cup goal, which secured a 1–1 draw with the stubborn Danes and continued Senegal's eye-opening run in the tournament, will endure in Diao's memory forever, his participation in the game lasted only another 28 minutes. Not content to bask in the glow of his stunning goal, he inexplicably went studs-up on Denmark's René Henriksen and was shown a red card. Today, it is difficult to know what to take away from this game—those electrifying 13 seconds that once again appeared to herald the arrival of African soccer, or the kind of reckless defense that at least partly explains why Senegal hasn't qualified for the World Cup since.

RONALDO
Brazil: 1998, 2002, 2006

Ronaldo's career has been like a Weight Watchers infomercial in reverse. He morphed from a powerful and swift superstar into a bloated, injury-prone playboy who looked like he had been locked in a pie factory. Perhaps everyone should have known something was up when he named his first son after Ronald McDonald. But when it came to the World Cup stage, Ronaldo proved that looks were irrelevant. In three campaigns he consistently tormented teams with his goal-scoring exploits, netting 15 in all, to become the most prolific marksman in World Cup history.

Buck-toothed and bug-eyed, Ronaldo looked more like a cartoon character than a world-class athlete when he debuted internationally as "Ronaldinho," or Little Ronald, to distinguish him from a veteran teammate with the same name. By 1998 he was Ronaldo again, the golden boy on a Brazilian team that made it to the World Cup final, only to implode amidst controversy and confusion. Rumors began to circulate on the day of the game

that the pressure of expectations, coupled with whispers of his girlfriend's infidelity, had led him to suffer convulsions. He was left off the original team sheet, only to appear on the field, rumor has it on orders of Nike, which demanded that its poster boy show off its new line of boots, named the R9 in his honor. He obliged in body, but not spirit, and the French team was willed to victory by the home crowd.

What happened may never be known. An extensive investigation by the Brazilian Parliament was inconclusive. The only certainty was that Ronaldo's reputation was severely tarnished, his durability suspect. In the words of one Brazilian commentator, "When he moves on goal he is like a beautiful thoroughbred, but we must still wonder if he is made of glass."

Ronaldo had to wait four years to redeem himself. After two operations on his damaged right knee and almost two unhappy years of rehabilitation, he returned just in time for the 2002 World Cup,

where he buried the mental and physical traumas of the past with a resplendent performance. Almost as staggering as his eight goals was his haircut—a triangle fade that shamed the mohawks, dye jobs, and cornrows also on display. His two goals in the final capped one of the most prolific performances in World Cup history and transformed him from footballer to icon.

By 2006 he had put on more than a few pounds, causing even the Brazilian president to exclaim, "Isn't Ronaldo fat?" when he addressed the squad in training. Although Ronaldo took the field with the physique of a washed-up heavyweight, he still scored three times to claim the all-time goal record. His club career deteriorated amidst injury, continued weight problems, and a reported appetite for transvestite prostitutes, but his goal-scoring feats had by then cemented his place alongside Pelé and Garrincha in the pantheon of classic Brazilian heroes.

IT'S ONLY BIZARRE WHEN IT DOESN'T WORK

Classic World Cup Superstitions

It's too bad that Landon Donovan and Sergio Goycochea never faced each other in a penalty-kick showdown. The world would have witnessed the collision of two of soccer's all-time weird superstitious rituals. On one side, you'd have Donovan, America's marquee player with his interminable haunch-sitting, wrist-kissing, sign of the cross-making pre-shot routine. And staring him down would be Goycochea, the Argentine goalkeeper, who would simply hitch up his shorts and urinate on the grass, as he did so memorably in the 1990 World Cup semifinals, just before he made two acrobatic shoot-out saves to beat Italy.

Goycochea's defense of his public bladder-emptying sounded entirely reasonable: "By the rules of the game, until a match finishes you cannot leave the field of play. And if you have any natural human urges, you have to go on the field. So that is what happened in the 1990 World Cup quarterfinal against Yugoslavia, I went and we won. There was another shoot-out in the semifinal against Italy so I went again and we won again. It was my lucky charm and I went before every shoot-out. I was very subtle, nobody complained."

Tolerance for magic and superstition is nowhere greater than in South America and Africa. To the 1982 World Cup, Peru brought along a couple of "special" fans, named Augusto and Ramon Canales, whom the national team believed possessed supernatural powers. Casting spells, drinking elixirs, and brandishing voodoo dolls, the brothers attempted to put a hex on Peru's opponents. It didn't work; Peru was humbled by Poland 5–1 and was on an early flight home. Ecuador's resident shaman, Tzamarenda Naychapi, had better luck in 2006 when he traveled to Germany with the team. His pregame dances and chants on the field were viewed as part of the process that propelled Ecuador into the knockout rounds for the first time.

In Africa, several teams employ or consult with "muti-men," the religious specialists versed in witchcraft, who perform rituals to give the home side an edge. The rituals may or may not work, but stiffing the voodoo specialists always brings bad luck. After winning the African Cup of Nations in 1992, Ivory Coast neglected to compensate their witch doctors. A curse followed until 2004, when the debt was finally squared away with a $2,000 payment enhanced with several bottles of whiskey. Lo and behold, the Elephants qualified for the 2006 World Cup. South of the Sahara, African soccer giants Ghana, Nigeria, and Cameroon seek to establish themselves as legitimate international threats without the aid of arcane hoodoo, and yet during the 2002 African Cup of Nations, assistant Cameroon coach Thomas Nkono was arrested for trying to embed a magic charm into the grass before a game. As a spokesman for the Confederation of African Football put it, "We are no more willing to see witch doctors on the pitch than cannibals at the concession stands."

Most players have more conventional ways to protect themselves from misfortune. Romania's Adrian Mutu favors a one-size-fits-all approach: "Curses cannot touch me," he says, "because I wear my underwear inside out"—although, for good measure,

Zagallo's horror when Brazil lost in the quarter-finals to France on a goal scored by a man with a 12-letter name (Thierry Henry).

Then again, Henry was playing for a team coached by the nutty professor himself, Raymond Domenech, who has famously admitted that he consults astrological charts when selecting his lineup. Thus, he rarely selects Leos due to their fiery temperament and he never picks Scorpios because he doesn't trust them. "When I have a Leo in defense," he explained, "I've always got my gun ready as I know he's going to want to show off at one moment or another and cost us." Because of his Zodiac-dependency, many great Frenchmen have missed out on international success (most notably winger Robert Pirès), and only a select few Leos have been included in Domenech's plans (Henry and William Gallas among them).

And yet when Domenech was asked if he was concerned that France would be playing Holland on Friday the 13th of June, 2008, he replied without a hint of irony, "I don't believe in superstitions. They bring bad luck."

he reportedly once drank the blood of his Transylvanian girlfriend. In contrast, England's John Terry employs an arsenal of preventive tricks, up to 50 by his count. "I am so superstitious," he has admitted. "I've got to have the same seat on the bus, tie the tape round my socks three times, and cut my tubular grip for my shin-pads the same size every game. I also drive to games listening to the same Usher CD in my car."

To maintain hot streaks, some players go to extraordinary lengths. English striker Gary Lineker, the recipient of the Golden Shoe for top scorer at the 1986 World Cup, never practiced his shooting during warm-ups "because I didn't want to waste a goal. I wanted to save those for the game. I'd always change my shirt in the second half if I hadn't scored in the first, but I'd keep wearing the same shirt if I had scored. If I ever went on a bad run, I'd always get a haircut." And if a new 'do fails to ensure success, there's always an appeal to a higher authority. The Republic of Ireland's goalkeeper, Shay Given, places a vial of Lourdes holy water in the back of his net, believing that its power will exorcise any evil spirits, keep him personally safe, and lead to

a shutout. But Given's lucky water couldn't prevent his country from crashing out in his only World Cup stint in 2002, losing on penalties to Spain. Other players live in fear of less sacred fluids. Before a decisive World Cup 2010 qualifier against Ireland, French defender Patrice Evra swore off his favorite soda, Sprite, because the can is green.

Even members of Brazil, a nation synonymous with World Cup glory, have been known to succumb to bizarre acts of faith. The number 13 is a staple of superstition, but legendary former coach Mario Zagallo developed anti-triskaidekaphobia because his wife was devoted to St. Anthony, whose feast day is July 13. The number of visits Zagallo made to St. Anthony's shrine to help him recover from stomach cancer surgery? Thirteen. The number of World Cup victories he recorded in his four stints as national team coach? Thirteen. Imagine his delight when Brazil's first match against Croatia took place on June 13. And imagine

ROGUES, PART II:

DIVERS

Experts of the Extracurricular

Diving is the province of slender continental players with speed, flair, and superb stunt-falling skills who delight in taking advantage of an era when flagrant violence is frowned upon—and referees are easily impressed by drama-club theatrics. The Diver's signature trait is the ability, when merely brushed by a defender, to crumple to the ground as if riddled by a Kalashnikov. (Think Didier Drogba's operatic death spiral against Argentina in the 2006 World Cup, which was the equal of Willem Dafoe's slo-mo demise in *Platoon*.) If a furtive glance at the referee indicates that a diver's acting has been rewarded with a yellow or red card to the opponent, he springs to his feet, not only unhurt, but totally rejuvenated. Because of its proven success, diving has gained momentum and turned some of soccer's most artful practitioners into shameless thespians. Sadly, this behavior proliferates in the World Cup, where so many flustered referees struggle to cope with the pace and chicanery of the players.

CRISTIANO RONALDO, PORTUGAL

Ronaldo, the FIFA 2008 World Player of the Year, has virtually no peer in the biathlon of athleticism and histrionics. As with everything else he does on a soccer field, Cristiano Ronaldo dos Santos Aveiro is nonpareil at the art of diving, but his propensity for play-acting diminishes his stature in comparison with other once-in-a-generation players like Pelé or George Best, who went down only when opponents took their legs out from under them. Ronaldo is so melodramatic that he sometimes appears to be imploring the ref to make the call even before he hits the ground.

On most occasions, Ronaldo *has* been hacked, but it's his constant writhing, pouting, and finger-pointing that taxes a referee's sympathy. Jorge Larrionda, the Uruguayan referee assigned to the center slot in the 2006 France-Portugal semifinal, was wholly unimpressed by Ronaldo's whirling dervish collapse minutes after Zidane's penalty kick had put France ahead 1–0. His dive in the box, jeered by the fans, was all the more egregious after he responded to England's Wayne Rooney's red card in the quarterfinal with a self-satisfied wink.

Justice was ultimately served, though. Portugal lost in the semis and, while fans voted overwhelmingly for Ronaldo, the award for the Best Young Player of the 2006 World Cup went to Germany's Lukas Podolski.

JÜRGEN KLINSMANN, GERMANY

During the course of his illustrious career, the lanky blond striker was so fast and lethal that he earned the nickname "the Golden Bomber." In Italia '90, though, they should have dubbed him "Stuka" for all his dives. He unveiled his face-planting talents early in the tournament against an overmatched United Arab Emirates. Although the Germans won easily 5–1, Klinsmann went into death throes when a blade of grass grazed his ankle. On the biggest stage of all, the World Cup final against Argentina, Klinsi sank to the occasion again. Marauding down the right wing in the 65th minute of a hard-fought, deadlocked game, he was challenged by substitute defender Pedro Monzón, who slid, studs high, across his path. Looking like he had just stepped on a grenade, Klinsmann flew four feet through the air, kicking out his legs in a spasming jackknife and tumbling to earth like a rag doll. The game was stopped for several minutes as medics debated whether to summon a priest to administer last rites. In homage to Klinsmann's antics, the referee swiftly and subserviently red-carded the befuddled Monzón instead. Thanks to a late penalty kick before another Argentine was sent off, Germany lifted the trophy. Klinsmann, who had seemed close to death just minutes before, pogo'd along with his giddy teammates on the victory stand.

Years later, coach Berti Vogts proved Klinsi wasn't the only accomplished actor on the German team when he came to the defense of his star striker. "Jürgen Klinsmann was not a diver," Vogts said. "No. Never."

SLAVEN BILÍC, CROATIA

In 1998, Laurent Blanc, known as "Le President" for his commanding presence at the heart of the

Didier Drogba strikes a familiar pose.

Diverse divers: Portugal's Ronaldo and Germany's Klinsmann in arch agony.

French defense, had scored the golden goal to help his team eliminate Paraguay in the round of 16, and was but 24 minutes away from realizing his childhood fantasy—to represent Les Bleus in the World Cup final in his nation's capital.

Enter the Croatian pratfall artist known as Slaven Bilíc. In a tense and tight semifinal at the Stade de France, Blanc and Bilíc became entangled while awaiting a 75th-minute free kick into the Croatian box. There was a blur of bodies and then there was Bilíc rolling on the ground, clutching his eye, as if he had been struck by a meteorite. In fact, Blanc had tapped Bilíc lightly on the chin with an open hand, but Bilíc grabbed the opportunity to hoodwink the Spanish referee, José García-Aranda, into brandishing a red card. It was the only sending off in Blanc's 97-match international career and his ejection meant that the 32-year-old was ineligible for the final.

The incident during the game changed nothing except the course of Blanc's life. The French defeated Croatia 2–1 and went on, four days later, to their epic glory in the City of Light. But Blanc was left behind. "I was sorry for Laurent," said French coach Aimé Jacquet. "The referee's decision was unjust. It took the shine off our victory celebrations."

Ever the gentleman, Blanc later said, "Of course I resented what he did and I always will resent it, but it's one unfortunate episode of a long journey that we all went on together. Today I forgive him."

Ever the Croatian clown, Bilíc was remorseless, "He didn't hit me like Mike Tyson," he said, "but he gave me a push. . . . The bottom line is that he made a mistake. Nobody can say he didn't and that was a red card, but because it was the final, and because it was in France, blahblahblahblah, it's a big story."

It was a big story, too, when Bilíc was appointed manager of Croatia's national team in 2006. Known more for his rock star aura, complete with tattoos, diamond ear stud, and his own band, named Rawbau, as well as for his incessant smoking on the sidelines, he had little coaching experience but was beloved by his players for his maverick ways. In return, they could do no wrong in his eyes. When the Brazilian-born Croatian striker Eduardo, playing for his club team Arsenal, triggered a firestorm of controversy for appearing to dive in the box against Celtic in a 2009 Champions League qualifier, Bilíc rushed to his defense. "We are talking about a player who is a role model of a sportsman," he said. "I simply cannot understand how he can be punished."

Maybe he should ask Laurent Blanc.

RIVALDO, BRAZIL

While Rivaldo may have been the 1999 FIFA World Player of the Year, he will forever be remembered as the Jerry Lewis of soccer vaudevillians.

Deep into extra time of a group match in which Rivaldo's 87th-minute penalty had given Brazil a 2–1 lead over Turkey, Brazil won a corner and Rivaldo, in the eyes of the agitated Turks, wasn't exactly rushing to put the ball in play. In frustration, Turkey's Hakan Ünsal kicked the ball at Rivaldo from about 10 yards away. Rivaldo could have easily caught the ball, placed it down, and taken the corner. Instead, he let it glance off his right thigh, whereupon he threw his hands up to cover his face as though he had just been splashed with battery acid and crumpled backward to the ground in the kind of writhing pain more commonly seen in triage units. Korean referee Joo-Kim Young wasted no time in red-carding Ünsal.

Ironically, the 2002 World Cup featured FIFA's much ballyhooed crackdown on what they euphemistically called "acts of simulation." Although unable to do anything about the unjust red-carding, the sport's governing body couldn't laugh off Rivaldo's theatrics.

"Such behavior," said FIFA's disciplinary chief Marcel Mathieu, "means that everybody is cheated, not only the opponents, but also the referee and particularly the fans."

"I'm leaving the referee to the Koreans," said an embittered Haluk Ulusoy, the president of the Turkish FA. "We sacrificed 1,000 soldiers to defend Korea and one Korean has killed 70 million Turks with this decision."

Brazil went on to win the World Cup, and Rivaldo earned the first-ever fine for simulation—a paltry $7,300, probably less than he paid for his acting lessons. For his part, Rivaldo's poker-faced statement after the match showed him to be a man ready for high political office.

"I am not a player who fakes fouls," he said.

CULT FIGURES

JOSÉ LUIS CHILAVERT, PARAGUAY

"I want to get through to the knockout stages and then go all the way to the final. I also hope to score the goals that help take us there."

If this sounds like the usual gibberish that players spout before a big tournament, then why did the soccer world snap to attention at Korea/Japan 2002 when it came out of Chilavert's mouth? Well, for starters, Chilavert was a goalkeeper. And then there's this: He scored an astounding 62 goals during his career, including eight for Paraguay.

A goal-scoring keeper is as much an oxymoron as a benign dictator—except in Chilavert's case. Loud, defiant, and possessed with terrifying leg strength, the Paraguayan realized early on in his career that he had the most powerful shot on his team and he quickly became the penalty and free-kick taker for both club and country. His rise through the food chain of Paraguayan soccer to become not only the captain of the national team but also, to many minds—most especially his own—the best goalkeeper in the world, owes as much to his strutting self-confidence as to his fearsome shot-stopping abilities.

His eccentricities, however endearing they seemed to his countrymen, often incurred the wrath of opposing teams. In 2001, before a World Cup qualifying match with Brazil, Chilavert declared that Brazil return land that was taken from Paraguay during a 19th-century war. Brazilian coach Luiz Felipe Scolari responded by mocking the rotund goalkeeper's "400 kilos of fat." After the game, Chilavert triggered a mass brawl by spitting in the face of Brazilian fullback Roberto Carlos, who he claimed had aimed racist comments and obscene gestures at him. "At the first corner kick, after Carlos was called for a foul, this dwarf shouted to me, 'Get up, Indian,' " Chilavert stated. "After that, when they scored he touched his genitals to provoke me."

Though he played his club ball in Argentina, he was only popular in that country with the fans of his team, Vélez Sársfield. In fact, rival supporters seated behind the goal made a sport of hurling lit firecrackers at Chilavert. He once accused the entire Australian national team of being on drugs, and in a 1997 game against Colombia, where both Chilavert and a Colombian player were ejected for the usual boorish behavior, Chilavert proudly recalled, "In the tunnel, when nobody was looking, I punched him in the head."

But in Paraguay, "El Chila" could do no wrong. A small nation of 7 million nestled between the twin South American titans Argentina and Brazil, Paraguay had wandered in the soccer wilderness, making only one World Cup appearance between 1962 and 1994. In Chilavert, they found their Moses. Under his guidance and prodding, they not only qualified for consecutive World Cups in 1998 and 2002, but remarkably advanced to the second round in both. In a qualifying match against their immense rivals, Argentina, Chilavert scored a spectacular left-footed, around-the-wall free kick to earn the Albirroja a valuable point in a 1–1 tie in Buenos Aires. It was a goal Chilavert had *predicted* he would score. At home he was called a hero, but he received multiple death threats from enraged Argentinian fans. After the 1998 World Cup, FIFA named him the tournament's top goalkeeper, along with France's Fabien Barthez.

During Paraguay's surprising run through 2002 qualifying, he scored four times, and while he never added to his tally in either World Cup, his free-kick prowess meant that opposing coaches had to construct strategies to thwart him at both ends of the field. After all, they knew the answer to the trivia question: "Has any goalkeeper ever scored a hat trick?"

Chilavert was as grandiose a figure off the field as on it. When Paraguay was awarded the honor of hosting the Copa América in 1999, he refused to play because he felt it shameful for his country to spend its money on new stadia when there were not enough hospitals or schools. When he went to France near the end of his career to play for cellar-dwelling Strasbourg, he refused to sit on the substitutes bench. He felt that it would embarrass his countrymen and tarnish his status. As his agent put it: "Chilavert is a sub on the worst team in the French league—can you imagine the impact that would have on his image at home?"

By World Cup 2006, Chilavert's famous girth had caught up to him and his involvement was limited to his role as a commentator for Univision. But even there, the peacock flashed plumage. "The footballing environment misses me," he said. "Nowadays there are no forceful personalities. There seems to be a real dearth of characters in the game."

Goalkeeper Gianluigi Buffon embraces Italy's fourth World Cup championship.

2006
Germany

ITALY KEEPS ITS HEAD

Germany hosts ze best,

ze wurst, and Zidane.

GERMAN HISTORY IS RIFE with attempts to grab the world's attention—most often by force. The 2006 World Cup managed to succeed in forcing the world to admire all things German, though it was achieved not by might, but with politeness, sausages, and its own inimitable sense of humor. Thanks to its remarkable hospitality, as well as the plucky play of its national team on the field, Germany accomplished the impossible and

rebranded itself as a cuddly underdog, triggering a wave of self-love within the country that had not been experienced since World War II.

Even such mighty powers as corporate America were brought to their knees by this new Teutonic self-confidence. Budweiser, which had spent $40 million to ensure that the King of Beers was the only one on tap in World Cup stadia, was sued by German brewer Bitburger, plucky manufacturers of the Bud rival known as Bit. The German press whipped up the conflict into a foamy head. *Der Spiegel* asked, "What is this U.S. beer? An amber-colored cold drink that gives you a headache without making you drunk," and demanded to know why an American brew was the only one on sale in

German stadia in a country that was famed for its *bier*. Under local pressure, Bud was forced to relent, permitting its local rival to be available on tap as long as it was sold in unmarked cups.

This hiccup was an aberration for a corporate side of the tournament that ran like never before. Within the venues, global advertisers plastered their names on anything that did not move; it almost seemed as if HDTV had been invented primarily so viewers could see logos and taglines in brighter, crisper detail. But the vast majority of fans never got near the stadia. Crowds of up to 750,000 people packed into official "Fan Zones," which were the great innovation of the tournament, enabling ticketless fans to soak up the atmosphere, watch-

ing the games live in front of jumbo jumbotrons. Fan Zones elevated just being there to the status of actually attending the matches.

This was the World Cup in which soccer's "New World Order" was expected to upset the traditional powers, but although Australia, Ghana, and even Switzerland had their moments, they fell away, leaving the usual suspects—France, Italy, Germany, and Brazil—to dominate the later rounds. Mirroring this, the most highly touted young stars, including a just turned 19-year-old Lionel Messi, failed to deliver, leaving oldies but goldies to have one last day in the sun: the seasoned Miroslav Klose, Zinedine Zidane, and Ronaldo were all among the leading scorers.

(left) Rooney stomps on the crotch of Portugal's Ricardo Carvalho; (right) Brian McBride takes one for the team from Italy's Daniele De Rossi, who was duly red-carded.

Brazil, led by Kaká and Robinho, arrived as favorites, despite the fact that their star striker, Ronaldo, looked so lardy he seemed to be wearing a custom-tailored husky-size shirt. When asked whether it seemed as if Ronaldo was being given playing time so he could become match-fit, a Brazilian commentator quipped, "At the rate he is going he won't even be ready for the 2010 World Cup." The team never found its natural rhythm, progressing into the quarterfinals, where it was rolled over by the French. The roots of their awkward performance were accidentally uncovered when a team of deaf students, who had been employed by Brazilian television to read the German coaches' lips during games, discovered that those on the bench spent the game spewing a stream of obscenities instead of offering tactical observations.

ROONEY GOES NUTS

England was also sluggish. The players arrived encumbered not only with the usual unrealistically high expectations, but with their high-living wives and girlfriends (*see The WAGS That Tail the Dogs, page 232*), book deals, and an army of fans whose idea of fun was to use permanent markers to decorate their bodies with swastikas. Portugal and Holland squared off in the round of 16 in a game that became known as the "Battle of Nuremberg." The teams ignored FIFA's Fair Play campaign as they served up an old school game of violent soccer, kicking lumps out of each other in front of a jittery Russian referee, who awarded a startling 16 yellow cards and four reds. Portugal survived and proceeded to eliminate England, which predictably wilted under the pressure of penalty kicks after their young prodigy, Wayne Rooney, had been red-carded. Rooney, who had been goaded by the veteran Portuguese Ricardo Carvalho throughout the game, lost his cool and booted the defender in the nuts. While Rooney was being sent off, his then Manchester United teammate Cristiano Ronaldo was caught on camera winking at the Portuguese

bench, revealing to the world that baiting Rooney had been an official part of the team's game plan. Portugal became the tournament heels and were booed by fans from that point on. After they were eliminated by France in the next round, Ronaldo returned to Manchester to link up with Rooney again, and former English legend Alan Shearer told a live British viewing public that "I think Wayne Rooney should go back to the Manchester United *training* ground and 'stick one' on Ronaldo."

The German team became the darlings of their own party, led by their coach and *motivation-meister,* Jürgen Klinsmann, their former striking hero who now patrolled the sidelines clad head-to-toe in Hugo Boss. Having lived largely in

self-imposed exile in California since 1998, Klinsmann had been a controversial selection, but the physical and mental training techniques he had learned from American sports scientists equipped the squad to play the positive, plucky soccer that Klinsmann—more management guru than soccer manager—demanded. The French were also a delightful surprise. They were much maligned at the outset for their advanced average age, and their own fans were slow to warm to them as they progressed. But the country became believers once Zidane slotted home the only goal of the semifinal against Portugal from the penalty spot, triggering a frenzied night of national celebration in which at least one person was killed.

Materazzi (below, in goofy hat) receives a congratulatory hug from partially disrobed teammate Gennaro Gattuso after successfully inducing Zidane (left) to lose his head—and the Cup.

In the final, the French met an Italian team that had arrived in Germany beleaguered after a match-fixing scandal had rocked their domestic league. In a now-familiar story line, the Azzurri demonstrated they are never more dangerous than when their backs are against the wall. The team was led by 5'8" defensive dynamo Fabio Cannavaro, yielding only a single own goal as they emerged from a tough group that included the disappointing United States, which had proved only that their fourth-place FIFA ranking, awarded in April before the tournament, was recklessly optimistic.

The final itself was the stuff of legend, soccer as reimagined by Vince McMahon. Zidane dominated the game as both hero and villain, opening the scoring with a cheekily chipped penalty kick be-fore succumbing to his moment of madness, butting Marco Materazzi and launching a thousand YouTube parody clips in the process (*see Fraternité, Egalité, Stupidité: What Materazzi Said to Zidane, page 227*). The act of violence was so shocking that even French protests that the referee had missed it and needed to be alerted to the assault by the fourth official (FIFA has eschewed instant replay) were muted. The Italians won on penalties and the game ended in slapstick fashion as midfielder Gennaro Gattuso ran around the field pantless and Mauro Camoranesi had his hair cut on a folding chair in the middle of the field. They were surreal details that on any other day would have become memorable, but thanks to Zidane's forehead have hardly been remembered at all.

2006 RESULTS

QUARTERFINALS
Germany 1 Argentina 1 (4–2 PKs)
Italy 3 Ukraine 0
Portugal 0 England 0 (3–1 PKs)
France 1 Brazil 0

SEMIFINALS
Italy 2 Germany 0
France 1 Portugal 0

THIRD PLACE
Germany 3 Portugal 1

FINAL
Italy 1 France 1 (5–3 PKs)

Zizou bids his career adieu after being red-carded.

FRATERNITÉ, EGALITÉ, STUPIDITÉ:
What Materazzi Said to Zidane

Zinedine Zidane's cranial coldcocking of Marco Materazzi was as extraordinary for its bizarre timing as its unorthodox technique. Zidane, who had announced the game would be the last of his brilliant career, was a mere 10 minutes away from retiring as one of the greatest players to ever grace the tournament. Even though Materazzi was known as "The Matrix" for his on-field mayhem, what on earth could he have *said* to goad Zidane to self-destruct so spectacularly that he would tarnish his legacy while the world looked on in disbelief?

Both players maintained their silence in the weeks following the final, forcing the world's broadcasters to hire a battery of lip-readers to crack the mystery. Results were regrettably inconclusive, ranging from an attempt by Materazzi to debate the virtue of Zidane's mother ("You're the son of a terrorist whore!"), question the résumé of his sister ("I would rather have your sister who is a prostitute!"), or demonstrate an impressive knowledge of obscure historical slurs ("You're the son of Harkis!") referring to Algerians who fought on the French side in the War of Independence.

Zidane remained coy, revealing only that the insult consisted of "very hard words" about his mother and sister, adding, "I am a man and some words are harder to hear than actions. I would rather have taken a blow to the face than hear that." Materazzi protested that he "did not bring up Zidane's mother; for me a mother is sacred." Nor, he insisted, did he mention terrorism. "I am ignorant," he pleaded. "I don't even know what an Islamic terrorist is." He added as he gestured toward his 10-month-old daughter, "My only terrorist is her."

Lacking closure, Zidane's battering-ram moment became a cultural phenomenon and creative muse for chart-topping pop songs, bestselling books, a fashion line, and a deluge of digitally altered YouTube clips until Materazzi broke his silence two months after the incident—on the eve of an Italy-France rematch in a qualifier for Euro 2008. Neither man was playing; Zidane had retired and Materazzi was still suspended for his role in the confrontation. Yet the Italian put the world out of its misery by revealing that all it took to turn Zidane's skull into a weapon of crass destruction was the common Italian insult, *"preferisco quella puttana di tua sorella."* "I prefer the whore that is your sister."

Perhaps to mitigate the widespread sense of anticlimax, Materazzi proceeded to write a book in aid of UNICEF entitled *What I Really Said to Zidane,* listing 249 creative provocations he *could* have said, including "Do you want to know what happens in the season finale of *Lost*?"; "Where exactly is the sternum, Zizou?"; and the author's favorite: "French philosophy just hasn't been the same since Foucault died."

The book became an instant bestseller.

ESTEBAN CAMBIASSO
Argentina vs. Serbia and Montenegro, First Round

Proud doesn't begin to describe the Serbia and Montenegro players who took the field that day. With the dissolution of Yugoslavia, they were playing under their national colors for the first time in the World Cup. Moreover, they had compiled a remarkable nine shutouts in their 10 qualifying matches, giving up a single goal. Entering the tournament, the Serbs were, statistically, the most impenetratable defensive team in the world, and yet it took Argentina only 60 seconds to leave them in ruin. In one mind-boggling sequence of 24 passes involving eight different players, Argentina pinged the ball around as if they were controlling the movements on a PlayStation rather than on a real live soccer field. The Serbia and Montenegro defenders seemed hypnotized by the interplay until Esteban

Cambiasso snapped them back to reality with a left-footed blast into the roof of the net.

Not since the Dutch team of 1974, the storied progenitors of Total Football, had the World Cup seen such mesmerizing ball possession. How ironic that it was Argentina, long renowned as a collection of brilliant individual talents, that produced this enduring homage to teamwork.

It started off harmlessly enough. Argentina's Javier Mascherano won possession deep in his own half, and from there, the ball glided from foot-to-foot with the team's playmaker, Juan Riquelme, always at the hub, slowing or speeding up the flow as he saw fit. With each pass, the Serbian defenders appeared more and more immobilized, until they finally resembled a string of orange traffic cones on a training field.

Before they knew it, the ball had nestled at the feet of Argentine striker Hernán Crespo inside the box. It was the 23rd pass of the sequence and everyone, knowing Crespo's predatory instincts, expected him to shoot. But Argentina had one remaining surprise. Instead of turning and rifling a shot on goal, Crespo dragged the ball across the box from left to right, taking two defenders with him and opening up the space behind him. Suddenly, he played a delicate back-heel into the path of the on-rushing Cambiasso. This would be the midfielder's fourth—and last—touch on the ball since the play started. Cambiasso's powerful finish lifted the Argentinian fans out of their seats and they hugged and danced for far longer than it had taken Argentina to pass the ball two dozen times the length of the field and straight into World Cup lore.

"THE WORLD CUP IS EVERY FOUR YEARS, AND SEX IS NOT"

An Alternative History of Scoring

There are few venues that can boast a higher concentration of testosterone than a convocation of some 736 soccer players from 32 different nations packed into a single country for one intense month of competition.

When asked by a French newspaper what he would be taking to the tournament in 2002, Belgian defender Eric Deflandre replied, "My soccer boots and a blow-up doll because a month without a woman will be difficult."

Monitoring carnal activity—only occasionally with women of the inflatable variety—has characterized the World Cup ever since the first one in 1930, when Uruguay's starting goalkeeper, Andrés Mazali, was dropped shortly before the opening game after he was caught sneaking out of the hotel for a "conjugal visit." (In those days, teams were cruelly sequestered for two months.)

Sixty-four years later, German coach Berti Vogts was still instituting a ban on sex, forcing the wives of goalkeeper Bodo Illgner and midfielder Stefan Effenberg to book rooms in a hotel just down the street, then spiriting their husbands away from an official team function. When Vogts learned of the scheme, he was furious, igniting a national debate during which Bianca Illgner snorted that "this rule is something out of kindergarten. The whole football world is anti-women." The German public promptly proved her point, when 67 percent of those polled by a national newspaper agreed with Vogts.

When Sven-Göran Eriksson, quite the horndog in his own right, was managing England a few years ago, he avoided personal hypocrisy by allowing his players to spend a day with their wives and girlfriends (*see WAGS sidebar, page 232*) after the team had qualified for the second round. This became known in the English tabloids as a "nookie pass."

Brazil, which plays the sexiest soccer in the world, struggles with the conjugal conundrum more than any other country. Coach Mario Zagallo issued a sex ban in 1998 and the team finished runner-up. Four years later, coach Luiz "Big Phil" Scolari banned women entirely from his team's training camp, claiming that "players who cannot control

themselves when it comes to sex are not human. They are irrational beasts." Some players balked. "We all have active sex lives," said Brazilian forward Edílson, "and it's clear that fifty days without sex will not be easy." However, the team's superstar, Ronaldo, showed more self-restraint. "It's not that sex isn't good," he explained, "but the World Cup is every four years, and sex is not."

Scolari's abstinence tactics paid off as Brazil won the World Cup, but his successor, Carlos Alberto Parreira, took a different position: "I don't think that sex one day before the game will have any harm on the player," he announced. "Just sex, no problem. The problem is, they don't eat, they don't sleep, they smoke and they drink. That is the problem. Sex? No, sex is always very good—always welcome." It's impossible to prove any cause and effect, but at the 2006 World Cup Brazil was knocked out in the quarterfinals by France. Much of the blame for the loss fell on the libido of their latest demigod, Ronaldinho, who was outed by his then-girlfriend for their late-night romps.

In the World Cup's early days, the sex police weren't so busy. The sport's history is littered with tales of philandering that didn't interfere with performance on the field. The great Italian striker of the 1930s, Giuseppe Meazza, (*see Cult Figures, page 15*) was known to go straight from the local brothel to a game, and Garrincha, Brazil's bowlegged hero of the '50s and '60s, spent just as much time fathering illegitimate children with multiple consorts as he did destroying opponents from the wing and winning World Cup MVP honors in 1962.

But the game has changed dramatically since the louche days of the '60s and '70s. In the modern era, with millions of dollars spent on keeping players at peak levels of fitness, the only happy endings coaches care about are on the field. Still, it would be wise to heed the warning of Cameroon coach Valeri Nepomniachi who, in announcing that he was giving his squad a day off with their wives before its 1990 quarterfinal match with England, reasoned, "If a man is in discomfort for long it can affect his work."

PORTUGAL 1, HOLLAND 0
Round of 16

The official slogan of the 2006 World Cup was "A Time to Make Friends," but when the Dutch and Portuguese squared off in both teams' first lose-and-you're-out match of the tournament, they re-tooled it to read, "A Time to Maim Friends."

By the knockout round of the 2006 World Cup, teams had been through almost two years of qualifying matches, untold hours of mental and physical preparation, and three nerve-shredding group-stage games. As the best 16 teams in the world moved into the single elimination round, each player knew that his team was a mere four wins from soccer immortality. While it's not unusual for play to turn physical at this stage of the tournament, it was shocking that one of the most violent Cup games in the last several decades would be played by two proud masters of artful soccer.

The ringmaster in this cage match, referee Valentin Ivanov, flashed 16 yellow cards and four red ones, the most ever seen in a World Cup game. As with the "Malice at the Palace" rumble between the Detroit Pistons and Indiana Pacers in 2004, this game richly earned its own, albeit not quite as catchy, nickname: The Battle of Nuremberg.

The mayhem began within 95 seconds of kickoff, with hard-charging Dutch midfielder Mark van Bommel getting a yellow card for a studs-up tackle on Cristiano Ronaldo. Not to be outdone by his teammate, Dutch defender Khalid "The Butcher" Boulahrouz then launched his cleats into Ronaldo's thigh, prompting the Portuguese star to limp off after just

half an hour. Ronaldo later described the tackle as "clearly an intentional foul to get me injured." The Portugese were not amused, and the rest of the game played out like kickboxing on grass.

In the second half, the brooding Portuguese captain Luís Figo would leave his imprint on the game—and on van Bommel's forehead. Squaring up to the Dutch midfielder in the 60th minute, Figo gave him the Portuguese version of the Glasgow kiss. Figo, being Figo, didn't have much force behind his effort but this did not prevent van Bommel from collapsing in a heap. The Dutch demanded that Ivanov eject Figo for the perceived head butt, but Portugal coach Luiz Felipe Scolari vociferously defended his star, who was shown only a yellow card.

"Jesus Christ may be able to turn the other cheek," bellowed Big Phil, "But Luis Figo isn't Jesus Christ."

Figo, however, was the closest thing that Portugal had to a savior—a swarthy, handsome icon who ignited a holy war between Spain's top two clubs when he moved in 2000 from Barcelona to Real Madrid for a then-record transfer fee of $62 million. So bitter was the feud that when Figo returned to Barca's stadium in 2002 as one of Real's so-called *galacticos,* the fans showered him with whiskey bottles, cell phones, golf balls, and, most famously, a pig's head.

But Figo was 33 now, and while his guile and dribbling skills were still to be feared, he was no longer the game-changer he was as World Player of

the Year in 2001. He had also become increasingly petulant with age and it was only a matter of time before he combusted. When Boulahrouz swung an arm in his direction, Figo clutched his face, presumably so no one could see him laughing, and sank to the turf. Ivanov promptly gave Boulahrouz a second yellow and sent him off.

Because a soccer game occasionally broke out amidst the smackdowns, Portugal had taken a 1–0 lead in the 23rd minute on a rapier strike from Maniche, and the Dutch, desperate to equalize any way they could, flopped to the ground like fish on the deck of a trawler.

"You would expect some dirty tricks from the Portuguese," the card-happy Ivanov said afterward. "They are known for time-wasting or hitting from behind. But I was unpleasantly surprised to see such things from the Dutch. What's more, the Dutch were the instigators."

For the soccer purist, this match was an embarrassment, a blot on the reputation of the game. While the World Cup's governing body, FIFA, has since installed plenty of rules designed to curb both violent conduct and excessive diving, for those who like a little bloodlust with their sport, this was a highly entertaining spectacle and a vivid reminder of the days when men were men and the ball was just something that got in the way of kicking your opponent.

Cavalcade of cards: Referee Valentin Ivanov dispensed 16 yellows and 4 reds in Portugal and Holland's orgy of outrageous behavior.

England's better halves in formation during extra time in Baden-Baden.

THE WAGS THAT TAIL THE DOGS

WAGS n. 1. acronym for Wives And GirlfriendS of players on English national team. 2. latest excuse for England's underachieving performance at World Cups

Not every team blows the World Cup championship because of too much shopping, champagne-swilling, and table-dancing, but if you believe the English tabloids, that's what happenned to England's national team in 2006. When the players' wives and girlfriends descended on Baden-Baden in their Prada heels, skin-tight jeans, and fake tans, all paparazzi hell broke loose in the German spa town, distracting the team from their inevitable march to failure.

"We became a bit of a circus in terms of the whole WAGS situation," said defender Rio Ferdinand. "Football almost became a secondary element to the main event."

Inspired by their spiritual leader, Victoria (Posh Spice) Beckham, these designer hooligans drank, shopped, and partied with a ferocity unmatched by their men on the field. Forget about *winning* the Golden Shoe—these women only wanted to know if it came in their size. And if it was real gold.

Laying siege to the town's boutiques, five of the WAGS reportedly spent $75,000 dollars in less than an hour. They later celebrated their spree by knocking back $3,000 worth of champagne and engaging in a drunken sing-along till 4 A.M. at one of Baden-Baden's tony nightclubs. When a group of German men began chanting that Germany would win the World Cup, Frank Lampard's then-model girlfriend Elen Rives waggishly retorted, "F*** off and leave us alone."

The Germans sheepishly retreated, which is more than can be said for England's opponents. After the Three Lions were eliminated in the quarterfinals, then-manager Sven-Göran Eriksson was pilloried for permitting the WAGS to spend so much time around their husbands and boyfriends, but new, hardline manager Fabio Capello vowed to limit conjugal visits to once a week. (Spoken like a true Italian coach—content with low scoring.)

However, by January 2010, he already had his hands full with a non-conjugal crisis, deciding to strip John Terry of his captaincy for sleeping with England teammate Wayne Bridge's girlfriend (and mother of his child), a former French lingerie model.

THE NEW NEW THING

THOSE WHOM THE GODS WOULD DESTROY THEY FIRST NAME "THE NEXT MARADONA"

Some are born great, some achieve greatness, and some have greatness thrust upon them.

Still others show prodigious early promise, are christened the new Pelé or the new Maradona, and then crumble spectacularly under the pressure. From the moment soccer's greatest legends retired, the world has been waiting for the game's messiah to come again. More often than not for a young player, being the anointed one has become the game's equivalent of the *Sports Illustrated* cover curse.

Ghana's striker Nii Lamptey is a case in point. He was hailed as the next Pelé by no less an expert than Pelé himself, an honor Lamptey justified by scooping up the Player of the Tournament award at the 1991 FIFA Under-17 World Cup, which triggered a scrum for his signature across Europe. Despite playing with verve in the Belgian and Dutch leagues, his career went into free fall after a disastrous move to England was followed by failure in the German second division, culminating in a couple of seasons in the backwaters of China and Saudi Arabia. Now in his mid-thirties, he breeds cattle on a farm outside Accra.

Sonny Pike became the definitive Next Maradona in the early 1990s when, at the age of seven, he was filmed destroying all comers on London soccer fields. The media fell in love with his soft curls and photogenic smile as his parents signed up an agent and whisked him off to train first with Chelsea, and then the esteemed Dutch youth academy at Ajax. The combined pressures of the media, club, and sponsors led to Pike's parents divorcing, followed shortly after by his own mental breakdown. After retiring from soccer, he pursued a psychology degree and toiled in the lowest semi-pro leagues of England.

The story's always pretty much the same. Only the names change. Take Ariel Ortega, the pacey Argentinian attacking midfielder who was the new new Maradona in the early '90s. He ended up matching El Diego's skills only in the carousing department. His best remembered on-field moment was the head butt he laid on Dutch goalkeeper Edwin van der Sar, for which he was sent off in the 1998 World Cup quarterfinals. He then proceeded to drink himself in and out of rehab before resuming his career back home.

Then there's the strutting Brazilian showpony Denilson, who became the next Pelé and the world's most expensive player after moving to the Spanish league in 1998 and declaring that he would wear the number 20, as he was twice as good as his legendary number 10–wearing predecessor. He too excelled at the extracurricular perks of the game more than the game itself, partying his way into the depths of the Saudi Arabian league, before washing out of MLS.

The latest name to watch out for is Jean Carlos Chera, from Campo Mourão in southern Brazil, who was proclaimed the "Next Coming of Pelé" as a nine-year-old in 2005 after his stunning highlight reel amassed over a million hits on YouTube, causing teams like Manchester United and FC Porto to salivate over his 4'6", 77-pound frame. His handlers would do well to learn the lessons of history. Only those who follow the three rules below realize their greatness, flying close to the sun yet keeping their wings intact:

1. **GIVE *YOURSELF* THE NAME:** True greats are self-appointed. French legend Michel Platini presciently signed all of his school assignments with the name "Peléatina."

2. **RETAIN A SENSE OF SELF:** Lionel Messi has inherited Maradona's number 10 shirt for the Argentinian national team, but his nickname in the Spanish press is a new creation: "Messidona," part mortal, part deity.

3. **ADD A QUALIFIER:** Add an adjective or modifier and you may dampen the expectation yet still thrive. Zico, the phenomenal Brazilian captain in the '70s and '80s, was known as "White Pelé"; Gheorghe Hagi, the stocky Romanian legend, was the "Maradona of the Carpathians"; Saudi star Saeed Al-Owairan ran through the entire Belgian team to score in the 1994 World Cup and was dubbed the "Maradona of the Desert"; Joe Cole, the feisty Chelsea and England star, plays up his London bona fides as the "Maradona of the East End"; and our favorite, Gary Doherty, a journeyman defender from the Republic of Ireland who, thanks to his striking red hair, was ironically hailed by his own fans as "Ginger Pelé."

THE NEW WORLD SOCCER ORDER

Before 1970, the term "World Cup" was barely more descriptive than the term "World Series" for an October Classic between Kansas City and St. Louis. Almost all of the World Cup participants were from either South America or Europe, a continental disparity best illustrated by the 1958 tournament, in which four teams qualified from the United Kingdom—England, Scotland, Northern Ireland, and Wales—without a single representative from Africa, Asia, or Oceania joining them in Sweden. Aside from North Korea's tenacious, freakish 1966 performance, no team from another part of the globe cracked the fraternity, and then its stay proved fleeting. Until 1970, the vast continent of Africa had been represented only once, by Egypt, who qualified in 1934 by beating Palestine for the honor. The team took four days to sail to Italy, only to be tossed aside by the Hungarians in the first round, and left to face the long journey home.

But in 1966, 17 African teams boycotted the English World Cup to protest their exclusion from the tournament. Their entire continent lacked a single direct qualifying spot, as their champion faced the ignominy of competing against an Asian or European team in a playoff. The protest was effective, forcing FIFA to slowly open the door to a more diverse field of entrants. Yet, for the most part, their representatives, as those from Asia and Oceania, arrived and departed all too quickly, like character actors cast to add a slapstick footnote to the greater World Cup drama. Be it the Israeli squad descending from the team plane sporting sombreros for the Mexico 1970 World Cup, or a Kuwaiti sheikh taking to the field to order his team back into the locker room to protest a French goal in 1982, the story lines were mostly comic.

The nadir was perhaps the performance turned in by the Mighty Leopards of Zaire, when they became the first team to represent sub-Saharan Africa in 1974. Zaire arrived as African champions, and expectations were high. President Mobuto Sese Seko offered every member of the squad a villa, automobile, and family vacation of their choosing if they brought glory to the nation. Their appearance proceeded to become the stuff of World Cup legend, but for all the wrong reasons. The team gave up 14 goals without scoring once in their three games. The circuslike quality of their performances was best captured by defender Mwepu Ilunga's attempt to defend a dangerous Brazilian free kick in a most original—and illegal—way.

He broke from the defensive wall to blast the stationary ball downfield while the stunned Brazilians were still preparing to take their kick. The team limped out of the tournament humbled and were berated in person by President Mobuto himself upon their return. His exact words have been lost to history, but should not be too hard to imagine. After all, this was a man who went by the honorific "The Warrior Who Knows No Setback Because of His Enduring Inflexible Will and Whose Power Spreads Fire and Conquers All."

Morocco became the first African team to do more than show up, qualifying for the second round in 1986 after drawing with England and Poland and shocking Portugal along the way. Cameroon wasted no time bettering Morocco's success at the Italian World Cup in 1990. Led by their venerable 38-year-old forward Roger Milla, who had been plucked from retirement (*see Greatest Players, page 171*), the Indomitable Lions physically battered reigning champions Argentina in the opening game, finishing with nine men on the field and a shocking 1–0 victory. In the second round, they joyously powered past Colombia and earned the right to take on mighty England in the quarterfinals—a battle of big cats as the Indomitable Lions faced up to the Three Lions.

In the 1990s, African soccer was still very much an unknown quantity, and the English knew very little about their opponents before the clash. English winger Chris Waddle later confessed that their scouting reports were thin: "All we knew was they could 'play a bit.'" When Roger Milla came on as a second-half substitute with his team down a goal, he quickly orchestrated a 2–1 lead before English talisman Gary Lineker scored a clutch penalty with seven minutes to go, and repeated the feat again in extra time to allow his heavily favored team to scrape by. After the game, their legendary coach Bobby Robson channeled Yogi Berra. "We didn't underestimate them," he said, "but they were a lot better than we thought."

Cameroon's achievement signaled the emergence of a new world order, which reached its modern apotheosis in the 2002 World Cup, when Turkey and co-hosts South Korea battled their way into the semifinal, the former grinding out results, the latter willed along by the crowd and the occasional dodgy referee decision. From this point on, there was no longer such a thing as an easy game in the World Cup. The intensely organized Asian teams, effervescently courageous Australians, and the powerfully skilled West African powers of Cameroon, Nigeria, Ghana, and Senegal, made every squad feel they had been drawn in a Group of Death. The traditional power base of soccer, the established teams who had seen victory as a divine right, were left to scratch their heads and wonder just how this had come to pass. Here are the four factors that we believe leveled the field of play:

1. MORE ROOM AT THE INN: The most fundamental change has been the growth of the tournament itself. Up until the end of the 1970s the World Cup consisted of just 16 teams, half the size of the field in 2010. A single African team was welcomed in 1970. Six have qualified in 2010, including South Africa as hosts. As late as 1990, the three participants from Great Britain and Ireland trumped the two that represented the whole of Asia. In 2010, four Asian teams gained an automatic slot, and even New Zealand qualified via playoff. The expansion of the field has provided less hallowed teams with crucial regular tournament experience and the chance to become battle hardened.

2. THE SOCCER WORLD IS FLAT: Africa's greatest players of yore met the same fate as any rare colonial resource. They were quickly plundered and expatriated by European powers, never to be seen again. Eusébio was whisked from Mozambique as an 18-year-old, becoming a star on the 1966 Portugal team, many of whom were similarly born in Africa. In reality, African players had little choice since their own countries offered them few opportunities to develop their careers at the highest level. But now the game itself has gone global, and the leading club teams scour the earth to uncover great Ghanian defensive midfielders on a par with Michael Essien or Sulley Muntari, Ivorian strikers with the finishing skills of Didier Drogba or Bakari Koné, or Australian midfielders with the grit of Tim Cahill. Over 2,000 Africans now sharpen their skills in Europe. At the 2006 African Cup, over 70 percent of the talent on display played abroad. Similarly, all but two of Australia's squad of 30 who qualified for 2010 played outside of their domestic A-League. The Asian soccer diaspora is also emerging, as club powers such as Manchester United have discovered a lucrative link between employing Korean players like Ji-Sung Park and the deluge of replica shirt sales that his appearances trigger across the Far East.

The net effect has been that every nation is now able to summon a core of players whose games have been polished at the highest level of European club coaching and competition. This transition has not come without a downside, particularly for the African teams. After experiencing European professionalism and discipline, the players have trouble readjusting to the comparative disorder of the traditional African setups, with their low-security training sessions and unfettered press access. Togo's Manchester City

 In the 1990s, African soccer was an unknown quantity. Now over 2,000 Africans sharpen their skills in Europe.

striker, Emmanuel Adebayor, has had an unstable relationship with his national team, at times wearing the captain's armband, at others storming out of training camp and vowing never to represent the Sparrow Hawks again.

3. GREED IS GOOD: A national team's performance on the pitch can be influenced by many intangibles, but one of the most important and least understood is the economic climate. A rule of thumb over the long term: As a country's economy performs, so goes their soccer team. The more flush the economy, the more money directly invested in the soccer infrastructure. Witness the connection between the rise of the J. League in Japan or the A-League in Australia and the success of their national teams, then compare it to the frustration of former AC Milan star and FIFA World Player of the Year George Weah (*see Greats Who Never Made It to the Cup, page 209*), who was forced to personally fund the costs of Liberia's road games. Despite his dutiful generosity and peerless skills, the team never qualified.

Increased prosperity has other side effects. Dutch-born coach Guus Hiddink attributed his South Korean team's success in 2002 to the growth of the economy. Prosperity translated into healthier diets and improved body shapes and conditioning. In the 1930s, the average Korean male was only 5'4"; by the 1990s, he had grown four inches, and Hiddink could select his squad from a stronger, more physical, better-nourished population.

4. MAKING ORDER OUT OF CHAOS: Sometimes the reasons for a nation's defeat are not too hard to fathom. Senegal was eliminated from the 1994 World Cup because they simply forgot to enter it. Cameroon did qualify that year, but they seemed preoccupied with the mysterious disappearance of their bonus payments, along with the official who

had been delegated to administer them after their stellar 1990 showing. They were quickly eliminated in the opening round after giving up six goals to a mediocre Russian side. Australian soccer players in the 1970s historically saved some of their finest performances for the bar after the game, and many of their African counterparts were less interested in basics like strategy or tactics than the quality

The Socceroos of Australia take a bow.

of the juju or black magic surrounding their team. *African Soccer* magazine ran an exposé on the national teams dedicated to this aspect of the game, noting that "going off for a major tournament without consulting or taking a witch doctor is like sitting an exam without a pen."

Perhaps the signature improvement in the global game has been the professionalization of national team infrastructures, usually achieved by hiring a European coach who possesses sufficient confidence to change the culture surrounding the squad. The coaches typically introduce tactical nuance, replacing a reliance on silky skills with systems and organization. Off the pitch, they have enforced strict physical regimens, nutritional diets, and the kind of professional support infrastructure long taken for

granted by top European teams. Just as a foreign coach was at the helm of each of the six African teams to have emerged from the opening round, it took a European to transform Australia's fortunes. The Socceroos squad, which qualified in 1974, was all-amateur, a reflection of the game's lowly status in the country at that time. Even Johnny Warren, one of the country's greatest players and broadcasters, admitted that the game was enjoyed only by "Sheilas, Wogs, and Poofters." But once Dutch coach Guus Hiddink moved from South Korea to the Socceroos, he helped create a cohesive, tactically confident team that captured the popular imagination across the country. A crowd of 95,000 cheered them to victory in Melbourne on the eve of the 2006 tournament, where they charged into the second round before losing on a controversial last kick penalty against eventual winners Italy.

In South Africa, Hiddink would be absent after failing to lead the Russians into the tournament, then leaving the team, but a slew of European coaches will police other nation's squads. The Dutch and Italians in particular will supply the tournament with almost as many coaches as they will players. But the foreign coach's lot remains a tough one. Lose and they are fired. But if blame is rampant, credit can be elusive; as Frenchman Bruno Metsu discovered after taking Senegal to the quarterfinals in 2002, fans were quick to attribute his achievement to the witch doctor selected to accompany the team.

The rise of minor teams in the World Cup has been a slow march. It took 60 years for an African team to make the quarterfinals and 80 for an African nation to host a World Cup. Come July 11, 2010, do not be surprised to see one of these nations complete this journey and break the final barrier by etching a new name on the base of the trophy.

 Perhaps the signature improvement in the global game has been the professionalization of national team infrastructures.

FRANCESCO TOTTI, ITALY

Francesco Totti walks into a bar.
"What did you do on your vacation?"
the bartender asks.
"I went waterskiing," he responds.
"Was it good?"
"No!" Totti says, "I couldn't find a
downhill lake."

That was just one of hundreds of jokes that the Italian media have made about their country's most illustrious soccer player of the last decade, mocking him for his heavy Roman accent, his dopey slang, and for having the brainpower of Jessica Simpson. But as far as Totti is concerned, bring on the ridicule.

In 2003, he collected all the punch lines about himself, published them in a book entitled *All the Totti Jokes,* sold 600,000 copies, and donated most of the proceeds to UNICEF, for whom he's an ambassador. Who's laughing now?

Shy and awkward in interviews, Totti has never had any trouble expressing himself with the ball at his feet. Voted Italy's Best Player five times since 2000, he operated as the *trequartista* for both club (Roma) and country, a kind of point guard equally adept at creating goals for his teammates or himself. For a midfielder, he had a phenomenal strike rate, winning Italy's Golden Boot in 2007 with 26 goals.

But the best part of Totti is that he loves being Totti. When he was caught expectorating on a Danish player in Euro 2004, he hired the lawyer who successfully defended three-time prime minister (and former Mafioso suspect) Giulio Andreotti. Totti's excuse? The Danes put extra cameras on him and goaded him into his response. This early attempt at the "Zidane defense" didn't impress FIFA, which hit him with a three-match ban, or one game for every loogie. His life off the field, though, continued to rivet the Italian public. His marriage to a former showgirl was shown live on TV for over four hours, and when she became pregnant, he celebrated a goal by stuffing a ball under his shirt and laying on his back while his teammates "delivered" the baby.

His showmanship, however, backfired in 2002, when Italy crashed out against co-host South Korea and Totti was pilloried by the Italian press for a controversial dive in the Korean penalty area that left the Azzurri with only 10 men on the field. He continued to dominate domestic soccer in the run-up to the 2006 tournament, but suffered a horrific broken leg four months before the Cup. His national coach, Marcello Lippi, was devastated; when asked whom he would pick in Totti's spot, he replied, "I'll wait for him as long as possible because he's the one player for whom we have no replacement." Living up to the tattoo of a gladiator on his arm, Totti played in all seven of the eventual World Cup winner's matches despite having a metal plate in his ankle. He even scored Italy's only goal in a dramatic win over Australia. While he was clearly lacking in match fitness and found himself overshadowed by others on the team, there was little doubt among his adoring fans that his presence enabled the Azzurri to win the title. A year after lifting the trophy, the oft-injured 30-year-old announced his retirement from the national team, but no one was surprised when he declared in early 2010, if healthy and invited, he would return to play in South Africa.

And this despite Totti's tragic news, that his library burned down. Both books were destroyed. Even worse, Totti hadn't finished coloring in the second one.

Welcome to the next 80 years of the World Cup.

WORLD CUP FACTS AND FIGURES

WINNING, LOSING, AND JUST SHOWING UP

ALL-TIME STANDINGS (Top 10)

Team	GP	W	L	T
Brazil*	92	64	14	14
Germany	92	55	18	19
Italy	77	44	14	19
Argentina	65	33	19	13
England	55	25	13	17
France	51	25	16	10
Spain	49	22	15	12
USSR/Russia	37	17	14	6
Sweden	46	16	17	13
Netherlands	36	16	10	10
Serbia**	40	16	16	8

*Brazil is the only nation to participate in every World Cup.
**Serbia's numbers include tournaments as Yugoslavia and Serbia & Montenegro.

TEAMS WITH MOST WORLD CUP APPEARANCES

1. Brazil	19
2. Italy	17
West Germany/Germany	17
3. Argentina	15
4. Mexico	14
5. Spain	13
England	13
France	13

TEAMS WITH MOST WORLD CUP CHAMPIONSHIPS

1. Brazil	5
2. Italy	4
3. West Germany/Germany	3
4. Argentina	2
Uruguay	2
5. England	1
France	1

PLAYERS WITH MOST WORLD CUP APPEARANCES, GAMES

1. Lothar Mätthaus, Germany	25
2. Paolo Maldini, Italy	23
3. Diego Maradona, Argentina	21
Wladislaw Zmuda, Poland	21
Uwe Seeler, West Germany	21

PLAYER WITH MOST WORLD CUP CHAMPIONSHIPS

1. Pelé, Brazil   3 (1958, 1962*, 1970)
2. 20 players with 2

*Pelé missed the final through injury, retroactively awarded a medal by FIFA in 2007 along with 122 other players who suffered similar fates between 1930 and 1974. World Cup winners' medals for all squad members were introduced only in 1978.

MANAGERS WITH MOST WORLD CUP GAMES

25	Helmut Schön (Germany): West Germany, 1966–1978
20	Mario Zagallo (Brazil): Brazil, 1970–1998
	Bora Milutinovic (Yugoslavia): Mexico, Costa Rica, USA, Nigeria, China, 1986–2002
	Carlos Alberto Parreira (Brazil): Kuwait, UAE, Brazil, Saudi Arabia, 1982–2006
18	Sepp Herberger (Germany): Germany, West Germany, 1938–1962
	Guus Hiddink (Netherlands): Netherlands, South Korea, Australia, 1998–2006
	Enzo Bearzot (Italy): Italy, 1978–1986

MOST GAMES LOST BY A WORLD CUP WINNER, TOURNAMENT

1   Argentina, 1978; West Germany, 1954; West Germany, 1974

NOTE: Italy, 1982, is the only team to win the World Cup despite not winning a match in the group stage

MANAGER WITH MOST WORLD CUP CHAMPIONSHIPS

2   Vittorio Pozzo (Italy): Italy, 1934, 1938

WORLD CUP CHAMPIONSHIPS AS PLAYER AND MANAGER

Mario Zagallo, Brazil (1958, 1962 as player; 1970 as manager)
Franz Beckenbauer, West Germany (1974 as player and captain; 1990 as manager)

MOST CONSECUTIVE WINS, TEAM, ALL-TIME

Brazil   11 (2002–2006)

MOST CONSECUTIVE LOSSES, TEAM, ALL-TIME

Mexico   9 (1930 and 1950–1958)

LONGEST STREAK WITHOUT A LOSS, TEAM, ALL-TIME
Brazil   13 (W 11, D 2, 1958–1966)

LONGEST STREAK WITHOUT A WIN, TEAM, ALL-TIME
Bulgaria   17 (1962–1974, 1986, 1994)

**HIGHEST AVERAGE PER-GAME ATTENDANCE BY TOUR-
NAMENT, ALL-TIME**
1. U.S.A., 1994   68,991
2. Germany, 2006 52,491
3. England, 1966   51,093
4. Mexico, 1970   50,124
5. Italy, 1990   48,391

HIGHEST SINGLE-GAME ATTENDANCE, ALL-TIME
1. **174,000:** Uruguay 2, Brazil 1
(Estadio do Maracanã, Rio de Janeiro, 1950)
2. **153,000:** Brazil 6, Spain 1
(Estadio do Maracanã, Rio de Janeiro, 1950)
3. **142,000:** Brazil 2, Yugoslavia 0
(Estadio do Maracanã, Rio de Janeiro, 1950)
4. **139,000:** Brazil 7, Sweden 1
(Estadio do Maracanã, Rio de Janeiro, 1950)
5. **114,600:** Mexico 1, Paraguay 1
(Azteca, Mexico City, 1986)
   114,600: Argentina 3, West Germany 2
(Azteca, Mexico City, 1986)

LOWEST SINGLE-GAME ATTENDANCE, ALL-TIME
1. **300:** Romania 3, Peru 1 (Pocitos, Montevideo, 1930)
2. **500:** Chile 3, Mexico 0 (Parque Central, Montevideo, 1930)
3. **800:** Yugoslavia 4, Bolivia 0 (Parque Central, Montevideo, 1930)
   800: U.S.A. 3, Paraguay 0 (Parque Central, Montevideo, 1930)
5. **900:** Paraguay 1, Belgium 0 (Centenario, Montevideo, 1930)

TOTAL TELEVISION VIEWING AUDIENCES OF LAST SIX WORLD CUPS
1986, Mexico: 13,506,689,000
1990, Italy: 26,692,759,000
1994, United States: 32,115,652,000
1998, France: 24,770,446,000
2002, South Korea/Japan: 28,843,581,000
2006, Germany: 26,288,753,000

SCORING

HIGHEST-SCORING TEAMS, ALL-TIME

1. Brazil	201 (92 GAMES)
2. West Germany/Germany	190 (92)
3. Italy	122 (77)
4. Argentina	113 (65)
5. France	95 (51)

HIGHEST-SCORING PLAYERS, ALL-TIME

1. Ronaldo, Brazil	15 (19 GAMES, 1998–2006)
2. Gerd Müller, West Germany	14 (13, 1970–74)
3. Just Fontaine, France	13 (6, 1958)
4. Pelé, Brazil	12 (13, 1958–70)
5. Sándor Kocsis, Hungary	11 (5, 1954)
Jürgen Klinsmann, West Germany	11 (17, 1990–98)

HIGHEST GOALS-PER-GAME AVERAGE, TEAM, ALL-TIME

(Minimum 25 games played)

1. Hungary	2.72 (87 GOALS IN 32 GAMES)
2. Brazil	2.18 (201/92)
3. West Germany/Germany	2.07 (190/92)
4. France	1.86 (95/51)
5. Argentina	1.74 (113/65)

LOWEST GOALS-PER-GAME AVERAGE, TEAM, ALL-TIME

(Minimum 25 games played)

1. Bulgaria	0.85 (22 GOALS IN 26 GAMES)
2. Mexico	1.07 (48/45)
3. U.S.A.	1.08 (27/25)
4. Chile	1.24 (31/25)
5. Belgium	1.28 (46/30)

MOST GOALS SCORED IN A SINGLE GAME, TEAM, ALL-TIME

1. Hungary (1982 vs. El Salvador)	10
2. Hungary (1954 vs. South Korea)	9
Yugoslavia (1974 vs. Zaire)	9
4. Sweden (1938 vs. Cuba)	8
Uruguay (1950 vs. Bolivia)	8
Hungary (1954 vs. West Germany)	8
Germany (2002 vs. Saudi Arabia)	8

MOST GOALS SCORED IN ONE GAME, ALL-TIME

1. Austria 7, Switzerland 5 (1954)	12
2. Brazil 6, Poland 5 (1938)	11
Hungary 8, West Germany 3 (1954)	11
Hungary 10, El Salvador 1 (1982)	11
5. France 7, Paraguay 3 (1958)	10

MOST GOALS SCORED IN A SINGLE TOURNAMENT, TEAM, ALL-TIME

1. Hungary, 1954	27 (5 GAMES)
2. West Germany, 1954	25 (6)
3. France, 1958	23 (6)
4. Brazil, 1950	22 (6)
5. Brazil, 1970	19 (6)

HIGHEST GOALS-PER-GAME AVERAGE, TOURNAMENT, ALL-TIME

1. Switzerland, 1954	5.4 GOALS PER GAME (140 GOALS IN 26 GAMES)
2. France, 1938	4.7 GOALS PER GAME (84/18)
3. Italy, 1934	4.1 GOALS PER GAME (70/17)
4. Brazil, 1950	4.0 GOALS PER GAME (88/22)
5. Uruguay, 1930	3.9 GOALS PER GAME (70/18)

LOWEST GOALS-PER-GAME AVERAGE, TOURNAMENT, ALL-TIME

1. Italy, 1990	2.2 GOALS PER GAME (115 GOALS IN 52 GAMES)
2. Germany, 2006	2.3 GOALS PER GAME (147/64)
3. South Korea/Japan, 2002	2.52 GOALS PER GAME (161/64)
4. Mexico, 1986	2.54 GOALS PER GAME (132/52)
5. Germany, 1974	2.6 GOALS PER GAME (97/38)

MOST GOALS SCORED IN A SINGLE GAME, PLAYER, ALL-TIME

1. Oleg Salenko, Russia (1994 vs. Cameroon)	5
2. Emilio Butragueno, Spain (1986 vs. Denmark)	4
Eusébio, Brazil (1966 vs. North Korea)	4
Just Fontaine, France (1958 vs. West Germany)	4
Sandor Kocsis, Hungary (1954 vs. West Germany)	4
Ademir, Brazil (1950 vs. Sweden)	4
Ernest Wilimowski, Poland (1938 vs. Brazil)	4

MOST GOALS ALLOWED, TEAM, ALL-TIME

1. West Germany/Germany	114 (92 GAMES)
2. Brazil	85 (92)
3. Mexico	82 (45)
4. Argentina	73 (65)
Italy	73 (77)
5. Sweden	69 (46)

MOST GOALS ALLOWED, PLAYER, ALL-TIME

Single Match: Luis Guevara Mora, El Salvador	10 (VS. HUNGARY, 1982)
Tournament: Hong Duk-Yung, South Korea	16 (2 GAMES, 1954)
All-Time: Antonio Carbajal, Mexico	25 (10 GAMES, 1950–62)
Mohammed Al-Deayea, Saudi Arabia	25 (10 GAMES, 1994–2002)

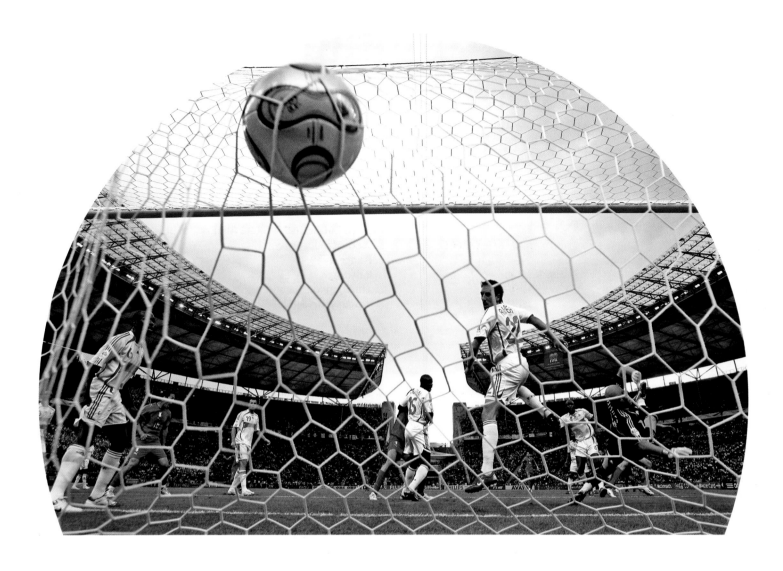

MOST CONSECUTIVE MINUTES BY A KEEPER WITHOUT ALLOWING A GOAL, ALL-TIME

Walter Zenga, Italy 1990	518

FASTEST GOAL, ALL-TIME

Hakan Sukur, Turkey (2002 vs. South Korea)	11 SECONDS

FASTEST GOAL BY A SUBSTITUTE, ALL-TIME

Ebbe Sand, Denmark (1998 vs. Nigeria)	16 SECONDS

PENALTY SHOOT-OUT RECORDS, TEAM, ALL-TIME

West Germany/Germany	4–0
Ukraine	1–0
South Korea	1–0
Bulgaria	1–0
Portugal	1–0
Belgium	1–0
Sweden	1–0
Argentina	3–1
Brazil	2–1
France	2–2
Ireland	1–1
Spain	1–2
Italy	1–3
Netherlands	0–1
Switzerland	0–1
Yugoslavia	0–1
Romania	0–2
Mexico	0–2
England	0–3

DISCIPLINE

MOST PENALIZED TEAMS, ALL-TIME

Team	Games	Yellow Cards	2nd Yellow	Red Cards
Argentina	65	93	0	10
Germany	92	91	1	6
Italy	77	79	1	7
Brazil	92	74	0	9
Netherlands	36	55	3	6
Mexico	45	49	2	6

MOST PENALIZED PLAYERS, ALL-TIME

Player	Games	Yellow Cards	Red Cards
Zinedine Zidane, France	12	4	2
Cafu, Brazil	20	6	—
Rigobert Song, Cameroon	8	3	2
Diego Maradona, Argentina	21	4	1
Lothar Mätthaus, Germany	25	5	—

WORLD CUPS WITH MOST RED CARDS*

1. Germany, 2006 — 28
2. France, 1998 — 22
3. South Korea/Japan, 2002 — 17
4. Italy, 1990 — 16
5. U.S.A., 1994 — 15

*NOTE: Cards have been in use only since 1970, and the tournament expanded to 32 teams in 1998.

TEAMS WITH MOST CARDS
Single Match
Portugal (vs. Netherlands, 2006): **16***

Single World Cup
Argentina (1990): **24****

All-Time
Argentina: **93**

*4 of which were second yellow cards, resulting in red cards.
**21 Yellow, 3 Red in 7 games.

MOST RED CARDS BY ONE REFEREE
Arturo Brizio Carter, Mexico: 7 in 6 games (1994 and 1998)

NOTE: Total includes, in his last World Cup game in 1998—Holland vs. Argentina—sending off two players with second yellow cards, as opposed to straight red cards.

FASTEST RED CARD, ALL-TIME
Jose Alberto Batista, Uruguay (vs. Scotland, 1986): **56 seconds**

NOTE: Claudio Caniggia of Argentina was sent off for swearing at the referee while still on the bench, without ever entering the game (vs. Sweden, 2002).

FIRST PLAYER EVER SENT OFF/DISMISSED
Mario De Las Casas, Peru (vs. Romania, 1930)

FIRST GOALKEEPER EVER SENT OFF/DISMISSED
Gianluca Pagliuca, Italy (vs. Norway, 1994)

SHORTEST WORLD CUP CAREER, ALL-TIME
Khemais Labidi, Tunisia (vs. Mexico, 1978): **2 minutes**
Marcelo Trobbiani, Argentina (vs. West Germany, 1986): **2 minutes**

FASTEST SUBSTITUTION, ALL-TIME
Alessandro Nesta, Italy (replaced by Giuseppe Bergomi vs. Austria, 1998): **4th minute**
Michael Owen, England (replaced by Peter Crouch vs. Sweden, 2006): **4th minute**
Bryan Robson, England (replaced by Steve Hodge vs. Morocco, 1986): **4th minute**

PLAYERS WHO HAVE APPEARED AT WORLD CUPS FOR MORE THAN ONE COUNTRY
Luis Monti (Argentina in 1930, Italy in 1934)
Ferenc Puskás (Hungary in 1954, Spain in 1962)
José Santamaria (Uruguay in 1954, Spain in 1962)
Mazzola* (Brazil in 1958, Italy in 1962*)
Robert Prosinecki (Yugoslavia in 1990, Croatia in 1998 and 2002)
Robert Jarni (Yugoslavia in 1990, Croatia in 1998 and 2002)

*Played in 1962 under his real name, José Altafini.

MANAGERS WHO HAVE TAKEN THE MOST NATIONS TO THE WORLD CUP
Bora Milutinovic: 5 (Mexico 1986, Costa Rica 1990, U.S.A. 1994, Nigeria 1998, China 2002)
Carlos Alberto Parreira: 5 (Kuwait 1982, United Arab Emirates 1990, Brazil 1994, Saudi Arabia 1998, Brazil again 2006, South Africa 2010)

YOUNGEST STARTING LINEUP, ALL-TIME
Yugoslavia (vs. Brazil, 1930): average age of players 21 years, 258 days

OLDEST STARTING LINEUP, ALL-TIME
Germany (vs. Iran, 1998): average age of players 31 years, 345 days

OLDEST PLAYERS TO PLAY AT A WORLD CUP

1. Roger Milla, Cameroon (vs. Russia, 1994):	42 years, 39 days
2. Pat Jennings, N. Ireland (vs. Brazil, 1986):	41 years, 0 days
3. Peter Shilton, England (vs. Italy, 1990):	40 years, 292 days
4. Lev Yashin, USSR (vs. Portugal, 1970):	40 years, 279 days
5. Dino Zoff, Italy (vs. West Germany, 1982):	40 years, 133 days

YOUNGEST PLAYERS TO PLAY AT A WORLD CUP

1. Norman Whiteside, Northern Ireland (vs. Yugoslavia, 1982):	17 years, 41 days
2. Samuel Eto'o, Cameroon (vs. Italy, 1998):	17 years, 99 days
3. Femi Opabunmi, Nigeria (vs. England, 2002):	17 years, 101 days
4. Salomon Olembe, Cameroon (vs. Austria, 1998):	17 years, 185 days
5. Pelé, Brazil (vs. USSR, 1958):	17 years, 235 days

SELECTED BIBLIOGRAPHY

WEBSITES

The Guardian (www.guardian.co.uk)
The Daily Telegraph (www.telegraph.co.uk)
The Daily Mail (www.dailymail.co.uk)
The Times of London (www.timesonline.co.uk)
Midfield Dynamo (www.midfielddynamo.com)
The official FIFA website (www.fifa.com)
Planet World Cup (www.planetworldcup.com)
BBC (www.bbc.co.uk)
Unprofessional Foul (www.unprofessionalfoul.com)
Soccernet (www.soccernet.com)

PERIODICALS

Four Four Two
When Saturday Comes
World Soccer
Soccer America

BOOKS

ABOUT THE WORLD CUP

Davies, Pete. *Twenty-Two Foreigners in Funny Shorts*. New York: Random House, 1994.

Douglas, Geoffrey. *The Game of Their Lives: The Untold Story of the World Cup's Greatest Upset*. It Books, 2005.

Freddi, Cris. *Complete Story of the World Cup 2006*. London: HarperSport, 2006.

Gardner, Paul. *The Simplest Game: The Intelligent Fan's Guide to the World Cup of Soccer*. New York: MacMillan, 1996.

Glanville, Brian. *The Story of the World Cup*. London: Faber & Faber, 1997.

Motson, John. *Motson's World Cup Extravaganza*. London: Anova Books, 2006.

Parnham, Tim and Haines, Steve. *22 Men and a Bag of Wind: The Ultimate History of the World Cup*. London: DSM, 2002.

Seddon, Peter. *The World Cup's Strangest Moments*. London: Robson Books, 2005.

Trecker, Jamie. *Love & Blood: At the World Cup with the Footballers, Fans, and Freaks*. Orlando: Harcourt, 2007.

Weiland, Matt and Wilsey, Sean, eds. *The Thinking Fan's Guide to the World Cup*. New York: Harper Perennial, 2006.

ABOUT SOCCER

Agnew, Paddy. *Forza Italia: The Fall and Rise of Italian Football*. London: Ebury Press, 2007.

Anthony, Andrew. *On Penalties*. London: Yellow Jersey Press, 2000.

Armstrong, Gary and Giulianotti, Richard, eds. *Football in Africa: Conflict, Conciliation and Community*. Basingstoke: Palgrave Macmillan, 2004.

Ball, Phil. *Morbo: The Story of Spanish Football*. London: WSC Books, 2003.

Bellos, Alex. *Futebol: A Brazilian Way of Life*. London: Bloomsbury, 2003.

Bennetts, Marc. *Football Dynamo: Modern Russia and the People's Game*. London: Virgin Books, 2009.

Bremner, Jack. *Shit Ground No Fans*. New York: Bantam Press, 2004.

Cohen, George. *My Autobiography*. London: Headline Book Publishing, 2005.

Davies, Hunter. *Boots Balls and Haircuts*. London: Cassell Illustrated, 2004.

Davies, Hunter. *The Second Half*. London: Pomona, 2006.

Downing, David. *England v. Germany: The Best of Enemies*. London: Bloomsbury, 2001.

Foer, Franklin. *How Soccer Explains the World: An Unlikely Theory of Globalization*. New York: Harper Perennial, 2005.

Foot, John. *Calcio: A History of Italian Football*. London: Harper Perennial, 2007.

Galeano, Eduardo. *Soccer in Sun and Shadow*. London: Verso Books, 2007.

Gardner, Paul. *The Simplest Game: The Intelligent Fan's Guide to the World of Soccer*. New York: Macmillan, 1996.

Glanville, Brian. *England Managers: The Toughest Job in Football*. London: Headline Book Publishing, 2008.

Goldblatt, David. *The Ball Is Round: A Global History of Soccer*. New York: Riverhead Books, 2008.

Hare, Geoff. *Football in France: A Cultural History*. Oxford: Berg Publishers, 2003.

Hawkey, Ian. *Feet of the Chameleon: The Story of Football in Africa*. London: Anova Books, 2009.

Herd, Mike, ed. *The 'Guardian' Book of Football: 50 Years of Classic Writing*. London: Guardian Books, 2008.

Hesse-Lichtenberger. *Ulrich. Tor! The Story of German Football*. London: WSC Books, 2003.

Honigstein, Raphael. *Englisher Fussball: A German View of Our Beautiful Game*. London: Random House UK, 2009.

Jennings, Andrew. *Foul! The Secret World of FIFA: Bribes, Vote Rigging and Ticket Scandals*. London: HarperSport, 2007.

Kapuscinski, Ryszard. *The Soccer War*. New York: Vintage International, 1992.

Kuper, Simon. *Soccer Against the Enemy: How the World's Most Popular Sport Starts and Fuels Revolutions and Keeps Dictators in Power*. New York: Nation Books, 2006.

Kuper, Simon and Szymanski, Stefan. *Soccernomics: Why England Loses, Why Germany and Brazil Win, and Why the U.S., Japan, Australia, Turkey—and Even Iraq—Are Destined to Become the Kings of the World's Most Popular Sport*. New York: Nation Books, 2009.

MacIntosh, Iain. *Football Fables: True Stories of Triumph and Despair from Football's Mavericks*. London: A & C Black Publishers, 2008.

Maradona, Diego. *Maradona: The Autobiography of Soccer's Greatest and Most Controversial Star*. New York: Skyhorse Publishing, 2007.

Martin, Simon. *Football and Fascism: The National Game Under Mussolini*. Oxford: Berg Publishers, 2004.

Match! magazine. Match!: *Best of the '80s*. London: Boxtree, 2008.

Mcllvanney, Hugh. *Mcllvanney on Football*. Edinburgh: Mainstream Publishing, 1999.

Mitten, Andy. *Mad for It: From Blackpool to Barcelona . . . Football's Greatest Rivalries*. London: HarperSport, 2007.

Montague, James. *When Friday Comes: Football in the War Zone*. Edinburgh: Mainstream Publishing, 2008.

Morris, Desmond. *The Soccer Tribe*. London: Jonathan Cape, 1981.

Murray, Bill. *The World's Game: A History of Soccer*. Chicago: The University of Illinois Press, 1998.

Murray, Scott and Walker, Rowan. *Day of the Match: A History of Football in 365 Days*. London: Boxtree, 2008.

Okwonga, Musa. *A Cultured Left Foot: The Eleven Elements of Footballing Greatness*. London: Duckworth Overlook, 2008.

Parkinson, Michael. *Michael Parkinson on Football*. London: Coronet Books, 2002.

Puskás, Ferenc. *Ferenc Puskás: Captain of Hungary*. London: Tempus Publishing, 2007.

Ricci, Filippo Maria. *Elephants, Lions and Eagles: A Journey Through African Football*. London: WSC Books, 2008.

Ruhn, Christov, ed. *Le Foot: The Legends of French Football*. London: Abacus, 2000.

Shaw, Phil. *The Book of Football Quotations*. London: Ebury Press, 2008.

Simons, Rowan. *Bamboo Goalposts: One Man's Quest to Teach the People's Republic of China to Love Football*. London: Macmillan, 2008.

Smit, Barbara. *Sneaker Wars: The Enemy Brothers Who Founded Adidas and Puma and the Family Feud that Forever Changed the Business of Sports*. New York: Ecco, 2008.

Snyder, John. *Soccer's Most Wanted: The Top 10 Book of Clumsy Keepers, Clever Crosses, and Outlandish Oddities*. Washington, D.C.: Potomac Books, 2001.

Unknown. *40 Years of Shite: The Unofficial History of the English Football Team Since 1966*. London: Atlantic Books, 2008.

Vialli, Gianluca and Marcotti, Gabriele. *The Italian Job: A Journey to the Heart of Two Great Footballing Cultures*. London: Transworld Publishers, 2007.

Wilson, Jonathan. *Behind the Curtain: Travels in Eastern European Football*. London: Orion Books, 2006.

Wilson, Jonathan. *Inverting the Pyramid: A History of Football Tactics*. London: Orion Books, 2008.

Winner, David. *Brilliant Orange: The Neurotic Genius of Dutch Soccer*. New York: The Overlook Press, 2008.

Winner, David. *Those Feet: A Sensual History of English Football*. London: Bloomsbury, 2005.

Acknowledgments

David Hirshey

World Cup squads are limited to 23 players but, fortunately, World Cup book acknowledgments aren't. There are so many people to thank that I just hope no one goes all Zinedine Zidane on me if I inadvertently leave them out. Let me start with the spine of my team. James Tyler may be the greatest English workhorse since Nobby Stiles ran the Germans into the ground in the '66 final—and James has all his teeth to boot. For the past 12 months, James has tirelessly researched, reported, and ransacked 80 years of World Cup history so that I could bang those through-balls into the back of the net. At the same time, my other midfield dynamo, Paul Kanarek, was marauding down the flanks to deliver perfectly weighted crosses for me to nod home—or shank wide, as the case may be. James and Paul may support crap teams (Liverpool and Chelsea, respectively), but that doesn't diminish the debt of gratitude—and beers—I owe them for saving my Arsenal ass on myriad occasions.

Special thanks also go to my old friend Michael Agovino, who helped choreograph the attack early on by providing invaluable knowledge about the more arcane aspects of the Cup—everything from the provenance of those shocking green-and-white-striped French uniforms to the dark side of Brazilian soccer. And to my long-suffering Board of Rabbis—Roger Director, Gil Schwartz, Alan Richman, Michael Solomon, Rob Fleder, Fred Schruers, and Guy Martin—who have indulged my soccer mania lo these many decades and never buckled under the barrage of e-mails and phone calls seeking their wisdom or the occasional elephant tranquilizer. Michael deserves an extra tip of the yarmulke for having to endure reading early drafts of gibberish before I hacked my way out of the thicket.

I am proud to call Paul Gardner my mentor, even if for the last two decades he has wanted to disown me for my Euro-snob view of the game. An unwavering supporter of American soccer and a fierce champion for the oft-ignored Hispanic players in particular, Paul has spent the past half century writing about the sport (his book, *The Simplest Game,* is my soccer Torah) with the touch of a poet and the acuity of a forensic scientist. It was Paul who introduced me to two of my journalistic heroes: the great Brian Glanville, who all but invented the art of writing about soccer, and Rob Hughes, whose smart, stylish prose has graced the *International Herald Tribune* for two decades and more recently, *The New York Times.*

When my father was traveling in Europe during my adolescence, he'd always bring me back a stack of newspaper clips and say, "Glanville and Hughes write like Pelé plays football." In my various guises covering the sport as a newspaper, magazine, and book writer for more than 30 years, I have been fortunate enough to have worked alongside some of the very best of the American soccerati—Jack Bell, Filip Bondy, Frank Dell'Apa, Grahame Jones, Michael Lewis, Jere Longman, Ridge Mahoney, George Vecsey, Grant Wahl, and Mike Woitalla.

From 2006–2008, I enjoyed the most fun perch in soccer commentary as a columnist for Deadspin .com, where I had total freedom to write about whatever I wanted (I'm sure I can think of at least three times over two years when the word "Arsenal" didn't appear), as long as I threw in a dick joke every two paragraphs. It's that kind of astute editorial acumen that accounted for the meteoric rise of Deadspin's founder, Will Leitch, in the blogosphere and beyond, and I, for one, am deeply grateful that he took a chance on an old-school guy like me, who still thinks Wii is something you do in the ocean. Writing for Deadspin opened up a whole new soccer universe to me and I spend far too much time wallowing in the first-rate blogs of Greg Lalas, Ives Galarcep, Jen Chang, Adam Spangler, Mike Cardillo, and all the lads at Unprofessional Foul. I look forward every day to the wonderfully incisive and entertaining coverage on the Guardian.com, which for me is the Brazil of soccer websites. In the course of my research, I hoovered up dozens of soccer books, all of which were helpful to varying degrees, but a few transcended the genre and took their place in my personal pantheon of sporting literature: Simon Kuper's *Football Against the Enemy,* Alex Bellos's *Fute-bol, The Brazilian Way of Life,* David Winner's *Brilliant Orange,* Musa Okwonga's *A Cultured Left Foot,* Franklin Foer's *How Soccer Explains the World,* and, of course, the *Official 2010 Arsenal Calendar* (did I mention I'm an Arsenal fan?).

My college coach used to bark "Stop pissing around in the penalty area, Hirshey" when I would attempt a blind back-heel where a simple square pass would suffice. Now, every Monday night I find myself shouting similar profundities to the players on HC United, eight-time champions of the Metro Co-ed Soccer League, and I'm happy to report they don't listen either, except when I say "Seven pitchers is the limit" at the bar afterward. Special thanks to co-captains Mike Signorelli, whose warrior spirit sets the tone, and Mary Choteborsky, who has been a rock of support both on and off the field. I first watched Gui Stampur play soccer in high school and such was his array of flicks and tricks, I thought he had picked up the game in the *favellas* of Brazil rather than on the Upper West Side of Manhattan. Gui went on to star at Columbia, where he played alongside a pugnacious Brit named Tommy McMenemy, who possessed the hardest shot I had ever seen this side of Roberto Carlos. The three of us later became friends and I was able to bribe them to play for HC United before they got a life.

All I know about coaching I learned from my role models—Emma Hayes, Ray Selvadurai, Wilson Egidio, Arnie Ramirez, Martin Jacobson, Ray Reid, Roby Young, Tony DiCicco, Anson Dorrance, Kevin McCarthy—and I thank them for putting up with my clueless questions over the years. There's a long list of people whose conservations with me have helped shape much of what I write about soccer so they deserve some of the credit/blame: Luke Dempsey, Karel Choteborsky, Gennaro Picone, Julie Foudy, Brandi Chastain, Ned Rosenthal, Tom Nash, David Friedman, Jeff Toobin, Mark Bryant, Aaron Spiegel, Dori Arad, Ted Howard, Sunil Gulati, Shep Messing, Clive Toye, George and Farrukh Quraishi, Ethan Zohn, Henk Spaan, Laura Burlacu, Julien Farel, Jeff Spiritos, Aaron Heifetz, Matt Weiland, Sean Wilsey, Will Kuhns, Aaron Guenther, Mike Packard, James Copland, Steve Quattrociocchi, Jack

Kogod, Robert Lewis, Dave Birnbaum, Gloria Averbuch, Roberto Abramowitz, Freddie Grgurev, Keith Miller, Ian Walker, Mal McHugh, John Kenney, Paul Kovach, Ralph Perlberger, Karim Abdul, and Arnold Zambrano. And, of course, my fellow Gooners: Andrew Arends, Tony Holden, Alan Samson (the brain trust of the legendary Crescuit Club in London), Greg Williams, Clive Priddle, Lawrie Mifflin, Brian Roth, Michael Hirschorn, Tom Dyja, Michael Bertin, and all the guys at the Arsenal end of the bar at Kinsale Tavern, my second home for the last five years. Thanks to Pauline, Shirley, Carolyn, and Frankie for keeping the bonhomie and Stella flowing even though I disapprove of them serving Spurs fans anything but cat piss.

The only reason you're reading this is that two years ago ESPN's John Skipper and Gary Hoenig approached me with the idea of writing a book about the World Cup. John is a smart and passionate soccer fan and the sport is lucky to have his creative and financial muscle (even if he has a criminally misguided love of Tottenham). Gary, meanwhile, wouldn't know a corner kick from a corner store but he's been a friend for 20 years and I've always valued his editorial wisdom—and Knicks tickets.

As an editor myself, I know what a daunting job it is to get your arms around a book with so many moving parts as this one has and I was fortunate to be working with a couple of talented mensches at ESPN Books, Richard Rosen and Steve Wulf, both of whom displayed heroic grace under fire throughout the whole quick and painful process. The entire editorial SWAT team at ESPN was a model of professionalism and I thank Jeff Bradley, Doug McIntyre, Taryn Wolf, Jim Surber, Henry Lee, John Glenn, and Gueorgui Milkov for their enterprise and forbearance. Thanks, also, to my old friend and former *Esquire* Art Director, Robert Priest, for inspiring the cover. I am grateful to Kate Lee at ICM, who represented this book with the craftiness and pit-bull tenacity of a top-notch defensive midfielder. I'd also like to thank my home team at HarperCollins, particularly Jane Friedman, Michael Morrison, and Jonathan Burnham, for allowing me to pursue this project and never

once commenting on my unshaven, bleary-eyed appearance in the office after a long night at the keyboard. Nobody sacrificed more for this book than my wife and daughter, Susan and Emily, whom I will never be able to thank enough for giving me the space and freedom to weasel out of countless weddings, bar mitzvahs, and vacations during the past two years. On one family trip to Spain, I disappeared for an entire day to watch my favorite Arsenal player, Thierry Henry, pull on his Barcelona jersey for the first time. I was one of 30,000 fans who had the same idea but I'm confident I was the only American. When I eventually returned from my hegira, Emily only half-jokingly said, "Sometimes I think you love soccer more than you love your family." "Nonsense," I responded, "I love you both the same."

If anyone could fathom that lunatic sentiment, it would be my father, who instilled in me a passion for the game from the time I was able to juggle my pacifier with both feet. I was never as good a player as my dad, who represented Switzerland in international competitions as a schoolboy, but I was every bit as devout about the sport, particularly the World Cup. I remember going to Madison Square Garden as a young boy with my father to watch the closed-circuit telecast of the 1962 final between Brazil and Czechoslovakia and crying when I found out that my idol, Pelé, wasn't playing due to injury. No matter how far our lives diverged over the intervening years, my father and I had a sacred pact to get together for soccer's High Holy Days. It didn't matter whether the games unfolded remotely on the screen or on the field in front of us, everything else—wives, children, girlfriends, work, essentially the world outside the stadium—ceased to exist during the World Cup. To this day, one of the most joyful moments of my life was conga-dancing through the streets of Madrid with my father and thousands of delirious fans after Italy crushed Germany for the title in 1982. I won't be dancing with my dad in South Africa or anywhere else during the upcoming tournament because he passed away last July as I was finishing up my sections of this book. His death blew a soccer-ball–shaped hole in my heart,

but I still have more than 40 years of World Cup memories to cherish and I know that on June 11 when that opening whistle is blown, my dad will be smiling down on the greatest show on earth.

Roger Bennett

Albert Camus once claimed, "All I know most surely about morality and the obligations of men, I owe to football." Camus experts have long since agonized as to whether he was joking or not, but for me soccer is the singular vehicle through which I have come to understand pretty well everything from human nature to global sociopolitics. As a result, the World Cup has been a dominant force in my life, creating a spine against which I have come to mark time. Some of my earliest television-watching memories revolve around the delirious spectacle of the 1978 World Cup, as stadiums exploded with confetti whenever the Argentinian team took to the field. The most captivating image from 1982 was the intense Brazilian midfielder, Falcão, maniacally celebrating a goal against Italy with the veins in his arms bulging from the screen as if in 3-D, a move I spent the next twelve months perfecting whenever I shinned in a goal on the schoolyard. Maradona's 1986 destruction of my English heroes by means foul and fair was a brutal crash course in ethics. My brother and I ran into the street to vent our grief by blasting a soccer ball straight through the window of our home. My parents, thankfully, understood our pain.

In 1990, I spent the summer as a counselor at a sleepaway camp in Maine and first encountered America's cruel indifference to the sport I loved. The day of England's semifinal matchup against West Germany was one of the most frustrating of my life. I spent an afternoon driving frantically from one sleepy rural bar to another. All were broadcasting the local minor league baseball game but not one was able to direct their massive satellite dishes toward a signal that could pull in the World Cup semifinal. In the pre-Internet age I had to wait for the next day's *Boston Globe* to discover the bitter result. Perhaps it was for the best.

Since I moved to the States in 1992, I have watched with wonder as the profile of the World Cup has ineluctably risen from tournament to tournament. When this country performed hosting duties in 1994, I viewed the majority of the games alone, courtesy of a Spanish network on an old television set in the corner of a deserted Jimmy's Woodlawn Tap in Hyde Park, Chicago, with only the barbacks for company. Between 1998 and 2002, I lived in D.C., and at that point the tournament had achieved cult status in that city. The cognoscenti had become clued-up and flocked to local Brazilian bars or Italian restaurants in Adams Morgan to digest the spectacle. I began to enjoy weekly English Premier League games with a small yet motley expat crew at Planet Fred's Bar. We would gather at 10 in the morning to feast on the likes of Southampton laboring against Leicester City as if it were Boca-River Plate. I happened to be back in D.C. for the U.S.A.-Italy game in 2006, and was shocked to see the bar was jam-packed with a line snaking around the block two hours before kickoff.

That line at the bar and the widespread sense of celebration surrounding the entire 2006 tournament gave me the idea for a book dedicated to framing the plotlines of World Cups past. The remarkable response I received when I blogged about Marcello Balboa's passionate but clumsy commentating style on Frank Foer's excellent *New Republic* World Cup 2006 website quickly cemented this notion. Executing the project triggered a wonderful return to my childhoood. My first step was to unearth the World Cup ephemera I came of age with in England: the 1978 Top Trumps cards, the 1982 Panini World Cup sticker book, and the three-volume set of *Football Handbook* that was published after the Spain tournament—the soccer equivalent of Topps baseball cards—and imagined writing a book that could enable the reader to develop the same emotional connection to the game I have had. Researching the book also neccessitated a long journey on the vast sea of exquisite football literature. To uncover story lines from the psychology of the penalty kick, the rise and fall of the Argentinian military junta, and the evolution of the game in Africa, I have immersed myself in book after book. Many of the tomes I have encountered over the past four years now feel like good friends. The works of David Winner, Simon Kuper, Chris Hill, Jonathan Wilson, and David Goldblatt have been particularly influential and can be seen all over this book. *The Guardian's Football Weekly* and *The Times's The Game* have been a podcasting feast, as has Bill Simmons's B. S. Report. (Bill, your support of the sport in this country is one of many reasons I feel as optimistic as I do about the future of American soccer.) The periodicals *Four Four Two*, *World Soccer*, and *When Saturday Comes* are all remarkable in their own way. The American writers Greg Lalas, Jen Chang, Jack Bell, Grant Wahl, the amazing Adam Spangler, and George Vecsey are all world class. On the Internet, *The Guardian*, *The Times*, Martin Samuel, The Spoiler, The Offside, and Toffeeweb have become looming presences in my life.

I want to thank all those who have let me talk their ear off over the past four years, especially fellow shareholder Jamie Glassman, Lenny Wolfman, Charlie Lander, Liverpool's Jonathan Abrams, Dana Ferine, Eli Horowitz, and assorted McSweeneys people, and Alex Goodman (the greatest insights from a *SportsCenter* sports guy) as well as Michael Cohen, Rob Stone of The Fader, the talented Etgar Keret, Eric Mourlot, Chris Isenberg and the team at No Mas, and Samuel Blumenfeld, who gave me very different perspectives when they were so desperately needed. Massive thanks to all those with whom I have watched games at Planet Fred's in D.C., and Nevada Smiths and the Kinsale Tavern in New York City, especially the gracious Pauline. Thanks as well to the Super Soccer Stars Premier Program and Coach Chip Wonderlin.

I am indebted to the dedicated Kate Lee and Larissa Silva at ICM, with whom I first discussed the idea of writing a book during the 2006 World Cup and who introduced me to my co-author David Hirshey. I have thoroughly enjoyed every conversation we have ever had at the Kinsale. Thanks to Robert Priest and Grace Lee for their creative design support. To eBay for allowing me to gather copies of every World Cup single ever released. And to the massive team at ESPN Books, especially the style of Henry Lee, the good humor and eye for detail of Jim Surber, the work of Doug McIntyre, and the unparalleled and remarkable encyclopedic knowledge of Gueorgui Milkov, as well as the organization and care of John Glenn and Steve Wulf. Some of the most enjoyable parts of the process have been the conversations I have had with Tim Scanlan, Russell Wolff, Seth Ader, Paul Grant, Barry Blyn, Mark Young, Grant Best, and Brendan O'Connor, among others, about the evolving place of the game within ESPN itself.

To borrow the words of David Winner (from the brilliant history of English football *Those Feet*), soccer "is a vehicle of love, especially between fathers and sons." To that end, while I am indebted to my entire family, especially my mum, my brother Nige, and sister Amy, as well as the entire Kroll clan, I want to especially thank my father, Ivor, and grandfather, Sam, for making me an Evertonian. Coming of age in Liverpool in the 1970s and '80s, I fell in love with the Blues when the Red Shite were dominant. Much of who I am today is because of the efforts, passion, humor, and humanity they have displayed on a weekly basis. I would particularly like to thank: Mick Lyons, the Mighty Bob Latchford, Dave Thomas, Colin Todd, Martin Dobson, Andy King, George Wood, Asa Hartford, Alan Irvine, Kevin Sheedy, Paul Bracewell, Duncan Ferguson, Kevin Campbell, Tommy Gravesen, Tim Cahill, Mikel Arteta, Phil Jagielka, Marouane Fellaini, Jack Rodwell, Anthony Bloch, and Mr. David Moyes. The story lines you crafted have never failed to thrill me.

I cannot describe the mix of joy and relief I feel now that my children share both my love of soccer in general and the Everton Football Club in particular. Thanks and gigantic love to Samson, Ber, and Zion for the inspiration they have provided on a daily basis. To my wife Vanessa: You were disgusted when I was red carded the very first time you saw me play. Despite this, you forgave me, allowed me to coach our kids, and permitted them to wear nylon soccer shirts to school practically every day, three acts that reflect the immense love, patience, and support you have given me, for which I will be forever grateful. Every morning when I wake up, the great love I feel for you is the first thing I think about, right before my mind turns back to 30th July, 1966—the day England last won the World Cup.

Photography and Illustration Credits

Page viii: Andy Clark/REUTERS/Landov • Page ix: Joe Kohen/WireImage • Page 3: Popperfoto/Getty Images (3); Offside; AP Images; Popperfoto/Getty Images • Pages 4–5: Popperfoto/Getty Images • Page 6: AFP/Getty Images • Page 7: EMPICS/Newscom; Popperfoto/Getty Images • Page 8: PA Photos/Landov • Page 9: Action Images/Zuma Press • Page 10: Popperfoto/Getty Images; L'Equipe/Offside • Page 11: Olycom/Sipa Press • Page 12: Popperfoto/Getty Images • Page 13: AP Images • Page 14: L'Equipe/Offside (2) • Page 15: Farabolafoto/Offside • Page: 16: fStop/Getty Images; Central Press/Getty Images • Page 17: EMPICS/Newscom; Central Press/Getty Images; AFP/Getty Images • Page 18: Popperfoto/Getty Images • Page 19: Mirrorpix/Newscom • Page 20: Popperfoto/Getty Images • Page 22: AP Images • Page 23: L'Equipe/Offside • Page 24: DPA/Zuma Press • Page 25: Picture-Alliance/DPA/Newscom • Page 26: AP Images; Popperfoto/Getty Images • Page 27: DPA/Zuma Press • Page 28: L'Equipe/Offside • Page 29: Popperfoto/Getty Images; L'Equipe/Offside • Page 30: Svenskt Pressfoto/SCANPIX/Sipa • Page 31: Popperfoto/Getty Images • Page 32: L'Equipe/Offside • Page 33: Offside (3) • Pages 34–35: Popperfoto/Getty Images • Page 36: Popperfoto/Getty Images • Page 37: Popperfoto/Getty Images • Page 38: L'Equipe/Offside • Page 39: L'Equipe/Offside • Page 40: Popperfoto/Getty Images • Page 42: SCANPIX/Sipa • Page 43: Lars Baron/Bongarts/Getty Images • Page 44: DPA/Zuma Press • Page 45: Bob Thomas/Getty Images • Page 46: Gerry Cranham/Offside • Page 47: Philippe Caron/Sygma/Corbis • Pages 48–49: Hulton Archive/Getty Images • Page 50: Hulton Archive/Getty Images; John Pratt/Keystone Features/Getty Images; L'Equipe/Offside • Page 51: Time & Life Pictures/Getty Images • Page 52: Popperfoto/Getty Images • Page 53: David Leah/Getty Images • Page 54: Hulton Archive/Getty Images • Page 55: Hulton Archive/Getty Images • Page 56: L'Equipe/Offside • Page 58: Action Images/Zuma Press • Page 59: Hulton Archive/Getty Images • Page 60: Hulton Archive/Getty Images • Pages 62–63: Sven Simon/Icon SMI/Newscom • Page 64: Popperfoto/Getty Images (2) • Page 65: DPA/Zuma Press; Popperfoto/Getty Images • Page 66: Popperfoto/Getty Images • Page 69: Gerry Cranham/Offside (2) • Page 70: L'Equipe/Offside • Page 71: Hulton Archive/Getty Images; Popperfoto/Getty Images • Page 72: Popperfoto/Getty Images • Page 73: Offside (2); AP Images • Pages 74–75: Popperfoto/Getty Images • Page 76: Picture-Alliance/DPA/Newscom; AP Images; DPA/Zuma Press • Page 77: DPA/Zuma Press • Pages 78–79: AP Images • Page 81: Popperfoto/Getty Images; Elisa Estrada/Real Madrid/Getty Images • Page 83: L'Equipe/Offside; Picture-Alliance/DPA/Newscom • Pages 84–85: John Varley/Offside • Page 86: Central

Press/Getty Images • Pages 88–89: Getty Images • Page 90: DPA/Zuma Press • Page 91: L'Equipe/Offside • Pages 92–93: Action Images/Zuma Press; Bob Thomas/Getty Images • Page 94: L'Equipe/Offside • Page 95: L'Equipe/Offside • Page 96: DPA/Zuma Press • Page 98: Mladen Antonov/AFP/Getty Images; Vladimir Rys/Bongarts/Getty Images • Page 100: Popperfoto/Getty Images; Oleg Popov/Reuters/Landov • Page 101: EMPICS/Newscom • Pages 102–103: Bob Thomas/Getty Images • Pages 104–105: DPA/Zuma Press • Pages 106–107: John McDermott • Pages 108–109: DPA/Zuma Press • Page 110: L'Equipe/Offside • Page 111: L'Equipe/Offside • Page 112: DPA/Zuma Press • Pages 114–115: Imago/Zuma Press • Pages 116–117: Bob Thomas/Getty Images • Page 119: David Cannon/Getty Images • Page 120: Bob Thomas/Getty Images • Page 122: Getty Images; Daniel Garcia/AP Images • Page 123: Offside (2); AP Images • Pages 124–125: Carlo Fumagalli/AP Images • Page 126: Bob Thomas/Getty Images • Page 127: AFP/Getty Images • Page 128: Bob Thomas/Getty Images • Page 129: Sergio Dorantes/AP Images • Page 130: DPA/Zuma Press; Action Images/Zuma Press • Page 133: Marcos Brindicci/Reuters/Corbis; Sygma/Corbis; Steve Powell/Getty Images; Zuma Press • Page 134: Florian Seefried/Getty Images; John McDermott • Page 135: Denis Paquin/Reuters/Landov • Pages 136–137: Bob Thomas/Getty Images • Page 139: Bob Thomas/Getty Images • Page 140: DPA/Zuma Press; Laurence Griffiths/Getty Images; Bob Thomas/Getty Images; Jonathan Daniel/Getty Images • Page 141: DPA/Zuma Press • Page 143: David Leah/Mexsport/Newscom • Pages 144–145: David Cannon/Getty Images • Page 146: AFP/Getty Images • Page 147: DPA/Zuma Press • Page 148: Billy Stickland/Getty Images • Page 149: Simon Bruty/Getty Images; PA Photos/Landov • Page 151: Getty Images (4) • Page 152: Farabolafoto/Offside • Page 153: L'Equipe/Offside • Page 154: Valery Hache/AFP/Getty Images • Page 155: Popperfoto/Getty Images; AP Images • Page 157: Billy Stickland/Getty Images • Page 158: PA Photos/Landov; Greg Wood/AFP/Getty Images • Page 159: Christof Koepsel/Bongarts/Getty Images; DPA/Zuma Press; Mark Leech/Offside • Page 160: L'Equipe/Offside; Mark Sandten/Bongarts/Getty Images; Nicolas Asfouri/AFP/Getty Images; Shaun Botterill/Getty Images; Mark Leech/Offside • Page 161: Eric Renard/TempSport/Corbis • Pages 162–163: Andre Camara/Reuters/Landov • Pages 164–165: Michael Probst/AP Images • Page 166: Romeo Gacad/AFP/Getty Images • Page 167: Luc Roux/Corbis; Corey Ross/Action Images/Zuma Press • Page 168–169: Bob Thomas/Getty Images • Page 170: AFP/Getty Images • Page 172: Toshifumi Kitamura/AFP/Getty Images; Chris Brunskill/ISI • Page 173: Alex Grimm/Reuters/Landov • Page 174: David Cannon/Getty

Images • Page 175: PA Photos/Landov; Lutz Bongarts/Bongarts/Getty Images • Page 176: PA Photos/Landov • Page 177: Kevork Djansezian/Getty Images • Page 178: John McDermott • Page 179: Imago/Zuma Press • Page 180: Susan Walsh/AP Images • Page 181: Offside; Getty Images (2) • Pages 182–183: Bongarts/Getty Images • Page 184: Alexander Hassenstein/Bongarts/Getty Images; Gerard Cerles/AFP/Getty Images • Page 185: Ross Kinnaird/Getty Images • Page 186: Courtesy Roger Bennett (5) • Page 187: Action Images/Zuma Press; Gerard Malie/AFP/Getty Images • Page 188: Popperfoto/Getty Images • Page 190: Jerome Prevost/TempSport/Corbis • Page 191: Stuart Franklin/Action Images/Zuma Press; DPA/Zuma Press • Page 193: Action Images/Zuma Press (3) • Page 195: Rob Tringali • Page 197: Doug Pensinger/Getty Images • Page 199: Pedro Ugarte/AFP/Getty Images; Witters/Offside; Bob Thomas/Getty Images (2); Popperfoto/Getty Images; Bob Thomas/Getty Images (2); Wilfredo Lee/AP Images; Martin Rose/Bongarts/Getty Images; Jonathan Daniel/Getty Images • Pages 200–201: Alex Livesey/Getty Images • Page 202: Roberto Schmidt/AFP/Getty Images • Page 203: Chung Sung-Jun/Getty Images • Page 204: Brian Bahr/Getty Images • Page 205: Gary M. Prior/Getty Images; Roberto Schmidt/AFP/Getty Images • Page 207: Etzel Espinosa/Mexsport/ISI • Page 208: Omar Torres/AFP/Getty Images; Andreas Rentz/Bongarts/Getty Images • Page 209: Gary M. Prior/Getty Images; Schalk van Zuydam/AP Images • Page 211: Bob Thomas/Getty Images • Page 212: NI Syndication/Offside • Page 213: Pornchai Kittiwongsakul/AFP/Getty Images • Page 215: DPA/Zuma Press • Page 216: Scott Bales/Icon SMI/Zuma Press; Getty Images (2) • Page 217: UPPA/Photoshot/Newscom; Martin Oeser/AFP/Getty Images • Page 219: JP Thomas/FEP/Panoramic/Zuma Press • Page 220: Philippe Laurenson/DPPI/Icon SMI/Newscom; Bob Thomas/Getty Images • Page 221: Reuters/Landov • Pages 222–223: DPA/Zuma Press • Page 224: Alex Livesey/Getty Images • Page 225: Wade Jackson/Icon SMI/Newscom • Page 226: Peter Schols/AFP/Getty Images; Lars Baron/Bongarts/Getty Images • Page 227: AFP/Getty Images • Page 228: Sipa • Page 229: Sipa • Page 231: AFP/Getty Images • Page 232: Chris Uncle/FilmMagic • Page 233: AP Images • Page 234: Laurence Griffiths/Getty Images • Page 235: Bob Thomas/Getty Images • Page 236: L'Equipe/Offside • Page 237: Patrick Hertzog/AFP/Getty Images • Pages 238–239: Victory Pictures (4) • Page 241: DPPI/Icon SMI/Newscom • Page 243: Ben Radford/Getty Images • Page 245: Alexander Heimann/Getty Images.

ABOUT THE AUTHORS

David Hirshey is the executive editor of HarperCollins Publishers and was a longtime editor at *Esquire* magazine. A former college player, he has been covering soccer for more than thirty years for a variety of publications, including *The New York Times,* the New York *Daily News, ESPN The Magazine,* and Deadspin. He is the co-author of two books, *Pelé's New World* and *The Education of an American Soccer Player,* and played himself (almost convincingly) in the acclaimed soccer documentary *Once in a Lifetime*.

Roger Bennett has written books about music, culture, and sports as well as articles for *ESPN The Magazine,* ESPN.com, *The New Republic,* No Mas, and *The Guardian*. His documentary film *Sons of Sakhnin United* followed an Arab soccer team made up of Muslims, Jews, and Christians that became cup champions of Israel.